I did it my way...

The Memoirs of HH Prince Andreas of Saxe-Coburg and Gotha

with Arturo E. Beéche

ISBN: 978-1-944207-00-7

EUROHISTORY.COM

6300 Kensington Avenue
East Richmond Heights, CA 94805 USA
Phone: (510) 236-1730 — Email: books@eurohistory.com

I did it my way...

The Memoirs of HH Prince Andreas of Saxe-Coburg and Gotha

©Arturo E. Beéche

ISBN: 978-1-944207-00-7

Artistic Design ©Arturo Beéche & David W. Higdon
Cover Design ©Todd Taubin

All rights reserved. No part of this book covered by the copyrights hereon may be reproduced or used in any form or by any means without prior consent of the publisher, except for brief passages covered by reviewers or fair use by other authors. Reproducing passages from this book by any means, including mimeographic, photocopying, scanning, recording, or by any information retrieval system is an infringement of copyright law.

The author and publisher of this book also wish to express their gratitufde to
the following individuals and entities for supplying illustrations for this publication:

We also wish to thank everyone else who helped us with this project, especially those who were instrumental in encouraging this book. In particular we appreciate the contributions of:

HM King Simeon of Bulgaria
Dr. Jürgen Aretz

We would like to express our appreciation to Count Hans Veit zu Toerring-Jettenbach for allowing use of some cf one of his photos. Other friends whose encouragement and support Eurohistory wishes to acknowledge, include:

Annet Bakker at Hoogstraten English Bookstore, Nicolas Fouint at Librairie Galignani, Joe Little and Jeannie Pittard-Whitmarsh at MAJESTY, Ted Rosvall at Rosvall Royal Books, Maria Smith (Thomson-Shore), Ian Shapiro, Seth Leonard, and Henry Wong.

Table of Contents

Table of Contents	i
Introduction	iii
Preface, by HM King Simeon of Bulgaria	vii
Forword, by Dr. Jürgen Aretz	viii
Family Tree: The Coburgs of Europe	x
Chapter I: Birth – 1943	1
Chapter II: My Parents' Doomed Marriage	8
Chapter III: A Messy Succession	25
Chapter IV: Grandfather Coburg's English Roots	40
Chapter V: Grandfather Coburg's Complicated Life	55
Chapter VI: Grandfather Solms and Omo	84
Chapter VII: The War's Aftermath and Divorce	95
Chapter VIII: 1946	100
Chapter IX: An Officer and A Gentleman	111
Chapter X: Mother's Second Marriage	116
Chapter XI: An American Life	123
Chapter XII: First American Chistmas	126
Chapter XIII: Army Life Across the USA	131
Chapter XIV: The 1950s and Unsavory Truths	138
Chapter XV: The 1960s, College, and A Return to Germany	149
Chapter XVI: A German Life	154
Chapter XVII: The Fall of the Berlin Wall and the Quest for Fair Restitution	165
Chapter XVIII: Happy Hour	174
Endnotes	215
Bibliography & Sources	217
Index	219

Für meine Kleine Prinzessin,

Andreas

Introduction
Why My Life Mattered

My life has been one of great contrasts. I was supposed to be born in Berlin, but instead I was born at my grandfather's estate in the countryside. I was supposed to be raised near my father's Coburg family, but instead my mother and her American husband raised me. German was supposed to be my mother tongue, but instead I spoke English with a certain Southern twang became the first language that I dominated completely. I was supposed to grow surrounded by the castles and palaces I would one day inherit, but instead I grew up playing in tide pools while barefoot and without a care in the world. I was expected to marry within the circles in which my family was prominent, but instead I married for love a beautiful girl of my own choice. I was expected to follow a pre-chosen path, but instead, I did it all my way. Germany was my destiny at birth. Yet, America kept a watchful eye over me as I matured from a fun-loving boy to a thoughtful young man.

I was a wartime child, one whose early years were decidedly affected by the madness that brought Germany to its knees. By the time I celebrated my fifth birthday, however, decisions unknown to me made the United States my home. Behind, I left my past, my family, all that was later in life going to shape my destiny. Ahead of me stood an amazing experience that began when we boarded a steamer and sailed across the Atlantic Ocean on our journey to a country that at the time stood victorious above all other world powers.

In Coburg with Queen Paola of Belgium.

Opposite page: In Gotha at Schloß Friedenstein during the time when we were negotiating with the authorities.

Spending my childhood in the United States was quite an adventure. We were not restrained by the heavy burden posed by social position, history and wealth. We were just a small military family formed by a father and a mother with two blonde cherubic children, a boy and a girl. At

With my wife Princess Carin, 1998.

home, my mother made sure that we refrained from communicating in German since she wanted us to become acclimated to America. She also did not want her second husband, Richard Whitten, to feel left out, nor did she want us isolated from his welcoming family. Since my new American family did not speak German, neither would we. Years later, in fact, when obligations brought me back to Germany, I, the heir to a considerable German legacy, had to learn the language, all while performing military duties. It was a challenge, no doubt, but like all the other challenges I have faced in life, not one which I shied away from.

I do believe that growing up in the United States, a country for which I hold to this day a special place in my heart, stamped my spirit with a different attitude. Americans are versatile, industrious and unstoppable. They believe that everyone can make it; everyone has a God-given right to pursue happiness. They are not restrained by old customs. No, they see life as a vast array of possibilities, a sea in which every fish has the capacity to make it to old age. This "can-do" approach, perhaps foreign to many people in the Old Continent, allowed me to rebuild that which was war, political sacrifices, erroneous choices and lackluster management nearly destroyed. I was never encumbered by attachments that seemed impractical, all while being mindful of the legacy I inherited, for after all I was not its owner, but its caretaker for the sake of my children and their own descendants.

Carin and me with my cousin Prince Georg Friedrich of Prussia. His grandmother, Grand Duchess Kira Kirillovna of Russia, was a frequent guerst at Grandfather Coburg's home and was a good friend of my father and his siblings.

My life has been one of great excitement, no doubt. However, I would like to think that mine has been a life dedicated to achieving something. As I approach my 75th year, I can look around and think that I was able to achieve most of what I set out to do during those halcyon days when the Coburg legacy was placed on my young and inexperienced shoulders. I did my best not to disappoint. I kept my word for I believed that a man's honor is his most prized possession. I was a dutiful son, a loving husband and an adoring father. I always treated those who worked for me with deep respect. I always negotiated with my counterparts with honesty and as equals. I worked diligently to rebuild my House and restore its presence among the other European dynasties. I sacrificed a lot to achieve what I thought was expected of me. History may, or may not, agree with how I achieved all the goals set in front of me. I suppose that will be left to historians to chronicle and analyze.

In the meantime, my legacy stands as my ultimate judge … but I rest assured that whatever I did, *"I did it my way …"*

Their Majesties King Simeon and Queen Margarita of Bulgaria.

Foreword
by HM King Simeon of Bulgaria

There is no doubt that the story of the House of Saxe-Coburg Gotha is History with a capital H.

Without going back ten centuries to the Wettiner days, I would like to invite the reader to an easy test: just underline in history books names such as Saxony or Saxe, Coburg, Gotha, or the variety of hyphenated renditions such as Saxe-Eisenach, Saxe-Saalfeld, Saxe-Weimar. You will find these names time and again. Before going on, I will share a belief reached during my long and rich-in-experience life: history is not a subject exclusively for old professors or book-worms. No matter what professional field you may be in, you can find a situation or a precedent in history, to guide you. This said, it is my perception, that anyone interested in going into politics must have a fair knowledge of history, of his or her own country and preferably, more. This should spare coming generations, to trip over and over the same obstacles, i.e. make the same mistakes which have proven fatal in the past...

Now back to the theme of the book you have in your hands. Not meaning to sound pompous, in any way I consider myself rational, well-read, with wide experience, yet, I am unable to answer a simple question: how and why a small and not wealthy duchy like Saxe-Coburg has played to this day, such an important role in European history?...Was it because of the politically convenient marriages, or the sense of duty of serving, in our families? Was it due to the solid bonds linking most of Europe's royal families? I leave the answer to this riddle, to the reader of this book, authored by the Head of the House of Saxe-Coburg and Gotha, my dear cousin Prince Andreas.

A staunch supporter of a united Europe, of the values and ideals that have made our old continent so significant, I am proud to belong to a family that has contributed so much through the centuries to a supra-national vision of Europe. Actually much before the so-called founding fathers of today's EU, with all due respect and admiration, for them!

Finally history is by no means, a static or an abstract notion, so anyone is free to contribute to it by aiming to improve laws and human relations so as to make today's globalized world a better and more peaceful place to live in.

Simeon

Preface
by Dr. Jürgen Aretz

H.H. Prince Andreas of Saxe-Coburg and Gotha is the Head of a House that – together with his ancestors – had played an important role in Thuringia for centuries. Thuringia is in the heart of Germany. The role of the House Saxe-Coburg and Gotha traces back to the times of the Holy Roman Empire.

Due to historical developments the assets of this dynasty were neither economic nor military power – the House has been generating the patronage of education, science and research for many generations and has been serving as role model far beyond its domains. At the same time the Ducal Family has been appearing as a collector of fine arts. After the Second World War, swaths of Thuringia were first occupied by the US Army, but then – according to the agreements between the Allies – they were surrendered to the Soviet Union. The Soviet occupiers expropriated all aristocratic families along with many others. Thus the House of Saxe-Coburg and Gotha lost all their territories in Thuringia: vast estates, castles, prized art treasures.

Those measures of expropriation met with the ideological aims of the communist regime, but not with the constitutional principles unifying all democratic nations. Nevertheless this breach of law could not simply be repaired by restitution during the process of German Reunification. According to information of the then government of the German Democratic Republic, the Soviet Union made the acceptance of the reunification in 1990 dependent of the persistence of those expropriations.

Prince Andreas made clear in a convincing and poised way that he was not driven by an obsolete understanding of possession. He was headed by the consciousness that his ancestors had acquired the marvellous collections not least in terms of science and art. As to his intention the collections should now be given over to the new sovereigns, the citizens in Thuringia. The House and the foundation respectively finally agreed with a compromised settlement, providing the transfer of the prized works of art against a comparatively moderate financial compensation. It came up to only a fraction of the value estimated by experts, which at the time amounted to more than € 250 million.

Thus, Prince Andreas had proved in his – historically speaking – possibly last real political decision which the House of Saxe-Coburg and Gotha had to make his loyalty to Thuringia, as well as to the constitutional democracy based on the principal of liberty.

There can be no doubt in the basic democratic attitude of Prince Andreas: previously he had represented the interests of his fellow citizens as an elected member of the city council of Coburg. There he assumed his democratic responsibility like other citizens, artisans, tradesmen, graduates, representatives of all ranks.

Prince Andreas has never claimed to play a special role due to the historical achievements of his family. He has also been conscious of the ambivalence and dubiousness of political actions that some of his ancestors are responsible for. Nevertheless a special experience has touched him personally and made him happy after having agreed with the settlement between the House Saxe-Coburg and Gotha and the Free State of Thuringia. The royal couple of Sweden, relatives and friends of the House, made an official visit to Gotha in 2003. Eighty-five years before, republican revolutionaries, as Prince Andreas expressed, had chased his Grandfather away from Schloß Friedenstein, this huge and impressive testimonial of architecture of the early baroque. Now there was again the flag of the House of Saxe-Coburg and Gotha flying on top of the castle. The reconciliation of the Family with a difficult past and the compensation of tangible assets and its role in modern times found their visible expression on that day.

Prince Andreas is, what we may call in an unpretentious way, a good person, and a man for whom his word is his bond having the same value as an official contract. To friends he is a good friend; to opponents he is indulgent, but nevertheless consistent and assertive.

By his action, the House of Saxe-Coburg and Gotha succeeded in gaining respect and, more importantly after 1990, the personal affection of many people who would have been his "subjects" in the times of his ancestors. Now the citizens meet him, as it should be, on an equal footing, nevertheless with due respect and mostly with great sympathy especially in the former ducal residencies. It is absolutely suitable to state that Prince Andreas of Saxe-Coburg and Gotha achieved some great impact with respect to his House and the compensation of the citizens.

When Prince Andreas and I met each other, we came from different positions, representing superficially regarded conflicting interests. Nevertheless, we succeeded in creating in common important things in favour of Thuringia and its inhabitants. In doing this we became friends. Friendship remains one of the most important achievements on earth. This is a cause for gratitude. My best wishes shall go along with Andreas of Saxe-Coburg and Gotha for many years beyond the time setting an end to this biography.

Jürgen Aretz
Bonn – Bad Godesberg, September, 2015.

Family Tree – Saxe-Coburg and Gotha in Royal Europe

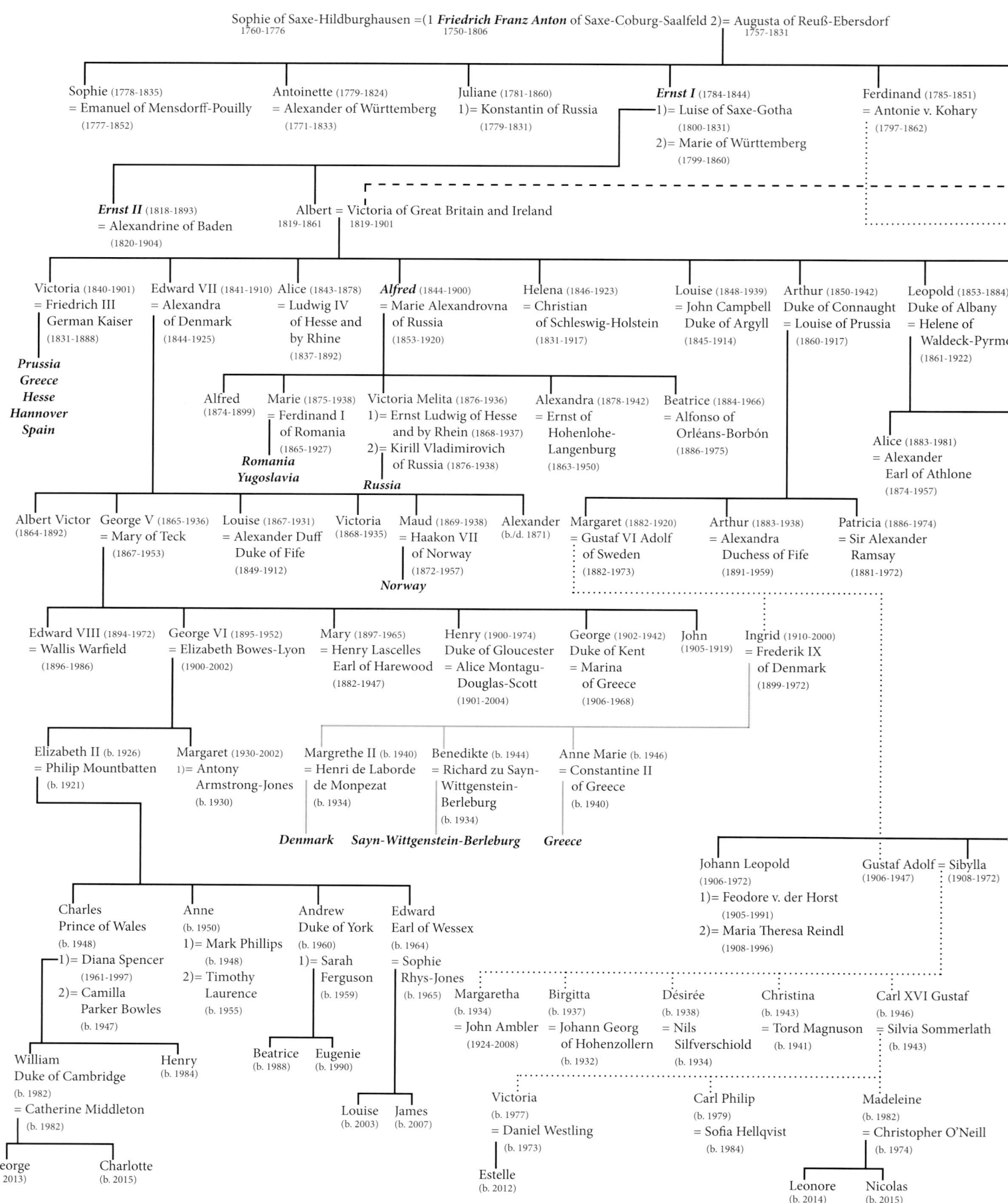

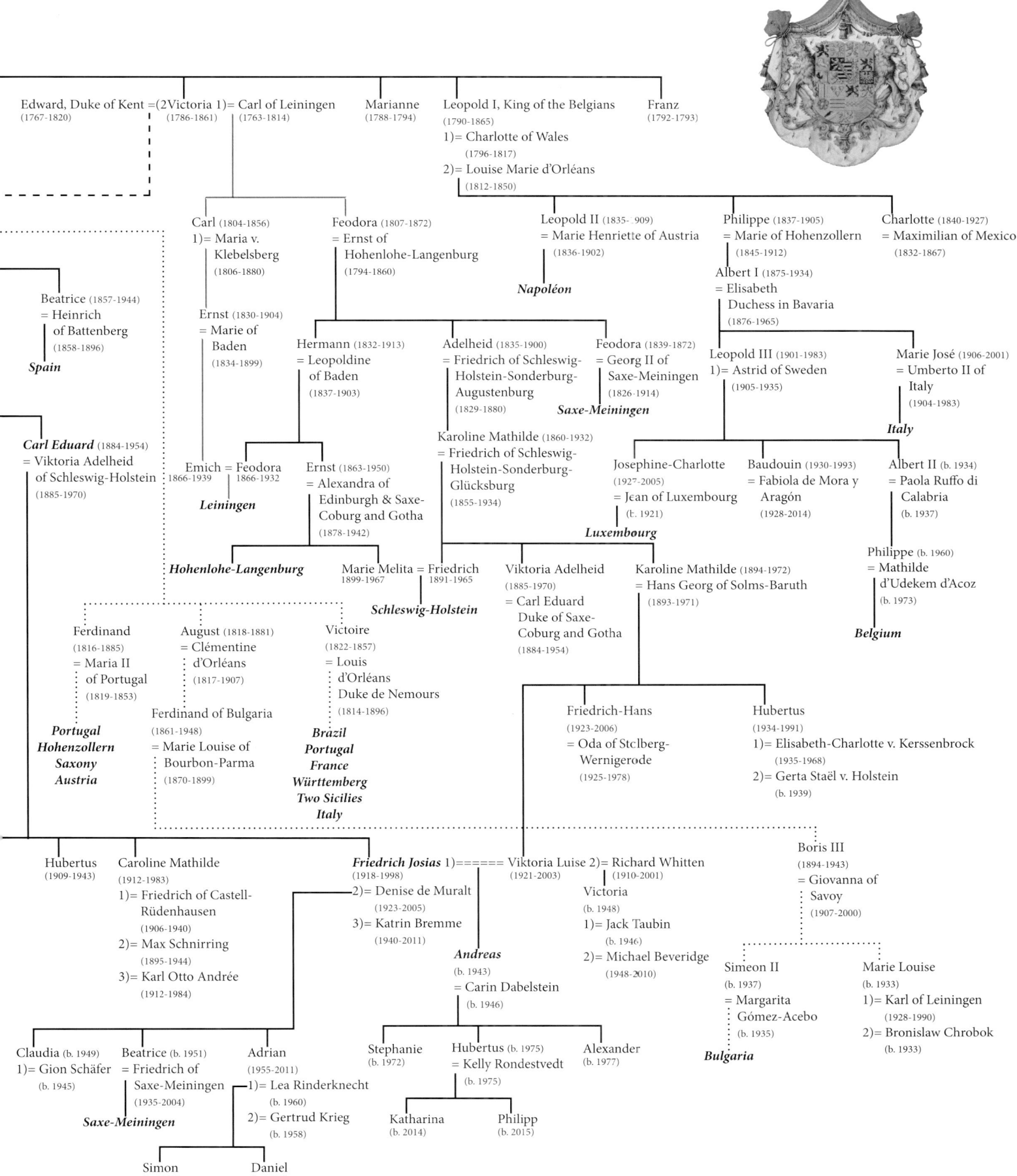

With my mother, Countess Viktoria Louise of Solms-Baruth, c. 1944.

Chapter I
Birth – 1943

Outside, the asphalt turned into a molten, deadly froth fueled by the never-ending barrage of firebombs raining from the skies over Berlin. When Hermann Goering's *"wunderhorns"*[1] began wailing that evening, Berliners never expected that the air raid would be so ferocious. Slowly, Berliners had become accustomed to the Allied bombings. It had become one of their daily routines. The sickening sound of the air raid sirens put everyone on notice that a raid was about to start. Everyone headed to the nearest shelter. Those who could not reach them sought underground rooms where they could wait out the announcement that the bombing was over.

This particular night, March 5, 1943, was quite different. The raid was the first such heavy aerial bombing. Security, already tenuous, was seriously disrupted on that fateful evening. The Reich's capital shook under the brutal pounding of Allied firebombs raining from the skies. One wave followed the next in a monotonous and deadly tsunami of infernal destruction.

The streets turned into fiery rivers that consumed everything in their paths. Venerable old buildings that had witnessed the history of the German capital were smashed to rubble. Little seemed to escape unscathed from the fury the Allies, now having gained the upper hand in the conflict, unleashed on once-proud Berlin. The war, no longer a faraway happening, had arrived and the capital began paying a ferociously tragic toll.

My parents.

I was expected to be born about March 5, 1943. The family gynecologist, Dr. Stoeckel, at whose clinic my mother wanted to give birth, had told my parents to prepare for my impending arrival. By his calculations, his patient would become a mother the first week of March. As it turned out, I delayed my arrival. Instead of arriving when expected, I kept my parents waiting. I wonder, perhaps, if the deluge of fire that descended upon Berlin that day subconsciously made me realize that staying inside my mother was far safer than appearing in the middle of the nastiest bombing Berlin had ever witnessed.

My parents had married the year before. My father was Prince Friedrich Josias of Saxe-Coburg and Gotha, third son and heir of the last reigning duke, Carl Eduard, a grandson of Queen Victoria. My mother was also closely related to Queen Victoria, albeit not directly since her great-grandmother was Fürstin Feodora of Hohenlohe-Langenburg (née Leiningen). Victoria and her elder half-sister were the daughters of the former Princess Victoria of Saxe-Coburg-Saalfeld, one of the children of Duke Franz Friedrich Anton and Duchess Augusta, perhaps the true great-grandparents of Protestant Royal Europe. Feodore was

I was born at Schloß Casel, the home of my Grandparents Solms-Baruth, on March 21, 1943.

Mother wanted to give birth in Berlin, as there were better doctors there than in rural Casel. However, daily air bombing raids in the German capital changed her mind and instead I was born in the country.

married off to the heir of a prominent mediatized dynasty, Ernst, a first cousin of Adelaide, the wife of future King William IV of Great Britain. Feodore settled in Langenburg in a massive castle that her husband's family had owned since time immemorial and there proceeded to raise a large family. One of her daughters was Adelheid (1835-1900), who in 1856 married Duke Friedrich of Schleswig-Holstein-Sonderburg-Augustenburg (1829-1880).[2] This couple had quite a few children, among them two of particular interest to my story. The couple's eldest daughter was none other than Auguste Viktoria (1858-1921), wife of the last German Kaiser, Wilhelm II, a first cousin of my Coburg grandfather. Karoline Mathilde was Friedrich and Adelheid's second daughter. Born in 1860, she married Duke Friedrich Ferdinand of Schleswig-Holstein-Sonderburg-Glücksburg (1855-1934), a nephew of King Christian IX of Denmark, famously known as the father-in-law of Europe due to the advantageous marriages of his children.

The Dukes of Glücksburg had six children, five daughters and the long-awaited heir, Friedrich, who married Princess Marie Melita of Hohenlohe-Langenburg (1899-1967), like her husband a descendant of the famed Fürstin Feodore.[3] Anyhow, Friedrich's eldest and youngest sisters are of particular importance in my story since they are my grandmothers. While Viktoria Adelheid, the eldest of the Glücksburg

Uncle Bertel, Uncle Leo, Grandmother Coburg and Father.

siblings, married Duke Carl Eduard of Saxe-Coburg and Gotha, her sister, Karoline-Mathilde (1894-1972), was married in 1920 to Count Hans zu Solms-Baruth (1893-1971).[4] This last pair were my maternal grandparents, a loving couple who played an important role in our lives for always providing a peaceful environment that shielded us from the violence and tragedy of the outside world.

My parents were first cousins. While this close kinship may raise eyebrows today, back when they married it was not so uncommon. Their wedding ceremony took place on January 25, 1942, in Casel, an estate owned by my maternal grandparents. Since Germany was at war, the celebrations were somewhat subdued, a far cry from the multitudinous royal gathering that took place in Coburg in 1932 when my father's sister, Sibylla, "Aunt Bylla," married the handsome and tall Gustaf Adolf, eldest son of the Swedish crown prince. Now, instead of Coburg witnessing another major gathering of the famed "royal mob," my grandfather, Duke Carl Eduard, had to content himself with a smaller affair in an isolated country estate away from his beloved former ducal capital. Surely he must have felt some degree of disappointment, but wartime conditions mandated that such events be conspicuously conducted. Once peace arrived, they must have felt that there would be plenty of time and opportunity to gather the extended family and celebrate like in the years of lore.

At the time of his wedding, my father was on a three-week leave from his military post. From Casel, the newlyweds headed to Berlin and stayed at the prestigious Hotel Bristol on the elegant Kurfürstendamm, the place-to-be in the capital. The establishment was a particular favorite of my mother's and her Solms relations. If they went to Berlin, the Hotel Bristol, it seemed, was their second home. From there, they traveled by train to Oberhofen, in Thuringia, where they spent ten quiet days in a cozy mountain hotel that belonged to the Coburg family estates.

Their short honeymoon continued with a visit to Coburg, where my father's sisters, Sibylla and Caroline-Mathilde, were still visiting their parents, Duke Carl Eduard and Duchess Viktoria Adelheid of Saxe-Coburg and Gotha. My mother, who was quite reserved for certain matters, always called them "Uncle Charlie" and "Tante Dicky," not "father" and "mother" as they had requested. Mother believed that word could only possibly be used to address her own mother, for whom she felt deep devotion.

Queen Victoria and Prince Albert, the Prince Consort.

After a short stay in Coburg, they all departed to Berlin, where my Coburg grandparents had some business to tend to. At the time, my grandfather served as the President of the German Red Cross, a post that brought him into dangerous contact with Germany's questionable overlords. Anyhow, my mother recalled their departure from Coburg: *"Arrangements were made for a special compartment to be reserved for us. We were all being taken to the train station in an official car. Sibylla, who always had difficulties with being on time, (in Sweden that was one thing, although her husband Gustaf Adolf always scolded her for it) was not ready to go when we were to leave, and so we got to the station about five minutes late! This was during the war, when all the trains were totally overcrowded and peoples' nerves were already on edge. People were hanging out the windows, wondering what the hold up was. And here we had to walk almost the whole length of the train to get to our comfy compartment with plenty of space! It was most embarrassing to say the least! Uncle Charlie and Aunt Dicky were furious with Sibylla, especially since many of the people recognized them."*[5]

Before settling in Berlin, close to where he was stationed, my father accompanied my mother back to Casel. She wanted to see her parents and collect some of her belongings. When they returned to the capital, they spent several days looking for a suitable apartment, which was no easy task in wartime. Finally, they settled on a furnished apartment not far from Stahnsdorf, my father's garrison. Since they expected that Father would be transferred soon, they did not want the move to Berlin to be permanent so as not to have to transport furniture and all that was needed to setup a more permanent residence. Transportation was dangerous in those days and trains were easy targets for aerial attacks. Mother, I believe, held deep hopes that their Berlin stay would be short, forcing them to return to Casel where she could once again ride her beloved horse "Jan," from whom she found it difficult to be away. My mother was a talented equestrian and she possessed immense passion for her horses, for they filled her with intense joy. Coincidentally, my own daughter Stephanie shares this same passion for her equine best friend.

Mother remembered later how difficult those early days of her marriage were. Berlin, as weeks turned into months, began suffering air raids: *"During the night we would often hear the air-raid sirens blaring their scary, shrill sounds and we would have to go down into the cellar to seek refuge. After about an hour of rumbling, bombs and anti-aircraft fire from the German guns things would usually calm down, and the all-clear sound was given. This would happen occasionally twice a night. Thank goodness these attacks were not as severe as they would become in the following years. Nevertheless, it is scary when you are on the receiving end, and are so totally unable to defend yourself. I found out very quickly that I was not made to be either a city – or an apartment dweller!! I really became quite homesick for the freedom of the country life with my horses and other animals and nature as a whole that had surrounded me all my life in Casel. I tried to busy myself with my household chores, and the interminable shopping for food with the ration cards, when one had to stand in line for hours for an eighth of a pound of butter, or four eggs, or whatever was available."*[6]

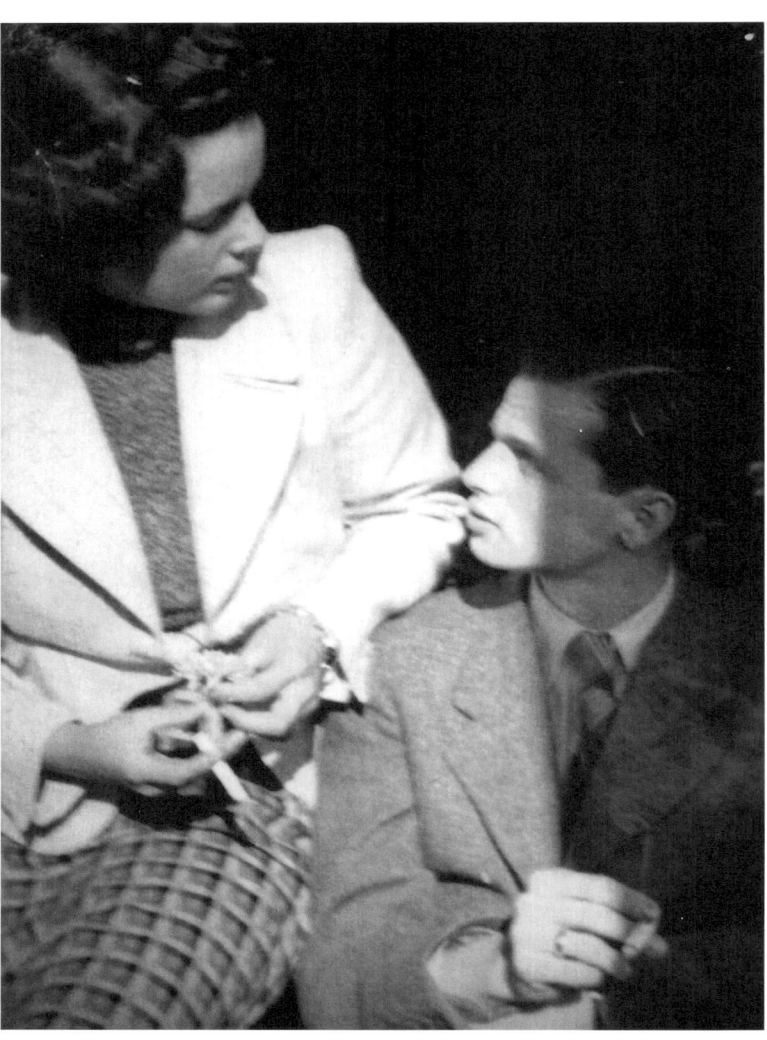

My parents, Viktoria Louise and Friedrich Josias.

At the same time, Berliners were given food rations. The war effort brought much sacrifice, and food was not as abundant as it once was. My parents, just like everyone else, received food rations and they had to do with what was available in the shops. Mother, always as resourceful as ever, found a way to supplement their meagre diet, while also finding an excuse to spend days with her beloved "Jan." Casel, not two-hours by train from Berlin, was her solution. In Casel, there was no shortage of vegetables and game. The estate's forests provided plenty of animals to hunt, while the house nursery was always amply filled with vegetables that enabled my Solms grandparents to continue enjoying a varied diet. Therefore, trips to Casel from Berlin became a fixture in my mother's schedule. Whenever possible, Father would accompany her.

That summer, my parents went to the seashore. It is quite likely that I was conceived while they were enjoying the relative peace and quiet of Westerland, on the lovely island of Sylt, where I have taken my family on many vacations. Anyhow, my mother recalled that this particular visit to Westerland made her realize how difficult times were for Germany. *"I found it not at all the Westerland I had known in my earlier years. It was totally overshadowed by the war! No bright lights at night,"* she recounted, *"no dance orchestras, and no delicious little goodies in the coffee shops that one could pick up and snack on in the afternoon. The meals had to be taken in the hotel where you stayed, and they were on the whole mediocre, to say the least. Naturally, you had to give the hotel your ration card for the time you were there. Everyone was assigned a particular time for breakfast, lunch and dinner, and you better be on time if you did not want to stand in line for a seat. We usually came right from the beach, as everyone else was doing. Fritzi and I had our swimsuits on under our slacks and shirts. Then most swimwear was made out of wool, and very snug fitting. We sat down at a table between the window and a long walkway on which the waiters used to bring the food to the tables. The first course was a HOT soup (probably liquefied leftovers from the day before), served in big soup plates, which were stacked one on top of the other on a tray that the waiter balanced over the heads of the waiting guests. Walking at a fast clip, he did not see a little boy running down the walk right into his way. Naturally, he lost his balance and the soup plates started to come down tumbling, emptying their hot contents. One of these ended in Fritzi's lap! He jumped up and tried to pull his pants and woollen swim trunks away from his body. It was a terrible experience, but thank the Lord he was not seriously burned. He, of course, left the table and went to our room to change. I had to stay there in order to save our place at the table. We finally broke off our vacation and went home. The vacation had been a terrible failure – as far as we knew then!"*[7]

Sometime after returning from her vacation in Westerland, mother accompanied her father on a visit to a family that owned a well-known racehorse farm. My mother had received a large sum of money as a wedding gift from one of her Solms uncles and with it she intended to buy herself another horse. She was not interested in more jewellery or dresses for she felt she had enough of both. A younger mare she could use for riding, now there was something she wholeheartedly wished to own. The fact that in wartime she was investing on a horse worried her not for a second. The new horse would be housed in the pristine stables of Casel, which had remained isolated from the conflict raging across Europe. War, surely, my mother believed, would never come to Casel. Oh, how mistaken she was going to be!

My parents on their wedding day, Casel, January 25, 1942.

Anyhow, it was during that trip that my mother felt a "bug," as she described what had gotten into her. She feared that she might have caught some illness that was causing considerable discomfort, *"mainly in the morning."* My Solms grandmother recognized the signs and told my mother that she believed her to be pregnant. That is how my mother first found out that I was on the way. Dr. Stoeckel at his clinic in Berlin later confirmed these suspicions. He had treated many of the Solms ladies and my grandmother venerated the respected doctor. My father, no doubt, was ecstatic with the news, just as were my Coburg grandparents who longed for an heir in the next generation.

Soon after, father received orders to ready for relocation to North Africa. This news made my mother give up the Berlin apartment and settle in Casel until my arrival, which she planned to have, as I mentioned earlier, at Dr. Stoeckel's clinic. My father visited Casel when his duties permitted, but mother truly enjoyed being back at home where she could spend hours riding her new horse, which she had named "Irrlicht", or "Will-o'-the-wisp."

My father never understood his young wife's fascination for horses. He, in fact, did not care much for them and abstained from riding. Mother could not understand his rejection of horses. She only stopped because her beloved "Irrlicht" was

Mother and Omo Solms.

"*spooked by a field lark, that fluttered out of the field next to us. She jumped unexpectedly to the side and at the same time kicked out in the back, so that I lost my balance and slid off to the ground. I must say it scared me terribly, especially since I was already almost in my fifth month of pregnancy. But, thank goodness, I had no ill effects from it all. I was able to get back onto 'Irrlicht' and rode her home. But after that experience I did not ride again until after the birth of my little baby-boy! Of course I had to listen to an awful lot of 'I told you so' and 'maybe now you will listen' from my mother.*"[8] This difference in appreciation and love for equines was to be but one of the many differences that in due time made my parents realize that besides a shared ancestry, as well as their only son, they shared little else. Their wartime wedding, many believed, was doomed from the beginning. They were not mistaken.

As my birth approached, both families began making preparations. My mother was issued stamps for baby clothes, diapers and all the necessary things one needs when readying to receive a baby. As a token of the graciousness of the Third Reich's appreciation for new babies, my mother was also allowed *"two maternity dresses and an extra pair of shoes during my entire time of pregnancy!"*[9] Luckily, she was very handy and in no time she took to cloth and needle and made herself some extra skirts and tops out of clothes her mother had owned. As I said before, my mother was extremely industrious and as Americans always said, out of lemons she made lemonade!

The carpenter at Casel built my first pram. He made a stand with wheels and attached a large laundry basket to it. This basket mother had lined with felt and flannel, *"strewn with a little floral print."*[10] My Coburg grandmother gifted my mother some old linens, a little mattress and pillow, all of which made my makeshift crib a rather cosy place.

Hence, in early March 1943, mother travelled to Berlin and checked into rooms on the third floor of the Bristol Hotel. All seemed under control until that day when the air raid alarms wailed their painful cry notifying all that the capital was under attack. Mother later recalled that while the streets of Berlin turned into molten rivers of fire, she found refuge in the hotel's cellar. Unfortunately, the Bristol Hotel was not spared and several bombs lit the upper floors on fire. At one point my mother feared that the gushing water from the fire brigade was going to fill the basement and drown them *"like rats."*[11] After the sirens sounded the end of the air ride, Mother, Father and Granny Solms alighted to find the upper floors of the Bristol Hotel gone. All the windows in their own rooms were blown out and fire raged outside consuming everything in its wake. The smell of sulphur and smoke was overwhelming. It was then and there that my mother decided that her hope of giving birth in the comfort of the Stoeckel Clinic was at an end. The clinic itself, anyhow, had been hit by bombs and was barely functional.

Eventually, they made their way to Casel, where mother awaited with great patience for my arrival. She spent the last days of her pregnancy going for long walks, reading and writing to friends and relations. *"My tummy seemed to get bigger and bigger, but the baby obviously was not ready to make its appearance,"* she wrote many years later.[12]

Then, during the night of March 20-21, I decided that I had kept them all waiting for far too long. Mother began feeling rather uncomfortable and contractions began in earnest. The midwife was called, as was the local physician, Dr. Fricke. An obstetrician was also summoned from the hospital in Luckau, and even though my mother had never met the man, she had to do with him, as there was no one else to help with the birthing. After keeping my poor mother in excruciating pains for nearly a full day, I made my arrival at 8:30pm on March 21. My mother best tells the story of my entrance into this world. In her memoirs, a fascinating story I must add, she recalled, *"After a long hard day ... my little baby . . . BOY was finally born. When the doctor picked him up and gave him a couple of little spanks to make him cry, he did not only cry, but a little fountain turned on at the same time. We all laughed and the doctor said: 'Well, we know that works!'"*[13]

My mother, until her last days, loved telling that story ... what a wonderful woman she was!

Mother and Father.

My baptism at Schloß Casel, May 1943.

Chapter II
My Parents' Doomed Marriage

My parents' marriage was doomed from the start. Shortly before announcing their engagement, mother had already developed deep concerns regarding marriage to her first cousin, Prince Friedrich Josias of Saxe-Coburg and Gotha. These reservations she held deep inside her soul, only daring to express them to her mother, who cautioned her to be true to her feelings. Mother, however, even though she wanted to break off the engagement after it was announced, in the end agreed to go ahead with the wedding plans. The reason for her acquiescing to it all was nothing but fear of how father would react to her breaking off the engagement. Mother always thought of others before thinking of herself, a characteristic that I truly admired in her.

My father, at birth, was not expected to become his father's and the dynasty's heir. Father was born at Schloß Callenberg, near Coburg, on November 29, 1918. He was among the first children born to a former ruling German prince since the German Empire had fallen just about three weeks before grandmother gave birth to her fifth child, and third son. Father was, well, an "after thought" as these late children are commonly described. By the time he arrived my grandparents were in their thirties and nearly seven years had passed since the birth of their last child, a girl named Caroline Mathilde ("Calma"), who grew up to not only become a free spirit, but later the source of much concern, and yes, frustration, to the Coburg family. But that is another story better left for later …

My father during the Second World War.

Schloß Callenberg was one of Grandfather Coburg's favorite residences. The property has been owned and used by the Saxe-Coburg and Gotha family for nearly two centuries. It has evolved over time to reflect the stylistic and architectural preferences of generations of dukes and princes. However, it remains a constant link between the family's past and present, and the Saxe-Coburg and Gotha family proudly owns it today.

The family's historical connections among the nobility has resulted in an incredible guest list witnessed by Callenberg over the last two hundred years. One of the most notable historical visitors to Schloß Callenberg, Queen Victoria, my great-great-grandmother, memorialized the castle in her diary with the following quote: *"A little steep, the way up to Callenberg castle, but once you have arrived there, you can enjoy a nice cup of tea in a beautiful surrounding."*[14]

Schloß Callenberg has a long history. The earliest documents date back to 1122, when a certain "Thiemo de Chalwinberch" is mentioned in a document. This ennobled family can be traced back to Callenberg until 1231.[15] The last ennobled freed-man residing in Callenberg, Ulrich III, sold the castle to the bishopric of Würzburg in 1231. However, already in the following year the castle belonged to Count Poppo VII of Henneberg. In 1313, the knight Hermann Hunt (Hund) von Sternberg acquired "Fortress Callenberg" from Count Berthold VII of Henneberg and maintained it as feudal tenure.

My mother with one of her beloved dogs.

Eventually, through devolution the castle became the property of Duke Johann Casimir of Saxe-Coburg in 1588, after the death of the last von Sternberg, a family that at some point in history had acquired the castle in 1313. Until 1825 the ducal treasury and Schloß Callenberg were the property of the Dukes of Saxe-Meiningen, one of the many branches of the Wettin family that ruled over Thüringen. However, when in 1826 the line of the Dukes of Saxe-Gotha became extinct, the surviving branches, as was customary, reshuffled their territories to incorporate the Gotha inheritance evenly.[16] This is how my branch, rulers in Coburg since 1735 and in Saalfeld since 1680, came to acquire both Gotha and Schloß Callenberg. Saalfeld was traded away and in return the duchy my grandfather was to inherit in 1900 became a dual entity, the duke ruling in both Gotha and Coburg. Schloß Callenberg, traded by the Duke of Saxe-Meiningen, thus became part of the important real estate possession of the new Duke of Saxe-Coburg and Gotha.

Since then, and when finances permitted, and sometimes when they did not, the Dukes of Saxe-Coburg and Gotha have rebuilt and reconstructed Schloß Callenberg. In 1831, for example, my great-great-great-grandfather, Duke Ernst I, Queen Victoria's uncle and father-in-law, concluded the reconstruction of the upper castle. In charge of this building project was Carl Alexander von Heideloff. Some twenty-five years later, in 1856/57, under the reign of Duke Ernst II, the lower part of the castle was redesigned in Neo-gothic style. Until 1945 Callenberg, and its vast park and woods, served as the summer residence of the ducal family. At one point, there was even a man-made lake, called "Callenberg lido," used by the ducal family for swimming and fishing. Quite a few photographs in the albums of my grandparents attest to those halcyon days.

Grandfather Coburg died at Schloß Callenberg, in a small cottage at the foot of the hill on which rests the castle. He was there when the war ended with tragic consequences for Germany and the family. In fact, Grandmother Coburg had built a cemetery for members of the family on a hilltop overlooking Schloß Callenberg. Grandfather Coburg was laid to rest there in 1954 near his son Hubertus, a casualty of Second World War. In due time, Father, Grandmother Coburg and even Aunt Calma were brought to rest on that quiet hilltop in the woods of Callenberg. I take daily walks in those woods, steeped to this day in centuries of our family's history.

After my grandfather's death, the Coburg Family Foundation sold Schloß Callenberg, which at one point served as a school for girls. Eventually, the Coburg

Opposite page: As was the case with millions of young German men, my father went off to fight in the Second World War. While his brother Hubertus served in the Luftwaffe, father received a commission in a panzer division. During some time he was stationed in Berlin and at one point he was scheduled to serve in North Africa.

Schloß Callenberg.

Grandfather Coburg was a very good shot and also an avid hunter. His homes were filled with hunting trophies.

Family Foundation reacquired Schloß Callenberg and during my tenure as head of the foundation we invested heavily in its restoration. After extensive restoration projects the former summer home of the Coburg Dukes was restored and since 1998 Schloß Callenberg lodges the collection of ducal art treasures, with precious pieces of furniture, paintings, porcelain, traditional handicrafts and a selection of weapons from four centuries. I well remember the inauguration of the new Callenberg, a wonderfully sunny day when other members of the family traveled to Coburg to accompany us on such a meaningful day. Most prominent among them were our Belgian, Bulgarian and Luxembourg cousins, who have remained very close to us ever since. Some years later we were able to bring to Callenberg a museum sponsored by the German National Shooting Guild. This was a considerable achievement and it guarantees that Schloß Callenberg will remain viable for years to come!

Kaiser Wilhelm II at Schloß Rosenau, April 1894. The Rosenau, a ducal property, was the birthplace of Prince Albert, my great-great-grandfather. His son, Duke Alfred, died there in 1900. His widow, Grand Duchess Marie Alexandrovna, continued using it as a country house.

Anyhow, let's return to my parents after this diversion ...

Father was born, as I mentioned before, at a very difficult time. When the Kaiser, mistakenly, I might add, allowed his generals to plunge the German Empire into war, few, if any, expected that four years later the Fatherland would lay defeated. By no means can one blame just the German Kaiser for this enormous tragedy, for guilt must be equally shared all the belligerent nations. However, one cannot possibly exculpate Kaiser Wilhelm II, Tsar Nicholas II and Emperor Franz Joseph, along with the French government, from plunging Europe into a fratricidal war that erased an entire generation of young men and destroyed the world my grandparents were raised knowing.

I can well imagine that Grandfather and Grandmother Coburg were delighted, in the midst of the unhappy times consuming Germany at the time, to welcome a third son. In due time, Father, who was to be the ducal couple's last child, became everyone's favorite. The family happily spoiled him and all the siblings eventually found in each other sources of support to withstand the strict environment in which the parents raised the Coburg children. My late Aunt Alice, Grandfather Coburg's amazing sister, the Countess of Athlone, who happened to be a sister-in-law of Queen Mary, as well as a first cousin of King George V, truly believed that her Coburg nephews and nieces were in desperate need of living in a more "liberal" environment, one that would better

Tsar Nicholas II also visited Coburg. He was a nephew of Grand Duchess Marie Alexandrovna, while also married to a niece of Duke Alfred. In this image he is surrounded by: Hereditary Prince Alfred of Saxe-Coburg and Gotha, Grand Duke Ernst Ludwig of Hesse and by Rhine (Nicholas' brother-in-law) and Duke Alfred of Saxe-Coburg and Gotha

Chapter II: My Parents' Doomed Marriage

In the terrace garden at Schloß Callenberg. Standing in back: Uncle Leo, Aunt Bylla, Uncle Bertel. Seated, same order: Aunt Calma, Grandfather and Grandmother Coburg and my father. The photo was taken in 1925.

suit their future life in the fast-changing world in which they lived.

At the time of the revolution in November 1918, the Duke of Saxe-Coburg and Gotha was in Coburg. When presented with political reality, he agreed to renounce his thrones in Gotha and Coburg. Gotha, a far more activist part of the ducal realm experienced quite a bit of uprising and insurgency. Not so in Coburg, where the revolution was quieter and more matter of fact. Grandfather Coburg, however, wanted to keep his family safe and in order to do so, he moved what remained of his small court to Schloß Callenberg, close enough to Coburg, but at the same time well outside the town center, where political passions could explode. This is the reason behind my father's birth in that beautiful mountaintop castle.

His childhood was spent mainly in Coburg. There he was in constant contact with some of the children of relations of his parents who had deep connections to Coburg. Among father's childhood friends were Grand Duke Wladimir Kirillovich of Russia, youngest child of Grand Duke Kirill and his Coburg wife, Victoria Melita of Edinburgh, a first cousin of Grandfather Coburg. These Romanov cousins had already spent years in Coburg since Tsar Nicholas II, who was a first cousin to them, did initially not approve Kirill and Victoria Melita's marriage. The Russian couple's older daughters, Marie Kirillovna and Kira Kirillovna, were frequent guests at Grandfather Coburg's home and they remained good friends with my Aunt Sibylla, particularly. Marie Kirillovna, in fact, was not only Coburg-born, but in 1925 Coburg was also the site of her wedding to the Hereditary Prince Karl of Leiningen, a very nice man who years later had a most unfortunate end at the hands of the Soviets. Father's other close childhood friends included brothers Hans and Alfred, the two eldest children of Duke Friedrich of Schleswig-Holstein-Sonderburg-Glücksburg and of his very nice wife Marie Melita, née Hohenlohe-Langenburg. Sadly, Alfred Holstein died young, in 1926, and that must have been a grave loss to the family. Our friendship with the Holstein cousins has continued and the current head of house, Christoph, has visited several times. Interestingly, the Holsteins and the Romanovs were descendants of the previous Duke of Saxe-Coburg and Gotha, Alfred, Queen Victoria's second son. Grandfather Coburg succeeded his Uncle Alfred in 1900.

Grandfather Coburg's settlement with the republican authorities in Coburg and Gotha took several years to settle. In

Uncle Leo, Uncle Bertel and Aunt Bylla on a slope at Schloß Callenberg.

the end, he was able to retain use of the Prince's Bastion inside the Veste Coburg, as well as Reinhardsbrunn, a picturesque castle and hunting estate between Coburg and Gotha. Schloß Callenberg, deemed private property, also remained in his possession. Besides these properties, he was restored vast forests in and around Thüringen. The Austrian properties, among them Greinburg and Schloß Hinterris, as well as several hunting lodges and considerable forestry estates, since they were private property, were not affected by the fall of the Austro-Hungarian Empire.

All these properties, as well as the ducal family's large, massive art collection and investment portfolio, allowed Grandfather Coburg a life of considerable comfort in the new Germany. His children were raised in an environment of quiet privilege, not showy, but certainly with plenty of wealth and privilege plainly visible to anyone who came in contact with the family. Indeed, it is well known that among the former ruling dynasties, the Coburgs were among the ones who managed to retain a larger number of their former properties.

The family at large liked my father and his siblings. Aunt Alice

Grandmother Coburg with her three eldest children.

My father and his cousin Grand Duke Wladimir Kirillovich of Russia.

Athlone had a particular devotion to Aunt Bylla (Sibylla). They were to remain in close contact until 1972, when Aunt Bylla died, far too early. Another frequent visitor to Coburg, the famed Queen Marie of Romania, believed the Coburg children were nice, simple, natural children whose spirits remain 'unsquashed' in spite of how severe the parents were. Grandmother Coburg, particularly, was extremely strict, and this brought her into direct conflict with her children. At one point, Aunt Bylla was sent to Romania to stay with Queen Marie, who was quite fond of her. Of that visit, Queen Marie once recalled, "*I am very responsible for Sibylla who was very near running away from home and must keep her here as long as possible as she dreads her parents.*" It didn't help matters one bit that at the time Aunt Bylla had lost her heart to a young man whose social standing made him ineligible for her hand. She "*spent the night in tears, as she has a 'chagrin de Coeur,'*" Grand Duchess Victoria Feodorovna (Victoria Melita) once wrote to her sister Queen Marie of Romania.

In the end, matters worked themselves out and Aunt Bylla found much love in a promising young man who was destined, or so it was hoped, to one day sit on the Swedish throne. Well, more about them later, for although I did not really get to meet Uncle Edmund, Prince Gustaf Adolf of Sweden, I was quite fond of Aunt Bylla, and remain close to her children, particularly King Carl XVI Gustaf.

In due time, Father left the family home and went to school. By then, his position in the line of succession had improved due to the unfortunate marriage contracted by his eldest brother, Hereditary Prince Johann Leopold, "Leo," to the family. Then, just as Father approached his twenty-first birthday, war ensued and once again their world was thrown into an abyss of uncertainty.

On September 1, 1939, Germany invaded Poland. Within days Europe found itself in a generalized state

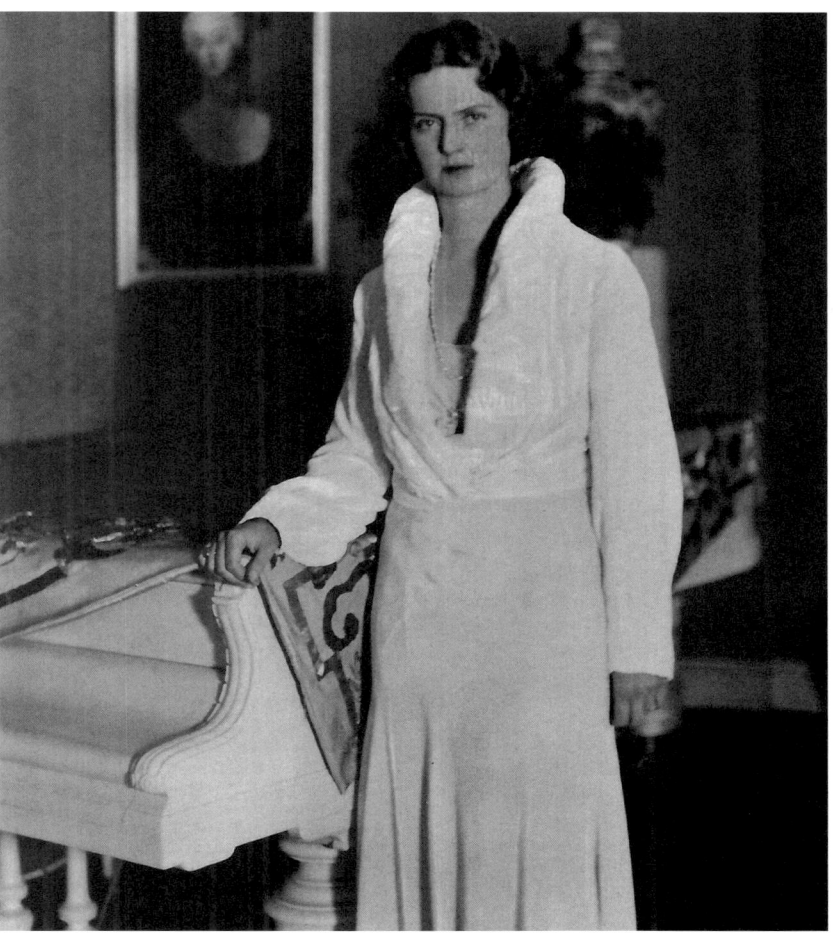

Princess Sibylla of Saxe-Coburg and Gotha, my Aunt Bylla.

From the left: Prince Harald of Denmark, Aunt Bylla, Grandmother Coburg, Uncle Bertel, Uncle Edmund and Grandfather Coburg, Schloß Callenberg, 1938.

I did it my way ...

Grandmother Coburg.

of war. Germany shocked everyone with its might. Within months German armies invaded Belgium, Luxembourg and the Netherlands. France fell like a house of cards and Paris was easily taken. Then, allied to Fascist Italy, Germany made the Balkan Peninsula its playground. Greece and Yugoslavia fell as Romania and Bulgaria quickly sided with unstoppable Germany. Denmark and Norway also fell to the German juggernaut, while Sweden declared its neutrality and was spared. Meanwhile, the Luftwaffe began conducting bombing raids over England, targeting not only strategic targets, but also the country's major cities. Adolf Hitler, my mother once wrote, *"saw that the English people were not going to give up that easily, he overestimated the actual military strength of the defenses and decided to postpone the invasion of England."*[18] In the meantime, Germany's advances in North Africa were crippling for the Allied efforts and victory seemed achievable. Then, the Führer made a strategic blunder and decided to invade the Soviet Union. Germany overstretched and the war, once the Americans became involved after

Grandfather Coburg in military uniform before the Great War.

16

the Japanese Empire bombed Pearl Harbor in Hawaii, was eventually lost with unimaginable consequences.

Meanwhile, Father, as was his duty, had joined the war effort, just as his brother Hubertus had. Uncle Hubertus, who had a deep passion for mechanics and machinery, entered the army and went off to the war. Father, who had a passion for automobiles, joined a tank battalion. In the spring of 1941, Father was stationed in Stahsndorf, south of Berlin. While there he served in a garrison for a tank unit and tank training facility. Being close to the Casel, Father would visit his Solms uncle and aunt frequently. My mother later remembered these visits by her cousin "Fritzi," particularly as, *"these visits seemed to become more and more frequent, and Fritzi became more and more flirtatious. I thought at first he was just playing around, and sort of went along with it, until I realized that he was much more serious, than having a flirtatious fling with me."*[19]

In due time, Father, who was a good talker when it came to these maters, convinced my mother that he really loved her. Mother worried *"how it would be to be married to someone so closely related to me…It seemed almost like a brother and sister relationship…"*[20] It was not a very auspicious beginning to what would become a short wartime marriage…

Mother, Countess Viktoria-Luise of Solms-Baruth, was born on March 13, 1921, in Casel-Golzig near Luckau, Niederlausitz, Germany. It was a little village some 50 miles south of Berlin. Casel, as we always knew this magical place, was in the middle of the area in which most of the vast Solms properties were located. The Solms family, a mediatized dynasty, owned estates that rivaled in size those owned by Grandfather Coburg.

The wedding of Grandfather Solms and Omo (Princess Caroline Mathilde of Schleswig-Holstein).

My maternal grandparents were Count Hans Georg of Solms-Baruth (1893-1971) and his wife Princess Caroline Mathilde of Schleswig-Holstein-Sonderburg-Glücksburg (1894-1972). Grandmother Solms was a younger sister of Grandmother Coburg,

My Solms great-grandfather, Fürst Friedrich.

both being daughters of Duke Friedrich Ferdinand and of his wife, the former Princess Karoline-Mathilde of Schleswig-Holstein-Sonderburg-Augustenburg, of the senior branch of the Holstein family. This last lady, my great-grandmother, had close connections to several of Grandfather Coburg's relatives. Her eldest sister, Augusta Viktoria, was none other than the first wife of Kaiser Wilhelm II, while her only brother Duke Ernst Günther married Princess Dorothea of Saxe-Coburg and Gotha, one of our Coburg-Kohary cousins. Kaiser Wilhelm II, as the reader may recall, was a first cousin of my Grandfather Coburg. I guess it all "stayed in the family."

Grandfather Solms was a very kind man, who also happened to be a devoted family man. Being with them always reminded me of a tranquil bay, a place of solace to where we all flocked in times of troubles. Count Hans Georg was the third of four sons of Fürst Friedrich Hermann of Solms-Baruth (1853-1920) and of his wife Louise, née Countess of Hochberg, Baroness of Fürstenstein, of the House of the Princes of Pleß. This connection with the Pleß family was to play an important role in the post-war era in keeping my Solms grandparents from being completely destitute after the Solms-Baruth lands were lost behind the Iron Curtain.

The family's firstborn was Tante Pink (1884-1945), who married Fürst Otto of Salm-Horstmar (1867-1941). Her youngest daughter was Marie Luise (1918-2015), wife of Prince Heinrich IV Reuß (1919-2012), their son Heinrich XIV being a good friend of mine and a frequent visitor to Coburg and Greinburg. Uncle "Dicky" Solms (Friedrich-Hermann) was born in 1886 and married "Aunt Ada," younger sister of my Grandmothers Coburg and Solms. They had five children and after the Second World War and the loss of the Solms properties they managed to settle in Namibia, where they acquired some land. Uncle Dicky died at Windhoek in 1951. Aunt Ada returned to Europe and died in Salzburg in 1964. Next came Uncle Hermann Solms (1888-1961), who married his aunt Countess Anna Hochberg, Baroness of Fürstenstein (1888-1966). Uncle Hermann and Aunt Anna settled in Salzburg after the war. They had three children, but all are dead now.

Grandfather Solms was a deeply loyal supporter of the Kaiser to the very end. The loss of the war in November 1918 was a serious blow to his morale. However, Uncle Dicky Solms placed his brother, my grandfather, in charge of the family's estate at Baruth. As their domicile, my grandparents were given a two-hundred-year old castle, Schloß Casel, built by Knobelsdorf, the same architect Friedrich the Great used in Sans Souci. Mother was born there. She always remained terribly fond of Casel and still in old age she reminisced about the happy times when she lived there. She once told me that the castle "*was really a manor house ... my parents were the*

Duke Ernst Günther and Duchess Dorothea of Augustenburg.

first ones to inhabit Casel permanently for a century, so they were forced to do much upgrading" to make it livable. "From the outside, the house had also a cosy comfortable look with four chimneys and a 'mansard roof,'" my mother recalled. Furthermore, "The upstairs rooms all had dormer windows. The walls were totally covered with ivy and from what my parents told us, the windows and doors had to be 'rediscovered' – so to speak – I only remember a beautifully manicured look with all the windows and doors trimmed out. Men standing on tall ladders and cutting the ivy around windows and doors with large hand clippers did this. They came twice a year to do this arduous job, which took several days. I always felt sorry for the poor little sparrows and their babies, many of whom lost their nests."[21] Mother thought of Schloß Casel as an idyllic place and she always felt much sadness when thinking of the estate's fate once it fell into the hands of the advancing Red Army.

As I mentioned before, my mother was born at Schloß Casel. Her brother, "Uncle Pety" (Friedrich-Hans), was born at Schloß Casel in 1923. Their youngest brother, Uncle Hubertus, was born in Berlin in 1934. In Casel, the Solms children were raised with a deep love of the outdoors. It is from that experience that my mother developed an abiding passion of horses and riding, a sport she and Uncle Pety practiced with devotion when they were young. They all loved animals and in future years their homes would always have more than one pet. Mother, for example, adored her endless list of dogs, which were simply part of the family. Mother wrote in her memoirs, "We had fish and birds in our playroom. My father had a little stable built behind the vegetable garden, where we had rabbits, guinea pigs, fan pigeons, guinea hens, bantams and my goat. The guinea hens, I remember, were a noisy bunch and laid thirty or more eggs into a hidden nest somewhere in the bushes and then would never sit on them so as to hatch the chicks. By the time we could find the nest half the eggs were spoiled. We often were able to rescue a few of them and sneak them under a chicken that just happened to be in the mood to sit on her own eggs. The guinea chicks were precious with red legs and beaks and a fuzz of brown and yellow stripes. Mother hen was just as proud of her adopted babies as of her own, and frankly did not know the difference! One Christmas we asked for a donkey, and when the doors were opened to the Christmas room, there he was wagging his tail and giving us a heehaw greeting. He was adorable, just what we had wished for: an all grey coat with a dark brown short mane that stood up and a stripe down the middle of his back to his tail. We had him many years and, later on,

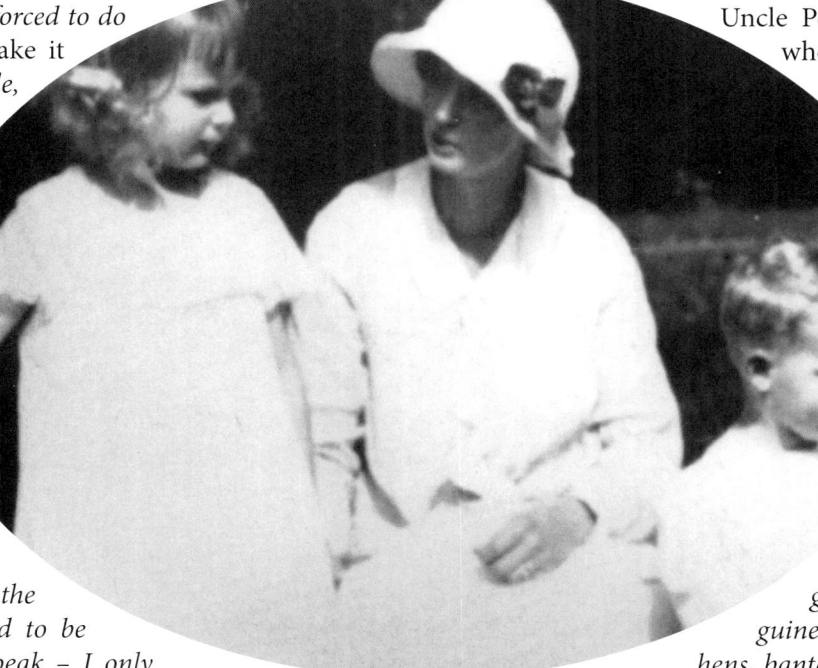

Omo with my mother and Uncle Pety.

Grandfather Solms and Omo at Schloß Callenberg, 1938.

My mother with her parents and Uncle Pety. This photo was taken at Schloß Casel.

he became a favoured companion of my little brother Hubertus!"²²

They also had riding ponies and the lake at Schloß Casel was filled with beautiful swans, which at times could be rather mean. Mother wrote that *"On the pond in the park we had Muscovy ducks (a large, greenish, black duck) and swans. Father and mother swan built a huge nest of sticks and leaves lined with downy feathers on the ground in the bushes near the bank of the little river 'Berste' every spring. Then they both took part in the hatching of the eggs. Father swan would not tolerate any one near the nest! My father one day saw that one of the big eggs had rolled out of the nest. Both father and mother swan were off of the nest, and my father tried to gently put the egg back into the nest, when father swan, half running and half flying, came out of the water and attacked my father, hitting him on the arm over the wrist with his wing and breaking his arm!"*²³

Besides caring for their many animals, the Solms children also swam, climbed trees, went on walks in the woods – they were raised in a carefree environment very different from that in which Father and his siblings were raised. It is no doubt to me that Grandfather and Grandmother Solms were much easier going than my Coburg side of the family. That difference in upbringing, I can well imagine, must have played an important role in the differences that eventually led to the total collapse of my parents' marriage.

Hence it was that these two very different people, tied by close family links, in 1941 became a couple. When Father asked Grandfather Solms for my mother's hand in marriage, he consented to the engagement but asked that the wedding be postponed *"until times were less uncertain and it was possible for us to have a normal family life together."*²⁴ While there were also some concerns about the fact that they were first cousins, it was also believed that Mother's Solms blood would add a new strain into the rather purified Coburg gene pool.

Before the fateful day when she walked down the aisle of the palace chapel at Schloß Casel, my mother had serious misgivings about her marriage to Father. In December 1941, Grandfather and Grandmother Coburg invited Mother to join them for a stay at Reinhardsbrunn, described as *"a lovely little Neogothic castle on the huge Coburg*

Schloß Casel, mother's childhood home and my birthplace.

estate in Thüringen."[25] Father was serving in Yugoslavia and my grandparents wished to spend some time alone with their future daughter-in-law. Mother had made the decision, before departing Casel, that she would put an end to the engagement. She was convinced that *"we were not suited to be married."* Mother, who cared very much for Grandmother Coburg, whom she called "Aunt Dicky," worried what effect her announcement would have on her. She later remembered the conversation she had with her Aunt Dicky: *"I would have to break the engagement before it was too late. I was really very fond of my Aunt Dicky and Uncle Charlie, and I knew how happy they were about Fritzi and my engagement and I hated to disappoint them. I was going to break the news to Aunt Dicky before we got to Reinhardsbrunn. I could see the expression of shock and disappointment in her face when I started on what I had to tell her. I felt very sorry for her and really hated to hurt her like that. She listened to me and my reasons for this decision. Then she begged me not to go forward with my plan for disengagement while Fritzi was in the field. She felt it would upset him so badly that he might not want to come back home! I knew Fritzi had a very sensitive personality and often became easily depressed. Although Aunt Dicky was a very strong woman, and was able to handle almost any situation, Fritzi was much more of his father's temperament."*[26]

Schloß Reinhardsbrunn.

The arrival at Reinhardsbrunn stopped my mother in her tracks. Father was there awaiting her, and she worried about his reaction. *"I still can feel the sensation I had when I saw him in the doorway to greet me,"* Mother later recalled. *"Frankly, I thought at the time that he had a premonition of what I was going to tell him. Our embrace was certainly not one of two people who are in love. There was shyness about it. We were in Reinhardsbrunn several days and I had this load over my head, but I did not seem to be able to talk about it. Every time I started, I had to think of the conversation I had with Aunt Dicky and what she told me. I know Fritzi must have felt that things were not right, and I felt very badly about it. Then on December 7th, a Sunday morning, came the news of the attack on Pearl Harbor."*[27]

Mother was derailed by events outside her control. Grandmother Coburg went to work on Mother. She had private talks with her niece and did everything possible to convince Mother to remain on course. She told my mother that they *"would grow together and learn from each other, even though we might not always share the same interests."* Wedding preparations continued in earnest and she convinced herself that once married, all things would, somehow, work themselves out. The eternal optimist that she was chided herself into believing that which was not there … the wedding date was set for January 25, 1942.

The only reminiscences left of my parents' wedding were authored by my mother. When reading them, one can easily notice how much she became involved in the planning of her wedding, for as uneasy as she felt, Mother hoped that in the end it would all settle itself, somehow. She remembered that it was a terribly cold January *"with an unusual amount of snow."*[28] She also remembered, with some degree of excitement, the more detailed preparations involved:

"My mother and I made several trips into Berlin where we bought pots and pans and other necessary things for my new household. Everything was rationed, and I had been issued stamps for the allowed amount of cookware and other household items. We

usually left Casel in the morning bundled up in heavy coats and felt boots to ride in a horse drawn sled, with Andreowich or Block as our coachmen, to the railroad station in Golsen, to take the train into Berlin. Often we had to wait for a long time for the train to come, because the tracks were snowed in or some other difficulty had arisen. It was a terrible ordeal and we would come home exhausted and half frozen. Getting the fabric for the wedding dress was also accomplished with only the greatest difficulties. But we finally were able to get everything together and Herta Hoeft made me a lovely dress."29

The day of the wedding came closer and closer. Wine and champagne arrived in crates. Some of the white wine had frozen and the bottles were broken during the transport and had to be reordered. All of this was involved with the greatest of complications due to the irregular availability and transport of such goods. "It is amazing how savvy one gets in such abnormal times. A week or so before the wedding, my grandparents Solms' old cook Huebner arrived from Silesia, where he lived in retirement near Klitschdorf. He was summoned by my parents to help our cook Frieda in the preparation of the dinner the night before the wedding, and the wedding banquet. Many of our relatives arrived, some of whom were staying in Baruth with my Aunt Ada and Uncle Dicky Solms, and in the castle in Golsen, which also belonged to our estate, and was occupied by the count and countess Castell. My Aunt Clea Castell was a cousin of my father's. Huebner had prepared a beautiful buffet dinner the night before the wedding which was served in the dining room. Both of the salons were filled with groups of people talking and eating and catching up on family news. We younger people had mostly gathered in the dining room. My father was strictly against dancing during the war, when so many young men were out in the field fighting and being maimed and killed. He insisted on that rule even at my wedding. Our younger generation did not agree with this view, although we had the same compassion for our troops as my father did. But we felt that most of the young men still at home, would also end up on the front one day, and why should they not have fun while still at home?" Mother wrote.30

She continued, "A few days before the wedding I felt a sore throat coming on, which became worse and worse. Doctor Fricke was called, and he gave me all kinds of pills to take and compresses to put around my throat. On the morning of my wedding day I had a full fledged tonsilitis. It had snowed some more that night and the temperature was down to 10 degrees Fahrenheit or less! There was no way to heat the church except with a little electric heater, set up close to the altar, to take at least some of the icy snap out of the air. The path from the house to the church went through the park. It was cleared the morning of the wedding, and almost formed a ditch with the snow piled up on either side of it. The wedding was set for eleven thirty. In the earlier morning I was asked by my mother to come to the small salon and look out of the window. There was Pety with my favorite horse 'Jan von Werth,' covered with a beautiful red plaid horse blanket and a big sign hanging on his side, 'Ich komme mit!' (I am coming with you!). Naturally I was so overcome that I broke out in tears. I had always been afraid that Jan would be sold or given away after I was gone from Casel. My father could not ride two horses and my mother, by that time, was not riding anymore. But now Jan was mine to keep! Naturally my father agreed to keep him there until I could take him with me, wherever I would be living. After a small breakfast with a few of our guests, I had to get dressed for the wedding. My mother and Herta Hoeft, who had made my dress so beautifully, assisted me in what became a hilarious affair! Due to the cold weather and my terrible sore throat I was bundled up almost like a

My parents.

My mother on her wedding day as she walked to the castle chapel.

mummy! Beneath my wedding dress I wore my father's hunting underwear - top and bottom - and in addition, a pair of white thick felt riding boots. My friend Birgit had a white lambswool coat that she lent me for the occasion. I was definitely dressed for the North Pole! My lace veil flowed over my polar bear figure, and I am sure Fritzi had to chuckle when he saw me like that, and, maybe, he even had second thoughts at the sight.

The church was beautifully decorated by my mother with white cyclamens and chrysanthemums tucked into dark green pine branches all around the altar. Superintendent Boelke officiated at the wedding, as he had done at my confirmation. Thanks to the temperature in the church his sermon was rather short this time. I could see his breath with every word, like a boiler letting off steam. After the church ceremony we all went back to the house where a very welcomed fire in the vestibule fireplace greeted us. I then had to undress and get all the 'under garments' off for the reception in the big salon and the following banquet which had been set up in the play room upstairs, the biggest room in the house. Huebner and Frieda had done themselves proud once again with their exquisite and delicious food. Huebner was a real artist in how to present things. There were a lot of speeches, toasting and well-wishes. When all was over, we went back downstairs to have cognac and a demitasse. I think it must have been the cognac that took care of my sore throat, or maybe my tonsils were frozen. At any rate it felt a lot better than before the wedding. Later in the afternoon Fritzi and I were taken by carriage to Golsen to board the train to Berlin. I remember kissing my teary-eyed parents goodbye and whispering to them that I would be back soon. They gave me a tight hug and managed a smile. I also had to hide a couple of tears!"[31]

As the reader knows now, I arrived nearly fourteen months later, making my entrance into the world at my mother's beloved Schloß Casel. By then, the war was not going so well for Germany and ominous clouds rose on the horizon … the approaching stormn was inevitable and our lives would forever change!

My parents after their wedding.

Chapter III

A Messy Succession

But from all sides I hear bad accounts of Alfred who has been ruining his health & looks dreadfully ill. Potsdam has been morally & physically most injurious to him, it is most grievous for he is the only son!"[32] – Thus wrote Queen Victoria to her granddaughter Victoria Battenberg what was the matter with the young, but terribly unhealthy Hereditary Prince Alfred of Saxe-Coburg and Gotha.

There is no question that the death of Prince Alfred Jr., as my Aunt Alice once wrote, *"brought about a dramatic change into our lives."*[33] As a nearly immediate consequence, Great-Grandmother Albany and her two children were forced to depart England and settle in Germany. But how so … why?

The matter behind this relocation was simple, yet extremely complex and important. Prince Alfred Jr. did not leave any heirs. Dying in his mid-twenties, Alfred had been unable to settle down because of the terrible illness his life of dissipation had gained him. Hence, without a male heir to inherit his succession rights to the ducal thrones in Coburg and Gotha, the succession was thrown into disarray. What ensued was a major confrontation between Queen Victoria and her sons, on the one side, against what they perceived was Kaiser Wilhelm II's meddling in what the English side considered a "family matter."

Opposite page: Hereditary Prince Alfred of Saxe-Coburg and Gotha.

Before getting into this incident, which mind you was a terrible mess, let us go back a few decades.

For a very long time, it was customary for the Wettins, the family that ruled the Saxon duchies, to divide a father's legacy among all living sons, or even act as co-rulers of a small duchy. However, this began changing in the early XVIII century when slowly each of the existing branches of the family began adopting the principle of male primogeniture. This meant that no longer would there be division of spoliation of a legacy once the ruling duke died.

My branch stems from Duke Ernst I of Saxe-Gotha (1601-1675), who began ruling cojointly with his brothers over the then duchy of Saxe-Weimar. In 1641, Ernst I and his two surviving brothers divided their father's large inheritance among them. He received the town of Gotha, along with the estate and monastery of Reinhardsbrunn, and several other important estates, villages and castles. Four years later his legacy was further enlarged when both Ernst I and his brother Duke Wilhelm of Saxe-Weimar divided among themselves the lands of their childless brother Duke Albert of Saxe-Eisenach. Duke Ernst I was extremely lucky due to the various inheritances he received during his long life. In 1660 he received the county of Henneberg, while three years later he purchased the lordship of Kranichfeld from the Counts of Schwarzburg. When the line of Saxe-Altenburg became extinct 1669, Ernst I of Saxe-Gotha stood to inherit an

Duke Ernst I of Saxe-Gotha.

even larger number of estates, forests, castles, art collections, towns and villages. One of these towns was Coburg.

Ernst I and his wife Elisabeth-Sophie, born a Saxe-Altenburg, had a total of seventeen children. Not all survived into adulthood, but the sons who did divided their father's large inheritance among them: Friedrich (1646-1691) inherited the duchy of Saxe-Gotha; Albert (1648-1699) inherited Saxe-Coburg; Bernhard (1649-1706) inherited Saxe-Meiningen; Heinrich (1650-1710) inherited Saxe-Römhild; Christian (1653-1707) inherited Saxe-Eisenberg; Ernst (1655-1715) inherited Saxe-Hildburghausen; and Johann Ernst (1658-1729) inherited Saxe-Saalfeld. Not all these dukes had descendants, so there were several further divisions every time one of the branches became extinct; hence, for example, my ancestor Johann Ernst received several domains and estates from Saxe-Gotha and later from Saxe-Römhild.

Duke Johann Ernst of Saxe-Saalfeld.

Johann Ernst, who died in 1729, was succeeded by two of his sons (Christian-Ernst and Franz Josias) who rule jointly over Saxe-Saalfeld. In 1735, the brothers received several territories, estates and towns in a further redistribution; among them was the town of Coburg, which from then on was to remain under my family's control until the fall of the German Empire in 1918. Since Duke Christian-Ernst died childless in 1745, his

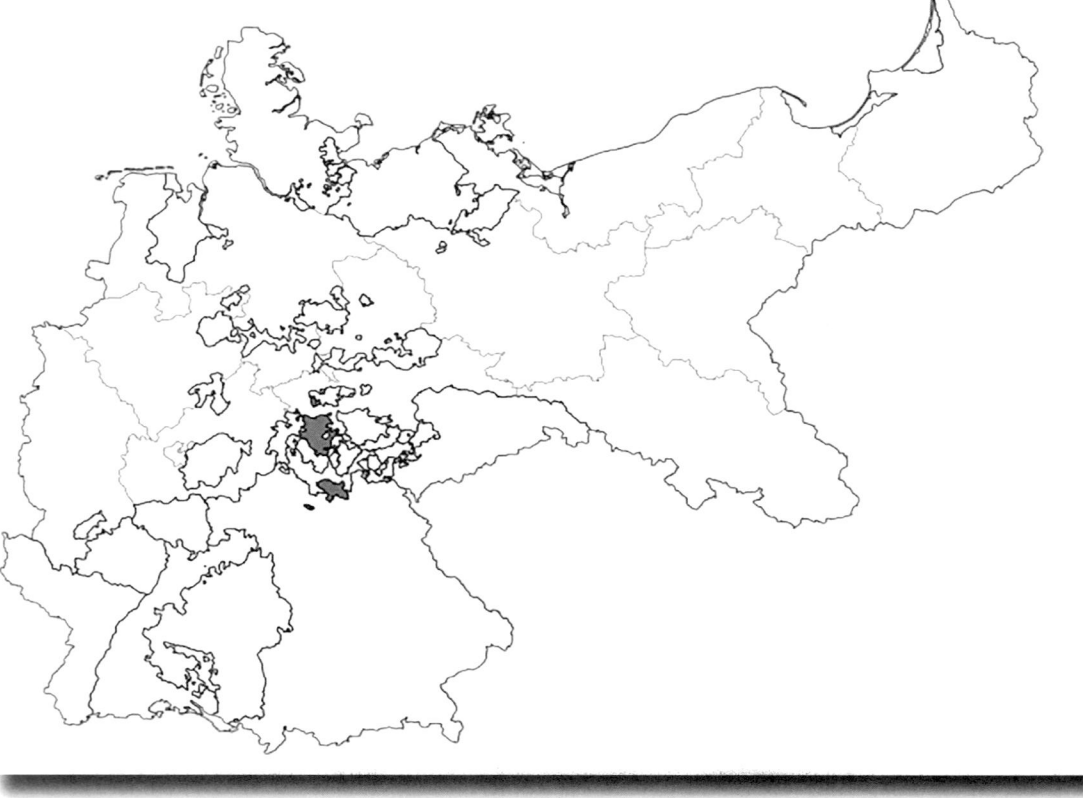

A map of the German Empire showing the political divisions of the various sovereign states. The darkened areas are the former dual duchy of Coburg and Gotha. My grandfather, Duke Carl Eduard of Saxe-Coburg and Gotha, ruled until November 1918.

inheritance went entirely to his brother Franz Josias, who was married to Princess Anne-Sophie of Schwarzburg-Rudolstadt. This couple were the parents of eight children, but only the firstborn and the youngest are of any interest to us. The firstborn, Ernst-Friedrich (1724-1800), was married to Sophie-Antoinette of Brünswick-Wolfenbüttel (1724-1802), whose father was Duke Ferdinand Albert II (1680-1735), whose descendants include most of Europe's royalty. The youngest son of Franz Josias and Anne-Sophie was Prince Friedrich-Josias (1737-1815), a well-known and very talented military leader who served under the Habsburg Holy Roman Emperor.

Duchess Sophie-Antoinette is best remembered in Coburg for the lavish lifestyle she led. In a way, she was doomed from the start of her marriage to Duke Ernst-Friedrich. Sophie-Antoinette was the poorest among a group of siblings who married extremely well. The middle child in a family of thirteen children, Sophie-Antoinette's brothers-in-law included: King Friedrich the Great and his brother Prince August of Prussia, and King Frederik V of Denmark. Her brother, Anton Ulrich, was the father of the ill-fated Tsar Ivan VI of Russia. Among such a distinguished and wealthy family group, poor Sophie-Antoinette simply could not compete, unless, that was, she spent beyond her husband's means, which she did. By the time Duke Franz-Josias died in 1800, the Duchy of Saxe-Coburg-Saalfeld, rich in property and art collections, was near bankruptcy. With war looming over the horizon, this was the nadir of my dynasty.

Duke Franz Friedrich Anton (1750-1806) succeeded his father at perhaps the most difficult time ever witnessed by Coburg. The duchy was bankrupt and the lack of resources seriously curtailed court life. Furthermore, Napoleon was preparing to invade the empire, and the German kingdoms, duchies and principalities were about to be defeated in battle and humiliated diplomatically. By 1806, Duke Franz Friedrich Anton, grandfather of Queen Victoria and Prince Albert, King Leopold II of the Belgians and King Ferdinand of Portugal, was a spent man. He died in Coburg on

Duke Franz Friedrich Anton of Saxe-Coburg-Saalfeld.

December 9, 1806. All around everything was destruction and desolation as the French overran Germany and the Fatherland was on its knees.

If one can argue that my ancestor was extremely unlucky in war and treasure, the same cannot be said, by any means, about his handsome children. Franz Friedrich Anton married firstly Princess Sophie of Saxe-Hildburghausen (1760-1776), from whom he did not have any descendants. One year later, he married Countess Augusta of Reuß-Ebersdorf (1757-1831), with whom he was to father one of the luckiest and best looking group of children royal Europe had ever witnessed until then, and arguably since. The children were: Sophie (1778-1835), married to Count Emmanuel Mensdorff-Pouilly; Antoinette (1779-1824), married to Duke Alexander of Württemberg; Juliane (1781-1860), married to Grand Duke Konstantin Pavlovich; Ernst I (1784-1844), married firstly to Princess Louise of Saxe-Gotha, and secondly to his niece Marie of Württemberg; Ferdinand (1785-1851), who married Princess Antonia Kohary; Victoria (1786-1861), firstly married to Fürst Karl of Leiningen, and

Duke Ernst I of Saxe-Coburg and Gotha.

secondly to Prince Edward, Duke of Kent; and Leopold (1790-1865), married firstly to Princess Charlotte of Wales and secondly to Princess Louise Marie d'Orléans. Leopold, as the reader may know, was the first Coburg to wear a royal crown. Presiding with a masterful eye over this brood was their mother, Duchess Augusta, who was the first of the formidable women that became such a distinguishable feature in our family!

When Duke Ernst I began his reign in Coburg, the family's fortunes were at their lowest ebb. His dukedom was occupied by Napoleon's forces and the French emperor had taxed the already broken treasury with high penalties to help pay for the enormous expenditures caused by his military campaigns. Napoleon truly had it out for the Coburgs, whom French considered treacherous and only too willing to betray their new overlord. In the end, Ernst I, accompanied by his brother Leopold had no option other than traveling to Paris in search of imperial pardon. During this journey the Coburg brothers became the toast of Paris, Leopold more so than his older brother. While there, Napoleon forgave them and at least for a short while all seemed back to normal, well, at least until the next major conflict when the Coburg brothers abandoned the French overlord at the first opportunity they had.

The Coburgs served in the armies that finally defeated Napoleon in 1814. For his cooperation and role in defeating the French emperor, Duke Ernst I received ample compensation from the Major Powers. *"Venture nothing … keep everything,"* one could safely argue, became Ernst I's motto and he followed this tenet religiously.[34] In the aftershock of the Napoleonic conflict, the Duke of Saxe-Coburg-Saalfeld sought to obtain as much benefit as diplomatically possible. Arguing, rightly so, that Coburg had suffered grave damages at the hands of Napoleon and his armies, he presented ambitious demands as compensation for the duchy's losses. Prussia, eager to please the Coburg duke, agreed and consequently some 404 square kilometers, formed mainly by the principality of Lichtenberg in the Saarland, were ceded to Coburg. These new territories yielded Ernst I a considerable yearly sum, which he lost little time in arguing was his and his alone, thus keeping Coburg politicians away from their administration. Disputes with the politicians immediately arose and these were not to disappear until Ernst I sold the principality to Prussia in 1834. The proceeds of the sale, the then Duke of Saxe-Coburg and Gotha claimed as his and used to acquire further personal property in Austria and Lower Franconia. Thus, Duke Ernst I planted the see of what was eventually to become the enormous legacy that Grandfather Coburg inherited in 1900.

Prince Ferdinand of Saxe-Coburg and Gotha.

Meanwhile, Duke Ernst I had married. His bride was one

of the most potentially advantageous alliances of his time, Princess Louise, only daughter of the extremely wealthy Duke August of Saxe-Gotha, who ruled his realm from within the large treasure filled rooms of Schloß Friedenstein in Gotha, one of Thüringen's largest palaces. Duke August was born in 1772 and he ascended the ducal throne in 1804. He firstly married Duchess Louise-Charlotte of Mecklenburg-Schwerin (1779-1801), by whom he had one daughter, Louise. The year following his wife's death, August remarried Caroline-Amalie of Hesse-Cassel (1771-1848), but this second marriage remained childless. As August only had one surviving brother, upon his death in 1822 Duke Friedrich IV succeeded him. The new ruler of Gotha, who had converted to Catholicism, was not to have a long reign. He died unmarried in Gotha in February 1825. His death, in fact, set off the last major partitioning and reapportioning of Saxon land among the remaining branches of the family: Weimar-Eisenach, Hildburghausen (Altenburg), Meiningen and Coburg-Saalfeld.

Negotiations over the Saxe-Gotha inheritance were lengthy and fraught with complicated diplomatic maneuverings. In the end, a treaty signed in November 1826 settled the matter. It is not surprising that Coburg came out the largest beneficiary since, after all, Duke Ernst I's two sons were the only grandchildren of the late Duke August of Saxe-Gotha. The bulk of the duchy of Gotha came to Duke Ernst I, along with the phenomenal and priceless ducal collections amassed over the centuries by that branch of the Wettin family. On top of these territories, Ernst I received in trade Königsberg and Sonnefeld from the Duke of Saxe-Hildburghausen (from then on known as Duke of Saxe-Altenburg), as well as the estates of Callenberg and Gauerstadt from the Duke of Saxe-Meiningen. Saalfeld, Duke Ernst I decided, was well worth ceding in order to build a more cohesive realm and not one that seemed a psychedelic patchwork of territories spread around Thüringen. Consequently, the ducal title was changed to Saxe-Coburg and Gotha and Duke Ernst I's realm now possessed two duchies with separate governance and administration but under one crown.

Dowager Duchess Augusta of Saxe-Coburg-Saalfeld, my great-great-great-great-grandmother.

Allow me to mention one more important acquisition made by my great-great-great-grandfather Duke Ernst I: Greinburg. He purchased this large domain earlier owned by the Counts of Dietrichstein in 1821, along with several other lordships: Kreuzen, Ruttenstein, Prandegg, Zellhof and Aich. The Greinburg was erected between 1488-1493. Its prominent position, seated atop a high promontory overlooking the Danube, gave it a privileged defensive and trade position. It was part of the dowry of Countess Anna of Meggau upon her marriage to Count Ludwig Sigismund of Dietrichstein. From that point in history onward, the Greinburg was closely related to the Dietrichsteins until they sold it in the early 1800s. Interestingly, Queen Victoria, as widow of Prince Albert of Saxe-Coburg and Gotha, briefly owned the Greinburg in 1893 after the death of her childless brother-in-law Duke Ernst II. Anyhow, along with the castle, the purchase made by Duke Ernst I included considerable forests and agricultural

Duchess Louise of Saxe-Coburg-Saalfeld. She was the mother of the Prince Consort as well as aunt and mother-in-law of Queen Victoria.

Hereditary Prince Ernst and Prince Albert of Saxe-Coburg and Gotha.

estates. These lands always provided a steady income to the private coffers of the ducal family, income that after the loss of the bulk of our properties after the Second World War was to play an important role in our efforts to rebuild what had been lost to Communist abuse and expropriations in what became the oxymoronically named German Democratic Republic (DDR), which was everything but democratic. The Greinburg has played an important role in our family history and I am personally quite fond of it. My father lived there in retirement and my youngest son, Alexander, currently lives and works there. I have spent long periods there as well and visit it quite frequently. In 2003 it was at the Greinburg where many of our royal and aristocratic cousins, as well as countless friends of ours, gathered to help me celebrate my 60th birthday. It was a fun party, one that has always remained quite vivid among the countless memories I have of my now long life.

Now, let us return to the unfortunate and poor Duchess Louise. She married Duke Ernst I in 1817 and at the time her mother-in-law, Duchess Augusta described her thusly, *"The poor little bride was so trembling and overcome when she entered the room that she could not speak for crying. She is a sweet little thing, not beautiful, but very pretty through her charm and vivacity. Every feature of her face is expressive; her charming blue eyes under their long black eyelashes often look so sad, and then she is suddenly a gay, wild child. She has a pleasant voice, speaks well, and is at the same time so friendly and intelligent that one must like her. I hope she is still growing, as she is very small."*[35] When the couple made their triumphant entry into Coburg, the people, as they have always done with us, received them with demonstrations of great joy. This reminds me, briefly, of the overall excitement when we witnessed in Coburg

Duke Ernst II of Saxe-Coburg and Gotha.

Prince Albert, the Prince Consort, my great-great-grandfather.

on the wedding day of my eldest son, Hereditary Prince Hubertus, in 2009. Worry not, for I will return to Hubertus and Alexander, as well as Stephanie (my daughter) later on.

Within a year of their wedding, Duke Ernst I and Duchess Louise welcomed their first child, a boy who one day would rule as Ernst II. One year later, on August 26, 1819, at Schloß Rosenau, Duchess Louise gave birth to a second son, Albert, who in due time would become the true architect of the Coburg rise to the highest echelons of European politics.

After the birth of Prince Albert, however, the differences between his parents became increasingly apparent. They, Ernst and Louise, in fact, had very little in common, other than their love for the children. He was fond of

Schloß Ketschendorf, Coburg.

Schloß Greinburg, our main Austrian home. It was acquired by Duke Ernst I nearly two hundred years ago.

A painting from 1887 depicting Queen Victoria with the Duchess of Albany and some grandchildren. From left: The Duchess of Albany and Aunt Alice; Grandfather Coburg; Princess Patricia and Princess Margaret of Connaught; and Queen Victoria.

hunting, a sport she abhorred; she loved dancing and parties, while he preferred entertaining within a small circle. Ernst found it impossible to find satisfaction in the arms of his inexperienced young wife, and did not remain faithful to her for long. Soon, he resumed his adventures with other ladies of the court. *"Ernst will go to Carlsbad,"* Louise confessed in despair, adding, *"How sad I already am you can well imagine, and mixed up with this is the tormenting feeling of jealousy. I am always afraid of the beauties there."*[36] Louise knew that her husband was untrue to their marriage vows and this pained her greatly. Alone and lonely inside the vast rooms of Coburg's vast Schloß Ehrenburg, Duchess Louise sought companionship and distraction in the company of others. *"Sensitive and romantic, her young heart fluttered easily in its thirst for love and with the attentions she received from handsome young officers."* The innocent flirtations soon turned serious when Alexander von Hanstein, a former Austrian cavalry officer attached to the Court Battalion, began courting her. Described as a *"good looking young man, with black, curly hair, shining bright eyes, and resolute manner … von Hanstein sighed and languished like a turtle dove."* Louise even confessed that he *"did a thousand pretty, amorous things that amused me very much."* Soon, the lonely Duchess of Saxe-Coburg-Saalfeld threw caution to the wind and made her feelings for von Hanstein known to him. Their obvious attraction soon sparked suspicions and led the couple into trouble. Duke Ernst was *"not the man to tolerate public cuckolding, notwithstanding that his own treatment of Louise had been largely responsible for this state of affairs. Separation followed soon after and Ernst moved into his summer palace at Ketschendorff, while Louise retired to her beloved Rosenau."*[37]

What followed was very tragic. The ducal separation caused quite a stir in Coburg, where the townsfolk blamed Ernst I and his misbehaving for having planted the seed of the couple's marital problems. In an effort to force the couple's reconciliation, Coburgers surrounded Schloß Ketschendorff,

Duke Ernst I of Saxe-Coburg and Gotha.

where Ernst I was (along with his mother and children) and forced him to return to Coburg. Another crowd had gone to Rosenau and asked Duchess Louise to return to Coburg. *"The people love me to a degree of worship,"* Louise later wrote, *"They went in thousands to Rosenau. As I stepped into my carriage they burst through the hedges and railings cut the ropes and harnessed themselves to the carriage and pulled me from Rosenau, with unceasing shouts and hurrahs, through the town and stopped before the castle. The love was most touching and they were all armed. When I arrived at the castle I went on the balcony and thanked them for their love. After shouts and hurrahs, they solemnly sang Now Thank We All Our God!"*[38] Forced to appear together on the balcony of Schloß Ehrenburg, that was the last time the public saw Ernst I and Louise next to each other. The couple divorced soon after and Duchess Louise, who departed Coburg quietly, was never seen again. She married von Hanstein, but her happiness was short as she died of uterine cancer in 1831. Duke Ernst I married again, his second choice being Duchess Marie of Württemberg, his own niece, but there were no children from this marriage. She was a close friend of her cousins, and stepchildren, and once installed in Coburg dedicated her efforts to the duchy's cultural life. She supported the construction of the new Landestheater Coburg and was a patron of Franz Liszt. She also was the leading force behind an institution for young girls called the "Gothaer Marien-Institut," while also donating funds to establish a refuge for young children in Coburg, the "Marienschulstiftung," still in existence today.

Duke Ernst I died in 1844. Behind him he left a conflicted and complicated legacy – new acquisitions, but large debts; two marriages, but many mistresses; two sons, but far more out-of-wedlock children. From London, when told of the news of his father's death, Prince Albert wrote to his brother Ernst II, *"How I should like to be with you* [his brother Ernst] *and see the beloved face once more, though it is cold. We no longer have any home. This is a break that you cannot feel in the same way. Poor subjects, be a father to them!"* [39]

The reign of Duke Ernst II was to last until 1893. A difficult man to his very core, Ernst II also was an avid politician with an incredibly ambitious personality. At one point, when the unification of the German kingdoms under one head was discussed, Ernst II believed himself to be the most viable candidate for the position. One can but imagine what the Hohenzollerns and Chancellor Bismarck must have thought of the Duke of Saxe-Coburg and Gotha's ambitions!

In May 1842, Ernst II married Princess Alexandrine of Baden (1820-1904). She was one of the daughters of Grand Duke Karl Leopold (1790-1852) and of his wife Princess Sophie of Sweden (1801-1865), of the old Vasa dynasty. Alexandrine's siblings included an interesting group of royalties: Grand Duke Ludwig II (1824-1858); Grand Duke Friedrich I (1826-1907), who married Princess Louise of Prussia, the only daughter of Kaiser Wilhelm I; Marie (1834-1899), who married Fürst Ernst of Leiningen, Queen Victoria's nephew; and Cäcilie (1839-1891), who married Grand Duke Michael Nikolaevich of Russia, this last union continuing Coburg's proximity to the Russian court, which began with the children of Duke Franz Friedrich Anton. Duke Ernst II, who had no children with his wife, was jokingly referred to as "the father of Coburg," and this name did not come for his prowess in matters of state, but for his countless adventures with willing ladies.

However, the childlessness of the ducal couple was a cause for concern, and not just to them. Monarchy needs an heir to provide security and stability to the following generation. A ruler without a clear heir is one who may potentially leave behind a succession mess, an entanglement to be avoided at all costs to protect

Duke Ernst II of Saxe-Coburg and Gotha.

the integrity of the realm. Hence, by the early 1850s, after a decade of childless marriage, Ernst II decided that something ought to be done about his successor. Next in line was his brother Albert, but since he was married to Queen Victoria, his succession in Coburg and Gotha was unfeasible. Albert, however, had several sons. According to the ducal constitution of 1852 and later, in 1855, the law of the Ducal House of Saxe-Coburg and Gotha, declared, once again, that the succession was mandated by male primogeniture. Therefore, in the absence of legitimate male sons from Duke Ernst II, the succession would pass to his brother Albert, from whom Albert's children had a stake on claims to the ducal throne. Albert's eldest son, the future King Edward VII, had renounced his rights as it would have been unthinkable that the English monarch would be the ruler of a German duchy. Therefore, the next son, Prince Alfred, Duke of Edinburgh, was chosen to succeed Uncle Ernst.

Prince Alfred, Duke of Edinburgh, later Duke of Saxe-Coburg and Gotha.

The Duke of Edinburgh entered the Royal Navy at an early age. He simply loved sailing and was going to develop the rough and tumble personality of a lifelong sailor. Whenever not on a ship, he found great joy in hunting and in due time he became one of Europe's best shots. In 1874 Alfred married, in St. Petersburg, Grand Duchess Marie Alexandrovna (1853-1920), the only surviving daughter of Tsar Alexander II and of his first wife, the former Princess Marie of Hesse and by Rhine. They had five children, among them one boy, Alfred Jr., whose untimely and unfortunate death in 1899 threw the succession back in the air since his father only had four daughters left, and women could not succeed to the ducal throne.

This is the point where Grandfather Coburg ceased to be an English prince and was forced by circumstances to become a German one!

The Coburg Succession became a matter of great confrontation between Queen Victoria and Kaiser Wilhelm II. Next-in-line came Prince Arthur, Duke of Connaught, followed by his only son Prince Arthur of Connaught. The Coburgs believed that the succession was a private family affair and in so believing they chose to ignore the Kaiser's opinion on the matter. This annoyed the powers at court in Berlin. Kaiser Wilhelm II, who always liked to be the "beau of every ball," believed otherwise. Negotiations between the Duke of Connaught, Queen Victoria and politicians

Grand Duchess Marie Alexandrovna of Russia.

German Kaiser Wilhelm II.

King Pedro V of Portugal.

in Coburg and Gotha soon were thrown for a loop when the Kaiser demanded to be a participant in the succession discussions. The Kaiser made it clear that *"foreign princes who publicly advance their claims to German thrones, as the Duke of Connaught had done, must sever their connection with foreign countries, acquire German nationality, have their principal residence in Germany, and arrange for their sons to have a German education."*[40] Although the duchy's politicians objected to such a stand, there was nothing that could be done to ignore the All-Powerful's line on the sand.

At Eton, however, two young cousins also discussed the matter. Well, one told the other what would happen if he did not go to Germany. Prince Arthur of Connaught, who had no intention of becoming a German ruler, threatened to either renounce the succession or the ducal throne at twenty-one if he were forced to succeed Uncle Alfred. He also threatened Grandfather Coburg *"with a thrashing if he did not at once offer himself as a candidate."* Queen Victoria was in an uproar over the entire complicated matter and one of her ladies-in-waiting later wrote: *"The Queen is rather overwhelmed by her family and the Coburg succession problems, endless discussions, some of them rather stormy."*[41]

In the end, the Duke of Connaught, unwilling to abandon his military career, made a fateful decision. Taking into consideration his own son's position, as well as the Kaiser's demands, he decided that the Connaught line would take itself out of the Coburg succession. Duke Alfred communicated the decision to his nephew Kaiser Wilhelm II, claiming that, *"to my great surprise, he* (Connaught) *has decided to stand down."* The renunciation not only concerned the Duke of Connaught. *"Unfortunately, it also seems that the resignation applies to his son* (Prince Arthur Jr.)." Duke Alfred asked his Imperial nephew to have a talk with the Duke of Connaught and help the family find a solution. Queen Victoria, wishing to have a final say in the matter, made her opinion very clear when she sent her Imperial grandson a letter in which she stated her position: *"Respecting the Coburg affairs, I will surely say that I entirely agree with Arthur and his views, which he will communicate to you."*[42] And with this the die was cast and the Connaught line took itself out of the running. The only candidate left to succeed Uncle Alfred was a young Etonian just a few weeks short of his 15th birthday: the Duke of Albany. It has also been repeated within the family that Prince Arthur Jr., who was also an Etonian, told Grandfather Coburg that he had better accept the ducal thrones or expect a thrashing from him. Hence, without a choice in the matetr, my grandfather was taken out of his comfortable English existence and shipped off to Imperial Germany to begin the long process of becoming a good German princeling.

One final word …

It is interesting to me how the Connaught cousins took themselves out of the succession and by doing so provided a more stable succession in Coburg. This is particularly when I think of what their ultimate fate became. Prince Arthur of Connaught married Princess Alexandra of Fife, a stunningly beautiful woman, who was the eldest daughter of his first cousin Louise, the Duchess of Fife. They, Arthur and Alexandra, had one son Alastair, who was their only child. Arthur Connaught also enjoyed a distinguished career in the Royal Army and fought with distinction in France and Belgium during the Great War. Later, Prince Arthur also served as Governor-General in South Africa, a position Aunt Alice's husband, the Earl of Athlone, would occupy as well. Upon returning from South Africa, Prince Arthur was very involved in charitable work and continued serving as a dutiful member of the Royal Family until his untimely death, caused by stomach cancer, in 1938. The Duke of Connaught, a venerable old soldier, survived his son by four years, dying in 1942 already his nineties.

Sadly, Prince Alastair of Connaught, who became the 2nd Duke of Connaught in 1942, did not survive very long. He also served in the army and was assigned as aide-de-camp to the Earl of Athlone, who served as Governor-General of Canada. Prince Alastair lived with Aunt Alice and her husband in Ottawa. It was there that he died in 1943 after freezing to death – apparently, the young man was inebriated.

This brings me to a sad set of circumstances affecting many members of the House of Coburg. Some historians have mentioned "the Coburg curse," a spell placed on our house because of some bad deeds regarding the Kohary inheritance and the role played by Ferdinand of Saxe-Coburg-Saalfeld in gaining the fortune of his father-in-law. I personally don't believe in such things. However, many Coburg princes have had to live through the unimaginable ordeal of outliving their eldest son. The list is large and ominous and seems never-ending as even my late cousin Johannes Heinrich, of the Austrian branch of the family, had to experience this terrible loss. I cannot begin to imagine what it would be to lose any of my children.

Yet it is food for thought when one looks at the ominous list of themale Coburgs who have lost their eldest son: King Leopold I of the Belgians lived through this experience twice: firstly with the stillborn child his first wife gave birth to at Claremont House in 1817, and secondly with the firstborn child, Louis Philippe, from his second marriage to Princess Louise Marie d'Orléans. Next came King Consort Ferdinand of Portugal who in 1861 lost his eldest son Pedro V, along

The Duke of Clarence.

Prince Arthur, Duke of Connaught.

Prince Arthur of Connaught.

Grandfather Coburg and Uncle Bertel.

with two other sons, all victims of a tragic epidemic that nearly wiped out the whole royal family. Our Belgian cousins, Leopold II and his brother the Count of Flanders, lost their sons Leopold and Baudouin in 1869 and 1891 respectively. In the early 1890s this awful "curse" came to the homes of the Prince of Wales, the future Edward VII, who lost his son the Duke of Clarence in early 1892; and to Prince Ludwig Gaston, who lost his eldest son (Peter August) to madness at about the same time. The young man, who had convinced himself that he could one day inherit the Brazilian throne of his grandfather Emperor Pedro II, lost his mind after the Imperial family's overthrow. Although he survived until 1934, Peter August was lost to the world the moment he entered the mental institution where he was placed to keep him from hurting himself.

This rash of untimely deaths visited the family again 1899 with the death of Alfred Jr., an event that had deep repercussions for my own branch of the family. Ten years later Prince August Leopold, the ancestor of my remaining Coburg-Kohary cousins, lost his own eldest son, August Clemens, when the boy was only fourteen-years old. Seven years later, while Europe was in the midst of the Great War, Prince Philipp of Saxe-Coburg and Gotha, Head of the Coburg and Kohary Fideikomiss located in the Austro-Hungarian Empire, lost his only son, Prince Leopold. This is perhaps one of the darkest episodes in our family's long history. Leopold, who had to marry equally in order to inherit his father's vast fortune, was involved with a Viennese actress who went a bit crazy when he ended their relationship. The young woman shot Leopold and poured acid on his face before committing suicide. He survived a few months and died during a surgery to repair his eyesight.

I already mentioned the death of Prince Arthur of Connaught in 1938, a great loss no doubt. Even worse, if there can be such a comparison of pain and loss, were the deaths of King Boris III and my Uncle Bertel, both taking place in 1943. The Bulgarian King died in August after returning to Sofia from a stormy meeting with Adolf Hitler. All sorts of rumors have been spread about these sad events, but I will not deal with them here. Suffice to say that this loss was a tragedy to his country and family, as well as for his father King Ferdinand, who lived exiled in Coburg's Burglaßschloßen, where he died in 1948. Three months later, nearly to the day, Uncle Bertel, who by then was Grandfather Coburg's heir since Uncle Leo had renounced his rights in the early 1930s, died in action over Romania. Uncle Bertel's death was deeply felt by all, one of them being my mother who liked him very much. Uncle Bertel joined the war effort to fight for the Fatherland, but also to escape troubles at home. Poor man, I can only think, to have such a death and so far away from home. His body was recovered and brought for burial in the family plot overlooking Schloß Callenberg.

Once again, an aerial tragedy struck the family when in 1972 Prince William of Gloucester, eldest son of the Duke of Gloucester died when his airplane crashed. The English cousins had changed the dynasty's name to Windsor in 1917, but for all intents and purposes they are Coburgs, of course. This should not matter whatsoever as the ancient origins of one's family play little role in one's patriotism. My cousin The Queen has demonstrated countless times, daily, and through her long life that she thinks of her people and realm above all else.

Fifteen years later, in 1987, an untimely end came to the only son of my cousin Johannes Heinrich, of the Coburg-Kohary branch. A promising young man, Johannes Albert was the only son of his father and his second wife, Princess Mathilde of Saxony. He was born in Innsbruck in 1969 and was quite an avid mountaineer. The youngster died in August 1987 when he fell off a mountainside. His death was a devastating shock to his desolate parents, as well as to his half-sister, my cousin Felicitas, who has visited Coburg frequently.

Fifteen Coburg princes have outlived their sons since 1817 – this is an awful chapter of our long family history. I truly hope it is just a tragic set of uncanny coincidences, for I as a father would not ever want to bury a child!

Prince Leopold of Saxe-Coburg and Gotha.

My cousins Felicitas and Johannes Albert of Saxe-Coburg and Gotha.

I did it my way ...

Chapter IV
Grandfather Coburg's English Roots

The story of Grandfather Coburg is one fraught with painful contradictions. I only met him a few times when I was still a child. He died when I was eleven-years-old and, thus, I cannot say that I had a deep relationship with him. What I know about him is what my family, particularly my mother, has shared with me. I have found it interesting that I do share many coincidences with Grandfather Coburg.

Just like Grandfather Coburg, at birth I was not expected one day to inherit the Coburg legacy. In his case, he was the only son of the youngest son of Prince Albert, Queen Victoria's husband. By the time Grandfather Coburg was born, in front of him in the Coburg line of succession stood two uncles and several cousins. In my case, when I was born as the eldest son of the youngest son in the family of the last reigning Duke of Saxe-Coburg and Gotha, my father had two living older brothers. Yes, my Uncle Johann Leopold had disqualified for entering what then was considered an "unequal" union, but there remained my Uncle Bertel, who could potentially have children in spite of his orientation. Sadly, Uncle Hubertus died later in the year of my birth and that cleared the way for me to one day inherit the Coburg Legacy.

Grandfather Coburg was raised in England until he was a teenager. In fact, he did not have to move to Germany until 1899. Much like him, I, although born in Germany, left my Fatherland at an early age to be raised in a foreign land across the tempestuous Atlantic Ocean. I only returned permanently to Germany when I was a teenager and it was not until then, like my grandfather, that the country became my home.

The Dowager Duchess of Albany with her children, Princess Alice and Charles Edward, Duke of Albany.

While Queen Victoria's family were polyglots, using English and German to communicate, Grandfather Coburg's birth language was English. It was not until 1899 that he had to shift mental gears and begin using German as his main language. This was due to his having to enter school in Germany and having to begin his preparation to assume the dual thrones of Coburg and Gotha. I was born in Germany and my first language was German. However, by 1949 Mother had relocated to the United States to start a new life with her second husband. I was raised speaking English in America for at the time there still prevailed a certain anti-German feeling because of the Second World War. On top of that, Mother did not want her second husband, Richard Whitten, to feel "outside the loop" because he did not know German. So, English it was what we used to communicate. It was not until I returned to Germany to perform my military duties that I had to learn German so I could function. I am sure that several of my superiors in the German army were quite frustrated with my initial inability to understand their commands, and I know for a fact that several of my fellow soldiers laughed heartily at my expense due to my general sense of disorientation in that new environment.

Opposite page: The Duke of Albany.

Grandfather Coburg was born four months after the tragic death of his father. A loving yet stern mother who wished to get the best out of her only son raised him. In my case, although I had a father, he was an absentee one at best. Father was a terribly complex man. At best he was a distant father, one who was far more comfortable leaving the raising of his children to others, while exempting himself from the arduous task of being father and mentor. I think my father wanted his children to see him as a friend, not a father figure. Hence, he was absent from our childhood. This same fate was suffered by my siblings (Claudia, Beatrice and Adrian), who lost him at too young an age when he simply gave up on his second wife and moved on to start life, a third time, with a new wife. I think that Father was a weak man; he was also a very complex human being.

Much like Grandfather Coburg, however, once given the responsibility of managing the Coburg legacy, I did my very best to pass to my children a solid enterprise, one that was healthy, growing, respected. While the two world wars seriously interfered with Grandfather Coburg's expert management of the Coburg estate, in my case I was tasked with rebuilding from the ashes what remained of the immense patrimony my grandfather had once inherited and cherished with such devotion. I do believe that if the wars had not ripped apart Grandfather Coburg's life, he would have been remembered by history quite differently and not for the terrible mistakes he made.

Opposite page: The Dowager Duchess of Albany with Aunt Alice and Grandfather Coburg, who is wearing a Scottish kilt.

Charles Edward was born a Prince of the United Kingdom and Ireland, and at birth he inherited the Dukedom of Albany, a title his father had received from his mother, Queen Victoria. In Germany, my grandfather was known by the Germanized version of his name, Carl Eduard, which is how I will refer to him from here onward. Grandfather Coburg was born at Claremont House on July 18, 1884.[43] His parents were the late Prince Leopold, Duke of Albany, Queen Victoria and Prince Albert's youngest, and erudite, son, and Princess Helene of Waldeck und Pyrmont, one of the many daughters of the ruler of a miniscule principality formed by lands in Hesse and Lower Saxony.

Great-Grandfather Albany was born in 1853. Soon after his birth, much to their horror, his parents discovered that their plump little son suffered from hemophilia. This is a dreadful genetic disorder that impairs the body's ability to control blood clotting, used to stop bleeding when a blood vessel is broken. Hence, even a bump could have catastrophic consequences, while cuts were usually deadly. Males, who can pass the gene to their daughters, suffer from Hemophilia – while females are carriers of the dreaded gene.

Queen Victoria with the Dukes of York, George and Mary.

Several historians have argued that hemophilia, an inherited condition, appeared in Queen Victoria's family because she married a first cousin, Prince Albert of Saxe-Coburg and Gotha. I personally do not think this was the cause of its appearance. Instead, I believe that in their case this was a mutation since no one in the family seems to have been afflicted by this disorder before. Several years ago, however, an English author alleged in her biography of Great-Grandfather Albany that hemophilia was already present in our distant Mensdorff-Pouilly relatives, descendants of our common ancestor Duke Franz Friedrich Anton of Saxe-Coburg-Saalfeld (1750-1806), but I doubt any real medical studies have been done to prove this very interesting theory.

Hemophilia, as I mentioned before, was quite present in

Schloß Rosenau.

Queen Victoria and Prince Albert's extended brood. While Great-Grandfather Albany was the only one of their sons to be a hemophiliac, several of their daughters apparently were carriers. Some studies point to the Princess Royal, Victoria, Kaiser Wilhelm II's mother, having been a carrier. Her next sister, Alice, Grand Duchess of Hesse and by Rhine, was indeed a carrier, as was their youngest sister, Princess Beatrice, the great-grandmother of my cousin King Juan Carlos of Spain.

It was through these family connections that hemophilia appeared, with tragic consequences, in the families of the last Tsar of Russia, Nicholas II, and King Alfonso XIII of Spain. Nicholas Alexandrovich, who was then Tsesarevich of Russia, became engaged to Princess Alix of Hesse and by Rhine at Schloß Rosenau, a small and quaint country residence that Duke Alfred of Saxe-Coburg and Gotha, Grandfather Coburg's predecessor, had in the outskirts of Coburg. The Rosenau, as we call it, still stands, a proud monument to a past long gone. Anyhow, the Royal Mob, as Queen Victoria used to call large gatherings of royalties, converged in Coburg in April 1894 to attend the wedding of Duke Alfred's daughter, Victoria Melita, to his nephew Grand Duke Ernst Ludwig of Hesse and by Rhine, one of the most artistic rulers any German estate ever had. Apparently everyone was delighted with the pairing of such a handsome couple, that is, everyone except the couple who got along well as friends and cousins, but not as spouses. This was the case with my own parents, frankly. My mother never uttered a nasty word about Father for she liked him as a cousin and a friend, but certainly not as a husband.

Anyhow, the curse of hemophilia had tragic consequences in both Russia and Spain. In St Petersburg, after the birth of four daughters the Empress finally gave birth to a son in 1904. Everyone was jubilant at the thought that Russia finally had an heir. What those outside the imperial circle did not know was that the Tsesarevich Alexis Nicholaevich was stricken with hemophilia. His constant attacks and near-death experiences made the Empress retreat from public view. The Tsar, who adored his wife and children, also suffered greatly witnessing his valiant son's condition. In their own little bubble of sycophants, Nicholas and Alexandra surrounded themselves with the worst possible intimates, people whose own self-interests hindered on the isolation in which the inhabitants of the Alexander Palace in Tsarskoe Selo lived.

When war broke out in 1914, Russia was completely unprepared. The German juggernaut made that quite apparent. Losses mounted at a tragic, infernally overwhelming rate. Every fallen soldier added to the Russian people's disillusionment with their once-beloved Tsar. Furthermore, the rumormongering machine was oiled with tales of misbehavior around Grigorii Rasputin, a pseudo monk, who somehow was able to calm the Empress and bring solace to the poor Alexis during his bleeding episodes. The entire house of cards came crashing down in February 1917 when revolution spread in the Russian capital and Tsar Nicholas II was forced to abdicate. Within eighteen-months his family lay bathed in blood on the floor of their prison house in Yekaterinburg. About a dozen other Romanovs suffered the same harrowing fate and with that butchery the dynasty was at an end.

In Spain, hemophilia afflicted the King's eldest son, the Prince of Asturias. Alfonso XIII had married Princess Victoria Eugenie of Battenberg, a first cousin of Grandfather Coburg, who at the time was one of Europe's most beautiful princesses. They were married in a spectacular wedding ceremony held in Madrid in 1906 and attended by the Royal Mob, leading them was Dowager Duchess Marie of Saxe-Coburg and Gotha, the Russian-born widow of Duke Alfred. Inside the church was a veritable who's who of European royalty and had the attempt on the couple taken place there, it would have been an even bigger tragedy. Instead, the anarchist who tried to assassinate the newlyweds launched a bomb at their carriage as the wedding procession returned to Madrid's vast royal palace, Oriente. Although the King and Queen of Spain escaped, her wedding dress was drenched in blood from the countless victims of the heinous act.

Tragedy was to pursue this couple, much as it haunted our Russian cousins. A year after their wedding, Victoria Eugenia, as she was known in Spain, gave birth to their first child, a boy named Alfonso, who as heir already received the title of Prince of Asturias. The family soon discovered his affliction after bleeding caused by circumcision would not stop. A second son, Jaime, was born healthy but later on suffered hearing problems caused by a botched surgery. Next came a daughter, Infanta Beatriz, who all evidence seems to point having been a carrier. Then the fourth child, Fernando, was stillborn. María Cristina, the next child, was healthy, as was the fourth boy, Juan, born in 1913. One year later, the Spanish queen gave birth a seventh time, her last child being another hemophiliac boy, Gonzalo.

King Alfonso XIII was advised that his bride could be tainted with the hemophilia gene, yet he insisted on marrying her. Later on he blamed Victoria Eugenia and their rift caused the king serious problems as he sought a life filled with swift passions and entanglements, all the while refusing to recognize the crown was in trouble. In 1931 the republicans obtained large electoral majorities in the urban areas and the King decided to leave Spain. He spent his exile in France and Italy, while his wife went her separate way and settled in Lausanne, Switzerland. In due time brothers Alfonso and Gonzalo died in car accidents, their

King Alfonso XIII of Spain.

Queen Victoria Eugenia of Spain (Ena of Battenberg).

Claremont House has a long royal history dating several centuries. It was the home of King Leopold I before he ascended the Belgian throne. Later it housed his queen's French relations when in 1848 they were overthrown. Eventually, it passed to the Duke of Albany, my great-grandfather. In 1884, Grandfather Coburg was born there.

hemophilia playing a fatal role in bringing about their sad and untimely end. King Juan Carlos, who assumed the throne in 1975 and reigned until June 2014, was the eldest son of Infante Juan, Alfonso XIII's only healthy son.

I do wonder how different matters would have been had hemophilia not killed Great-Grandfather Albany and afflicted the heirs to the Russian and Spanish thrones. In our case, it is quite likely that the Duke of Albany would have succeeded in Coburg instead of his son, thus giving Grandfather Coburg more time to prepare for the role future had in store for him. However, that was not the case as the Duke of Albany died when his wife was four months' pregnant with my grandfather when she became a widow.

Great-Grandfather Albany was a talented young man, perhaps the most intellectual among Queen Victoria's sons. His brother the future King Edward VII was a self-made diplomat, perhaps among Europe's most talented experts in international relations. Duke Alfred was a sailor to his very core – having to take the Coburg legacy at the death of his Uncle Ernst in 1893 was not a job change he took with joy. The ducal coffers were in disarray and Duke Alfred spent his short reign putting the ducal affairs in order, only to die in 1900. He was in his mid-fifties and his widow Marie felt cheated as all the work they had done to restore the ducal inheritance was now to be enjoyed by a nephew they barely knew, Carl Eduard, my grandfather. The third brother, Arthur, Duke of Connaught, was a military officer of great distinction. Great-Grandfather Albany was an avid reader and a very good student. He attended Oxford and traveled widely to further his knowledge. His mother the Queen relied on her youngest son to serve her as private secretary, a role the Duke of Albany both cherished and deeply disliked. He cherished it because of the access it provided him, but he also disliked it because it meant becoming his mother's constant companion. This he particularly battled, as he wanted to gain independence, set-up his own household, find a wife and become a father. He never accepted that hemophilia was to keep him from achieving his dreams.

Reluctantly, in 1880 Queen Victoria gave the Duke of Albany his own home. The beautiful property was Claremont House, a residence with a vast, and at times, sad royal history. Initially Lord Clive acquired the property of an aristocratic family, Claremont House with the fortune he made in India. Then he spent the astronomic sum of £100,000 on his time to build a Palladian-style residence on a park designed by the unequalled Capability Brown, the quintessential designer of English gardens.

Claremont House's royal history began when it was given to Princess Charlotte of Wales and Prince Leopold of Saxe-Coburg-Saalfeld, who married in 1816. She died at Claremont House the following year after giving birth to a stillborn son. Leopold,

The Duke of Albany in the reading salon at Claremont House. Among Queen Victoria's four sons, none other reached the intellectual standards of Great-grandfather Albany, a true Renaissance prince.

who in 1831 became King of the Belgians, retained Claremont House until his death in 1865, when it returned to Queen Victoria. In 1848, when the French Royal Family was exiled, King Louis Philippe arrived in England. There, his son-in-law Leopold I of the Belgians allowed him use of Claremont House, where the exiled monarch lived until his death in 1850. This was the second death to take place within the walls of Claremont House. The Duke of Albany was in awe of his new home and its sad past. Once when a guest informed him that his mother was born there when his grandfather owned Claremont House, Albany sardonically replied, *"I am very glad to hear of anyone being born here … The place is haunted with death; there is a tragedy in every room."*[44]

When his mother gave the go-ahead to find a bride, Leopold traveled to Germany, where the English royals traditionally found their spouses. Off his list of possible brides was one for whom he cared deeply, Friederike of Hannover, who had not responded to his approaches since she was already in love with one of her father's aides-de-camp. Along with Great-Grandfather Albany came a list of eligible princesses that included, among others: Elisabeth of Hesse-Kassel, Victoria of Baden, Karoline-Mathilde of Schleswig-Holstein-Augustenburg and the daughters of Fürst Georg Viktor of Waldeck und Pyrmont.

Elisabeth of Hesse-Kassel was initially interested, but in the end she chose to marry Hereditary Prince Leopold Friedrich of Anhalt (1855-1886), who seemed a physically stronger candidate. Sadly for the poor woman, her husband died young and she survived him, a widow, for nearly seventy years. Princess Victoria of Baden seemed a willing candidate, but her mother, Great-Grandfather Albany later said, made too much fuss and raised too many objections. She married Crown Prince Gustaf of Sweden, their grandson, Gustaf Adolf, married in 1932 my Aunt Bylla. The Augustenburgs also seemed just as unwilling to take a chance and my great-grandfather's chances to land the hand of one of their available daughters were unsuccessful. Interestingly, Karoline-Mathilde, who married Duke Friedrich of Schleswig-Holstein-Sonderburg-Glücksburg, was the mother of both my grandmothers. However, the more my grandfather was politely shunned, the more his efforts increased to find a suitable bride.

In July 1881, the Duke of Albany came to Coburg to represent his mother at the funeral of Prince August of Saxe-Coburg and Gotha, head of the Austrian branch of our house. The venerable old prince had married Princess Clementine d'Orléans, youngest daughter of King Louis Philippe of the French and one of the richest of royal brides. Her two sisters, by the way, Louise Marie and Marie, were both married to Coburgers: Louise was the second wife of King Leopold I of the Belgians, while Marie married Duke Alexander of Württemberg, son of Antoinette, a sister of Leopold's. This last marriage, in fact, began our family's long-standing relations with the Württembergs.

Albany had been visiting his motherless nephew and nieces in Hesse before coming to Coburg. He had always been very close to his sister Princess Alice and after her untimely death in 1878 he remained deeply concerned for the wellbeing of her devastated children and widower. After the funeral in Coburg, instead of meeting the Waldecks, the Duke of Albany returned to Darmstadt to be with the Hessian children.

Finally, in September, Great-Grandfather Albany finally mustered the energy to travel to Lake Constance. There he met the Fürstin Helene of Waldeck und Pyrmont (and some of her children), a Nassau by birth, who was a rather large lady with an even heftier presence. At the time, it was believed that the heftier the family, the healthier they were, particularly the women. In this respect, my Waldeck und Pyrmont ancestors won just about any competition – they were both healthy and hefty!

Two months after meeting Princess Helene, the fifth daughter of the Fürst and Fürstin of Waldeck und Pyrmont, and her mother's namesake, my great-grandfather traveled to Germany once again. The young princess had made a positive impression in him and the Duke of Albany, a title he was granted earlier that year, intended to ask for her hand in marriage. The news was kept secret so as to maintain the degree of discretion Albany preferred. Queen Victoria described her son's bride as *"very nice looking with the highest character ... I have heard very high and excellent character of her."*[45] To those who complained that Helen was *"plain,"* the Queen replied that Helene had *"charming character, excellent education, solid, sterling qualities!"* Both future King Wilhelm II of Württemberg and King Willem III of the Netherlands, who had married sisters of Helene, attested to the good health and solid education of the Waldeck und Pyrmont children. Queen Victoria was delighted with her son's choice and she wrote to her eldest daughter that the whole affair *"was entirely my own idea."* However, the Queen's youngest daughter, Beatrice, provided a more accurate summary of affairs in London when she wrote, *"Mama is after a momentary agitation quite calm, & I only hope she will remain so."*[46]

Queen Victoria, a highly superstitious woman, chose the date for my great-grandparents' wedding. She chose April because her Uncle Leopold's brief marriage to Charlotte of Wales had taken place in May. Not only was Great-Grandfather Albany the namesake of the first king of modern-day Belgium, but also Claremont House was the ill-fated Leopold and Charlotte's home. The fact that Albany had a bleeding episode just before his marriage only added to Queen Victoria's unease over the entire matter.

Leopold and Helene's wedding took place at Windsor Castle on April 27, 1882. The Waldecks left Arolsen, their beautiful and magnificent palace, five days earlier and traveled to England arriving in Vlissingen, the Netherlands, where the

Aunt Alice and Grandfather Coburg.

Royal Yacht awaited them. Great-Grandfather Albany, still recuperating from his latest bout with hemophilia, was lame at the time and he could not go to meet his bride and her family. However, on the wedding day his lameness *"was barely noticeable during the ceremony,"* although another witness wrote that he saw *"the cruel wrench of pain every time he put his foot to the ground."*[47]

That afternoon, Leopold and Helene left Windsor Castle and settled into Claremont House. Unfortunately, their honeymoon was going to be as short as their marriage. That same day Great-Grandmother Albany's sister Marie Württemberg gave birth to a stillborn daughter and three days the mother herself was dead. This untimely sad passing plunged the Albanys into mourning. *"Life lies open to you,"* the widowed Wilhelm Württemberg wrote to Leopold, *"you just start on your happy journey together, so do not look back too much and try to make Helen do the same; a young wife always (always) ought to look forward to the future with thoughts of hope."*[48] Great-Grandmother Albany, in fact, was to have an entire life of suffering guided by her endless pool of hope and indomitable will.

Less than a year after the wedding, Great-Grandmother Albany gave birth to their first child, a baby girl named Alice in memory of Great-Grandfather's late sister, Grand Duchess Alice of Hesse and by Rhine. Queen Victoria reacted to the arrival of this granddaughter by writing in her journal, *"I can scarcely believe that dear Leopold has got a child."* Furthermore, the Queen, who was *"not an admirer of babies,"* thought Aunt Alice was *"a beautiful child, so plump and so big with such neat little features and such a complete head of dark hair."* This dear child, our beloved Aunt Alice, Countess of Athlone, was destined to be the mainstay of our family during her very long, long life. Aunt Alice was one of the most hardworking members of the royal family and served with great admiration during five reigns stretching from that of King Edward VII to Queen Elizabeth II's. Aunt Alice, who was born at Windsor Castle under the watchful eye of her grandmother Queen Victoria, died at Kensington Palace, her London residence, in January 1981.

Late in 1883, Great-Grandmother Albany brought happy news to her husband: she was expecting another child. The doctors told them to expect the baby for later that summer and the family began making arrangements for the arrival of a new family member. Sadly, my great-grandparents Albany had very little time left to celebrate the news of the impending arrival of the baby destined to become Grandfather Coburg.

Ever since the onset of winter, Great-Grandfather Albany had been experiencing excruciating pains in his joints. These afflictions were all tied to hemophilia and the intense cold weather did little to improve his condition. The doctors recommended that he seek warmer climates, so off to Cannes he went, where he stayed at the Villa Nevada. The Duchess of Albany remained in England, at least for the time being. Great-Grandfather Albany wanted to be well enough to attend the wedding of his niece Victoria of Hesse and by Rhine to Prince Louis of Battenberg, who later became the parents of Aunt Louise Sweden and Earl Mountbatten of Burma.

Great-grandmother Albany.

After a few weeks in Cannes, Great-Grandfather Albany's health began improving. He felt stronger and looked forward to meeting everyone in Darmstadt. Unfortunately, two days before his scheduled return to Claremont House, he suffered a fall and hit his right knee very hard. Within hours an internal hemorrhage set in and he experienced incredible pains. His doctors later reported that he had convulsions just before dying. It was the early morning hours of March 28, 1884, and Great-Grandfather Albany died just a few days before his thirty-first birthday.

I can only imagine how painful and devastating the news of her beloved husband's death must have been for Great-

Grandmother Albany. The telegram notifying her of her husband's death was handed to Great-Grandmother Albany at Claremont House, where she was hosting her sister-in-law Helena and some other ladies. As discrete as ever, she did not break the news to her guests until she had began making arrangements to deal with the situation. Not only was she left a widow at the age of twenty-three-years old, but she also had a baby that was barely a year-old and was five months' pregnant.

Queen Victoria expressed the family's deep sorrow for Great-Grandfather Albany's death. In a letter she wrote to her daughter Victoria, she said, *"this is an awful blow. For him we must not repine; his young life was a succession of trials and sufferings though he was so happy in his marriage. And there was such a restless longing for what he could not have; this seemed to increase rather than decrease."*[49] To her granddaughter Victoria in Darmstadt, the Queen wrote, *"Your dear sad letter ... touched me very much! I knew what you wld [would] feel & what wld [would] be the loss of beloved 'Uncle Leo' to you & dear Papa! The whole, Country as well as ourselves are in deepest mourning – There is such sorrow! Darling Uncle was so beloved, people thought him so like his precious father, that he was following in His footsteps, the he wld [be] (& he was) a gt. Help to me – & now – all, all is ended & He is with Him & darling Mama!! Free from all his constant sufferings & trials! This dear Helen herself feels & says! Nothing can exceed her goodness, patience, unmurmuring unselfish resignation. It is too touching to see her. We were at Claremont on Saturday and yesterday."*[50]

The Prince of Wales (King Edward VII) brought back to England my great-grandfather's remains. Queen Victoria wanted to bury her youngest son in the Royal Mausoleum at Frogmore, where so many other family remembers lay, but Great-Grandmother Albany would not have it. Her husband had always told her he would like to be buried inside St.

Aunt Alice.

George's Chapel, where they had been married. Helene was intent on keeping true to her late husband's wishes. It was not the first time Queen Victoria would face her extremely honest daughter-in-law, who was not one to cave and turn over.

Claremont House, once again, was plunged into mourning. It was in this sad atmosphere that Grandfather Coburg made his entrance into this cruel world of ours. He received the names "Charles Edward George Albert," the first two as tribute to his late father's fascination with the Stuarts. The last, of course, nearly mandatory for Queen Victoria's descendants was given in memory of her late husband. The cabinet minister appointed to witness the birth, wrote to Great-Grandmother Albany, *"God has granted you a son of consolation in your great sorrow and I pray that the little child I was so happy to welcome into this world may grow up to be a comfort and support to you."*[51] Queen Victoria, delighted that it was a boy, wrote to her granddaughter Victoria Battenberg that Grandfather Coburg was *"quite a pretty healthy looking baby – very like dear Uncle Leopold. – his eyes quite remarkably so."* Everyone took note of the indomitable spirit of Great-Grandmother Albany, who *"was greatly tried but behaved so courageously, though she was nearly breaking down often, but she bore it till it was all over. Little Charlie is a fine, big boy,"* Queen Victoria wrote about Grandfather Coburg's baptism.[52]

Grandfather Coburg and Aunt Alice were raised in a disciplinarian environment. Aunt Alice recalled years later that their mother was a *"strict disciplinarian, sometimes too domineering in her anxiety to bring us very ordinary little urchins up as perfect beings. My brother even feared her, which was a great handicap, as it tended to make him evade independent decisions as he grew up."* On top of that, Grandfather Coburg was described as *"delicate, nervous and tiresome."*[53] He was an artistic child whose spirit was somewhat checked by the regimented environment in which he was raised. While his sister profited from this sort of upbringing, Grandfather Coburg certainly did not. For the rest of his life he was to be too prone to allow others to make decisions that should have been left to his discretion. Mother once said: *"Uncle Charlie was a highly cultured, gentle man, who liked books, poetry, classical music, good food and conversation. Born in England, the grandson of Queen Victoria of England, he was sent to Germany at the age of fourteen to be groomed as the future Duke of Saxe-Coburg and Gotha, under the watchful eye of his cousin, the German Kaiser. Uncle Charlie married my mother's sister Victoria-Adelheid, my Aunt Dicky … Uncle Charlie did not like difficulties with anyone and would try to avoid awkward situations as often as he could, by always saying: 'Oh Dicky, you can handle this so much better than I.'"*[54]

And yet, Aunt Alice always retained very fond and happy memories of her childhood. Princess Alice later wrote that life at Claremont House was very pleasant. Their mother, although the loss of her husband's income caused some worry, was still able to provide her children with an environment of "some style." The children also read and painted while she read stories to them. They were somewhat restricted when it came to the sort of children they could befriend, but since their Connaught and Battenberg cousins were of similar ages, they became childhood friends. The Duchess of Albany also believed in the therapeutic aspects of outdoor living. Grandfather and Aunt Alice, hence, were encouraged to climb trees, go on walks and develop a love of the outdoors. In this part of their development, the children were greatly aided by their nanny, Ms Potts, who believed that children ought to enjoy the countryside and engage in physical exercise. Aunt Alice, in fact, was an amazing walker and she enjoyed impressive stamina.

Grandfather Coburg in his youth.

The Duchess of Albany *"sought to instill into her son, and his elder sister, Alice, her own practical Christian faith and highly developed sense of duty."*[55] Both siblings, one cannot deny, spent their life fulfilling their duties with admirable devotion. Neither wanted to disappoint, both wished to be the perfect little beings their mother had hoped they would turn out. This, I believe, later played an important role in Grandfather Coburg's future role in Germany, both during the imperial era and after.

Queen Victoria was always very fond of her Albany grandchildren and held their mother in great esteem. The children certainly enjoyed visiting their august grandmother, whom they affectionately called "Gan-gan." Queen Victoria's role within her family was like a sun around which their young lives revolved. Princess Alice years later recalled what it felt to be in the presence of grandmother: *"There is something indescribable about Windsor Castle,"* she wrote, *"The moment we entered the door of the 'sovereign's Entrance' there was a special Windsor Castle smell – a smell like nowhere else – old furniture kept very clean, flowers and, altogether, a special delicious and welcoming smell that only now is fading away. There was an aura about the whole place – the dignified page who helped us, the housekeeper in black silk and a lace cap at the door, and, of course, the equerry-in-waiting; then the beauty and richness of the wide corridor with all its treasures which one accepted yet never noticed."* In the Queen's presence, the children were expected to behave like *"a flock of well-behaved little geese … Mind you curtsey at the door and kiss Grandamama's hand and don't make a nose and mind you are good."* Only once did Aunt Alice forget herself, her infraction eliciting a royal rebuke from Gan-gan who sternly said, *"You are a very naughty little girl!"* [56]

Meanwhile, Grandfather Coburg was sent to school. In

Grand Duchess Marie Alexandrovna, Duchess of Edinburgh and Saxe-Coburg and Gotha.

1895, he was enrolled at Eton, where he was to remain for several years. Also enrolled at Eton was his cousin Prince Arthur of Connaught. In fact, he was still an Etonian when in 1897 he participated in the celebrations for the Queen's Diamond Jubilee. Both youngsters rode in the same carriage and the crowd reacted with *"fresh outbursts of applause,"* when they saw *"the military salutes of the Duke of Albany and Prince Arthur of Connaught."* It was the grandest celebration Grandfather Coburg had ever participated in, but the day was to end embarrassingly for him. The combined effect of nerves, excitement, heat and a *"hasty breakfast,"* landed the poor young man in an ambulance for the sick. The Diamond Jubilee celebrations having ended, Grandfather Coburg returned to Eton.[57]

Whenever possible, the Albanys would travel to Germany, where they spent long periods with Great-Grandmother Albany's family at Schloß Arolsen, a beautiful castle that I have visited many times. The current Head of House Waldeck und Pyrmont is my cousin Wittekind and we have maintained family contacts for a long time. Anyhow, these old gatherings attracted the descendants of Great-Grandmother Albany's parents, who included, among others: Queen Wilhelmina of the Netherlands, the daughter of King Wilhelm II of Württemberg (Pauline), and the children of Fürst of Bentheim und Steinfurt. Also present were members of the Nassau (and Luxembourg) family, since after all Great-Grandmother Albany's mother was a sister of the Grand Duke Adolphe of Luxembourg. At one of these gatherings, for example, Grandfather Coburg and Aunt Alice were left at Arolsen while the adults travelled to Bohemia to attend the wedding of King Wilhelm II of Württemberg to his second wife, Princess Charlotte of Schaumburg-Lippe. These were happy gatherings spent with family. The children were able to establish strong ties with their continental cousins, particularly Queen Wilhelmina, who remained a life-long close friend of Aunt Alice.

However, as it often happened in the life of Grandfather Coburg, events outside his control were about to bring a sudden end to his halcyon existence in England.

Troubling news coming from Coburg was the cause of great misgivings for all involved, particularly Queen Victoria and Kaiser Wilhelm II, the Duke of Saxe-Coburg and Gotha and the Duke of Connaught. Great-Grandmother Albany, much to her chagrin, was also involved in this terrible episode for its outcome forever changed the life of her son. On February 6, 1899,[58] Hereditary Prince Alfred of Saxe-Coburg and Gotha, the only son of Duke Alfred and Grand Duchess Marie Alexandrovna, suddenly passed away. The

The Edinburgh children. From the left: Marie, Victoria Melita, Beatrice, Alexandra and Alfred Jr.

Grand Duchess Marie Alexandrovna was immensely wealthy. Besides a sizable dowry, she received large settlements from her father, Tsar Alexander II. Her financial independence allowed Marie Alexandrovna the possibility of purchasing her own residence in Coburg. The building was previously owned by an aristocratic family. In Marie Alexandrovna's time it was commonly known as the Edinburgh Palais.

wayward youngster was under medical supervision due to having contracted a terribly contagious illness, the product of his excesses and behaviour that caused his mother and grandmother untold worry and embarrassment. The only son in a family of five children, Alfred Jr. was the hope of the dynasty. His parents had hoped that he would marry one of the twin daughters of Grand Duchess Vera Konstantinovna of Russia. However, Alfred Jr.'s unfortunate illness mandated that any thought of marriage be archived for the time being. Instead, all efforts were directed to curing him of the devastating illness. Soon after his parents celebrated their Silver Wedding with a large gathering in Coburg, Alfred Jr. was taken to Meran, where doctors believed the climate would be of great benefit for the young man. However, his body spent and spirit consumed by the illness, Alfred Jr. lost the battle with his ailment and died.

This death, more than any other event in his life, was to have untold effects in the life of Grandfather Coburg … the disappearance of his first cousin meant that he now stood dangerously close to a legacy he was not prepared for, in a land whose language he had not yet mastered. Within months of Alfred Jr.'s sad end a new chapter began in the life of the Duke of Albany, now not only destined to inherit the Coburg legacy, but forced to abandon his comfortable life in England for one fraught with untold challenges in Imperial Germany.

Coburg's lost heir, Hereditary Prince Alfred.

Chapter V
Grandfather Coburg's Complicated Life

On an ominous day, June 28 (1899), the Duke of Connaught delivered important news to his nephew Kaiser Wilhelm II. At hand were the results a serious decision that all hoped would solve the succession crisis in Coburg. Armed with Queen Victoria's support, the Duke of Connaught explained to his nephew that the new heir would be his nephew the Duke of Albany. To further assuage the Kaiser's ego, Uncle Connaught informed him that *"what remained of the heir's education will take place in Germany under the guidance of his mother."*[59] The following day, Duke Alfred notified all the leading princes of Germany that Coburg, at last, had a new heir: Carl Eduard, Grandfather Coburg.

Before presenting this arrangement to the Kaiser, the Duke of Connaught, after discussions with his brother Wales and their mother, approached the Dowager Duchess of Albany and presented her with the facts: the Connaughts were taking themselves out of the Coburg succession and to avoid the prospect of an English prince having to always be provided, the family had chosen her only son to inherit the duchy and its vast legacy. Helene, dutiful to the end, accepted the fait accompli and agreed to leave Claremont House and settle in Germany for the Duke of Albany's schooling.

Since Grandfather Coburg was a minor, Hereditary Prince Ernst of Hohenlohe-Langenburg, the only German son-in-law of Duke Alfred, was asked to serve as regent if need be. Ernst was an effective regent and was to remain close to Coburg. Changes were made to the ducal constitution and on August 9, at Schloß Reinhardsbrunn, and in the presence of a visibly aged Duke Alfred, Great-grandmother Albany and Hereditary Prince Ernst of Hohenlohe-Langenburg signed the succession agreement in favor Grandfather Coburg.

Interestingly, the agreement did not take out the Connaught and Wales lines completely. If in the event that Grandfather Coburg died without direct eligible male heirs, all parties agreed that the succession would then pass to Prince Arthur of Connaught, *"and if he too died before his majority, the title should pass to Bertie (the Prince of Wales – Edward VII) who would confer it upon the nearest male descendant of his line."*[60]

In the meantime, since Duke Alfred, surprisingly, failed to offer Great-grandmother Albany a permanent home in

From the left: Grand Duke Ernst Ludwig of Hesse and by Rhine, the Duke of York (George V), Duke Alfred and Hereditary Prince Alfred Jr. of Saxe-Coburg and Gotha.

Opposite page: Duke Alfred of Saxe-Coburg and Gotha, the Prince of Wales (Edward VII) and the Duke of Connaught, Coburg, 1894.

Coburg, the Albanys settled in Stuttgart under the protection of the King of Württemberg, Helene's former brother-in-law. Duke Alfred wanted to adopt his nephew and raise him in his own home, but his sister-in-law would not have such a thing. She also declined Duke Alfred's suggestion that Grandfather Coburg attend a "*horrid, scruffy place,*"[61] near Reinhardsbrunn. Queen Victoria best expressed everyone's relief and admiration when she wrote to her daughter the Empress Friedrich, *"Poor dear Helen feels the uprooting of her happy and first home terribly and Charles feels leaving Eton very much. It is most stupid and ill judged of them both [Alfred and Wilhelm II] to take the poor boy away in the middle of his education and before he knows German enough to be able to learn in German. William, unfortunately, started this idea."*[62] However, no one expressed her misgivings more than Great-grandmother Albany, who Aunt Alice described as heart-broken that *"her small, blue-eyed, exceptionally handsome and highly strung young son was about to be transformed into a foreign princeling."* – *"I have always tried to bring Charlie up as a good Englishman … and now I have to turn him into a good German,"* she moaned.[63]

Soon enough, Grandfather Coburg's destiny was set in course by his cousin Kaiser Wilhelm II, who asked that *"his education be modeled on the education of our eldest; as the scheme has so well answered for him, it will doubtless be the same with little Albany …"*[64]

Accordingly, from Stuttgart, Grandfather Coburg was sent to Potsdam, where he entered the Lichterfelde military cadet school, one of the most prestigious such institutions in the old German Empire. In due time he was able to enter the First Regiment of Guards, one of the most prestigious units in the parade-loving, militaristic-embracing Prussian army.

During these years, Grandfather Coburg was, as one author best described it, *"steeped in the atmosphere of brash, boastful, self-confident militarism that characterized the Second Reich."*[65] I think that many of Grandfather Coburg's later problems stem from these years spent in such a pernicious environment. For too many years this impressionable youngster, who wanted to please all, was under the influence of Kaiser Wilhelm II, a self-righteous bully who relished playing questionable jokes on everyone around him. For his brash, pedantic and bombastic attitude, this *"brilliantly-uniformed monarch who seemed to delight in impressing his young cousin,"*[66] also teased him mercilessly, once even taking a picture of himself seated on Grandfather Coburg's stomach. The Kaiser, whose birth defect made him an extremely complicated man, was maddening and restless, punctilious and double-faced, apt to allow his bombastic personality get the best of him, all the while hiding his shortcomings behind his waxed mustachios and sparkling, medal-covered uniforms. Aunt Alice once wrote: *"It was not easy to understand everything William did because he was flamboyantly vain and temperamentally unstable. Without being blind to the consequences of his actions, he seemed unable to resist an opportunity of throwing his weight about if it helped to magnify his importance and the might of the empire*

The Empress Friedrich and Queen Victoria.

whose destiny, with God's connivance, it was his duty to shape. Invariably he regretted his impetuosity and tried, not often successfully, to repair the harm done by his rashness."[67] How anyone thought that Grandfather Coburg would prosper in such an environment is a source of bafflement to me.

Grandfather Coburg was a soft-spoken man who had been raised by an adoring mother in a well-protected environment. In his pre-Potsdam life, life was not one of endless display and consumption; life was one of dedication to duty and self-betterment. He was a cultivated man who loved the theater and was fond of music. He enjoyed reading and had a passion for history. Architecture was another of his great passions, the Coburg Theater being one of the main recipients of his largesse. Grandfather Coburg enjoyed traveling and when doing so also indulged in another one of his passions, photography. He was a good skier and a good shot, just as he was a good host and the sort of person who shied away from confrontations and uncomfortable circumstances. He simply hated to offend and wished to have everyone believe that they mattered. It was perhaps this fear to disappoint that later on let him come under the spell of stronger personalities who found him an easy follower.

This was the case with the Kaiser's role in Grandfather Coburg's life; it also was the case with how Grandmother Coburg influenced her husband's daily affairs; it would repeat itself with his dealings with National Sociliasm. Grandfather Coburg simply lacked the strength of character necessary to stand his ground and think for himself. He was easily pliable and even easier to be managed. The camaraderie he found in Potsdam's overblown atmosphere of militaristic masculinity captivated him. His wife's strong character he found addictive. The allure of playing an important role in the rise of a new Germany was frankly too powerful for him to resist. Aunt Alice once wrote that Grandfather Coburg was *"shattered"* by the outbreak of war. He was an English prince who was forced to become a German; during the Great War in England he was attacked for being a traitor, all the while in Germany he was accused of the same crime. In one country he was too German, while in the other he was not German enough. In an effort to fit in, Grandfather Coburg tried to please everyone and ended pleasing no one, all while losing himself in the mix.

Kaiser Wilhelm II in Death's Head Hussars uniform.

Aunt Alice years later recalled that when in Potsdam, the Albanys lived in close proximity with Kaiser Wilhelm II's family. *"Much of our spare time was taken up with the imperial family, because the Neues Palais was close by and not a week passed without our going there,"* she recalled.[68] The Kaiser's wife she thought *"delightful,"* as were the Imperial couple's six sons. The two eldest, Crown Prince Wilhelm and Prince Eitel Friedrich, who had ages similar to Aunt Alice and Grandfather Coburg, were like brothers to them. Years later, August Wilhelm, another complex human being, was to become close to Grandfather Coburg for besides having been friends since childhood, they married sisters. August Wilhelm, who seems to also have been quite an unsympathetic man, was also an ardent Nazi. Aunt Alice also thought the Crown Prince was a bit *"spoilt and very conceited."*[69]

It was into this maelstrom that Grandfather Coburg was plunged during the many years that he lived in Potsdam. We have many old photo albums in our archive in which his close relations with the Kaiser's children are catalogued. These include journeys to Greece and cruises onboard the *SMY Hohenzollern*, the floating palace Kaiser Wilhelm II built to compete with the Tsar's famed *Imperial Yacht Standart*. This proximity to the Kaiser and his wife, eventually led to

Grandfather Coburg finding a wife from among the Kaiserin's nieces.

Princess Viktoria Adelheid of Schleswig-Holstein-Sonderburg-Glücksburg, Grandmother Coburg, was born on New Year's Eve 1885 at Grünholz, an estate her father owned in Schleswig-Holstein. Her father, Duke Friedrich Ferdinand, was married to Princess Karoline Mathilde of Schleswig-Holstein-Sonderburg-Augustenburg, a sister of Empress Augusta Viktoria. The family grew to have five other children, apart from Grandmother Coburg. These included, besides Grandmother Solms: Alexandra Viktoria (1887-1957), who married Prince August Wilhelm of Prussia, the Kaiser's ardently Nazi son; Helena (1888-1962), who in spite of being married to Prince Harald of Denmark, a brother of King Christian X, also became an outspoken supporter of National Socialism, going as far as receiving German soldiers at her home during the occupation of Denmark, not a smart move one can certainly agree; Adelheid (1889-1964), who was married to my mother's Uncle Dicky Solms; Friedrich (1891-1965), who married Princess Marie Melita, eldest daughter of Coburg's regent Ernst Hohenlohe. The youngest daughter of the Dukes of Glücksburg was, as you may recall, my Grandmother Solms.

Although Grandmother Coburg descended from Queen Victoria's half-sister Feodora of Hohenlohe-Langenburg, she had very little contact with her future husband. That changed when he came under the aegis of Kaiser Wilhelm II and his wife. For the Kaiserin, whose nieces would greatly profit in the marriage market because of their Imperial aunt, Grandfather Coburg was a candidate that she intended to catch for her own family. Besides his good looks and exquisite education, the young Duke of Saxe-Coburg and Gotha was one of the most desirable bachelors of his time. The fact that the Coburg inheritance was his alone enhanced his already numerous attributes. Any princess, a German one it must be of course, who landed his hand in marriage would be secured of a life of considerable position and wealth. Once he arrived in Potsdam, Cousin Augusta Viktoria would not let go of Grandfather Coburg until he was safely in the hands of her own family's web.

Grandfather Coburg's photo albums catalogue his various visits to Grünholz and Glücksburg. In them there are countless photos documenting a budding romance between a smiling, attractive and young military officer and a rather serious looking girl who looks into the camera with a certain allure of mistrust and wonderment. Perhaps she wondered when it was all to end; perhaps she wondered what life would be like in quaint old Coburg. Whatever her thoughts were, Grandmother Coburg eventually accepted her beau's approaches and their engagement was announced to much merriment and joy, particularly in Coburg and Gotha. A member of the Kaiser's court described the situation thus: *"There is no doubt that the Duke has for some time been in love with the little Princess, but nonetheless, he was rather serious after the engagement. The mother-in-law, however, was beaming, and the Empress was very happy. But the truth is that, to put it in good homely language, the little Duke has been caught!"* My grandparents' engagement was announced on February 16, 1905 during a Court Ball at the Berliner Stadtschloß.

Grandfather Coburg in Scottish uniform.

While the Duke of Saxe-Coburg and Gotha was in Potsdam, and later attending school in Bonn and Berlin, his duchy was placed under a regency led by Hereditary Prince Ernst of Hohenlohe-Langenburg. One of the sons-in-law of Duke Alfred, Ernst, a grandson of Queen Victoria's half-sister Feodora, was highly respected by all who knew him. He was a dutiful, conscientious and dependable administrator who gave certainty that once tasked with a goal, it would be achieved. Besides his commendable character, Ernst, due to his family background as well as his wife, had been a constant visitor to Coburg since his early years. Hence, once Duke Alfred died in July 1900, the regency was set in place and for the next five years the duchy underwent a period of restructuring and cleansing of the ducal coffers. This all ensured that once Grandfather Coburg attained his majority in July 1905, he became a very wealthy man with thousands of hectares of forests and agricultural lands, as well as an innumerable collection of real estate, not to mention the ducal collections filled with priceless pieces. Besides the Veste in Coburg and Schloß Friedenstein in Gotha, which he used regularly, Grandfather Coburg owned Schloß Callenberg in Coburg, Schloß Greinburg on the Danube, Schloß Hinterriß in the Tyrol, and several other hunting lodges scattered throughout.

Grandfather and Grandmother Coburg were married at Schloß Glücksburg on October 11, 1905. Many family members attended the wedding ceremony, among them several members of the bride's extended family, as well as the Kaiser and Kaiserin and their children, except Crown Prince Wilhelm. In fact, Prince Eitel Friedrich's engagement to Duchess Sophie Charlotte of Oldenburg was announced during my grandparents' wedding ceremonies. Interestingly, representing the English Royal family was none other than Prince Arthur Jr. of Connaught, the same prince who had threatened Grandfather Coburg with a thrashing if he did not accept the Coburg succession. Grandfather Coburg's mother was present. Aunt Alice, had already married in 1904, her choice being Prince Alexander of Teck, who in 1917, when King George V changed the Royal Family's last name, became Earl of Athlone. Known to the family as Uncle Alge, he became a good and close friend of Grandfather Coburg and was fond of visiting the duchy. In 1905 when he attended Grandfather Coburg's coming of age, Uncle Alge went for a stroll with the Duke of Connaught. Dressed in one of his finest uniforms, the Duke of Connaught constantly returned the greetings of Coburgers who passed them. Surprised by this show of bonhomie, Uncle Alge asked the Duke who all these people were, *"Oh, they're just a few of Der Lieber, Gutte Ernst's* [Duke Ernst II] *illegitimates,"* he replied.[70] As I mentioned before, Duke Ernst II had been a "true father of Coburg."

Some time ago we found in the archives of *The New York Times* a report of the wedding festivities that took place in Glücksburg. Some *"fifty members of royal families,"* from Germany and abroad, attended the wedding ceremony. Schloß Glücksburg *"altogether too small to accommodate half the number of guests"* was beautifully decorated.[71] Many guests had to stay in country estates in the vicinity, while the *Imperial Yacht Hohenzollern,* sailed from Kiel, served as home to Kaiser Wilhelm II and his family. Furthermore, *"the civil ceremony took place in the wide hall of the castle."* After which, *"as many royal guests and their suites as could be accommodated went to the little chapel upstairs where the religious rite was performed."* Outside Schloß Glücksburg, an enthusiastic crowd cheered and waved when the newlyweds *"appeared on the balcony of the castle."*[71]

Postcard commemorating the engagement of my Coburg grandparents.

After a lengthy honeymoon, my Coburg grandparents settled in Coburg, although they were frequently seen in Gotha, where ducal affairs demanded Grandfather Coburg's presence. Soon enough, however, Grandmother Coburg discovered that she was pregnant and Uncle Johann Leopold (Leo) was born in August 1906. The second child, Aunt Bylla, was born in January 1908. In August 1909 Grandmother Coburg gave birth to Uncle Hubertus (Bertel) and three years later came Aunt Calma (Caroline Mathilde). The children were raised by nannies that were directly under the watchful eye of Grandmother Coburg. Their father enjoyed spending time with the children, particularly if it involved some sort of sport, whether it was skiing in Oberhof or swimming at the seashore or a lake. Theirs was a golden childhood isolated from the turbulent winds outside the palace walls.

Grandmother Coburg was very German. So much so that

The wedding of Prince Alexander of Teck and Princess Alice of Albany.

she did not visit England as much as her husband, who many times traveled to London and Claremont to spend time with his mother and sister, as well as other family members. In fact, when war broke out in 1914, Grandfather Coburg found himself in England. The outbreak of war between his birth country and his country of adoption was the source of deep anxiety for him. In fact, he felt as if he was living in a nightmare. Hence, upon arriving in Germany, he decided that the idea of taking up arms against his birth country was simply unthinkable. He asked to serve on the Eastern front rather than lift a finger against British troops. He was posted to Galicia and carried numerous inspections and official visits. He was deeply concerned with lifting the morale of the strained troops and did his best to be of service to his adopted Fatherland. In November 1914, Grandfather Coburg narrowly escaped death when a Russian *"shell exploded near where he and his staff were standing."*[72] Although the explosion killed one of his officers and wounded two others, the Duke of Saxe-Coburg and Gotha cheated death. However, illnesses, starting in 1915, played an increasing role in preventing him from playing a more important role in the war effort. In 1917, he was stripped of the title of Duke of Albany, as well as of the Order of the Garter, both deeply saddening him as these two distinctions reminded him of his English roots. It was very hard for him to accept that in England he was considered a "traitor peer," when he had never lifted a finger against his country of origin and had only gone to Germany by events out of his control. No wonder that Aunt Alice fervently believed that the war shattered him, leaving Grandfather Coburg a rudderless ship in search of a safe harbor. Unfortunately, instead of finding one with pleasant, calm waters, he entered the dragon's lair not realizing how much his mistake and naiveté would cost him.

The fall of the Second Reich in 1918 was a great shock to most Germans, particularly the ruling princes. My grandfather being no exception, he tried to do what he could to avoid the loss of his realm, position and properties. On November 11, the war came to an end after more than four years of fratricidal killing. Nothing remained of the once elegant world that welcomed the summer of 1914. In Russia, the Bolsheviks had done away with the Romanovs, even going as far as butchering nearly twenty members of the Imperial family, including Tsar Nicholas II, his wife and their innocent children. In Berlin, the revolution forced Kaiser Wilhelm II and Crown Prince Wilhelm into exile and not even the efforts of the very popular Crown Princess Cecilie to have her eldest son placed on the throne were successful. Ferdinand of Bulgaria had fallen already and in due time found refuge in Coburg's Burglaßschloßen, where he lived with his brother Prince Philipp, whose once mighty fortune was about to ripped to shreds by the hungry and communistic governments that rose out of the ashes of the Habsburg Empire. In Vienna, in spite of their efforts to stem the tide of revolution, Kaiser Karl and Kaiserin Zita could not swim against the current and the Habsburgs, one of Europe's longest ruling dynasties, were no more. Hence, in this tide of revolution fueled by disillusionment with the failures of the old regime, Grandfather Coburg could do very little to save his duchy. Already on November 8, there had been a revolutionary outbreak in Gotha led by mutinous sailors, workers and soldiers. In Coburg, the people remained respectful while they awaited a solution to the crisis. However, when revolutionaries from Gotha arrived in Coburg, the situation turned and danger appeared in the streets of the once calm Coburg cobblestones. On November 11 large crowds gathered in the Schloßplatz and in front of the Town Hall, where Prince Albert's statue served as witness to the end of his grandson's reign.[73] Realizing that the skies over Gotha were a turbulent sea of fluttering red flags, Grandfather Coburg accepted political reality and on November 14 released all public officials from their oath of loyalty. In doing so, his reign came to an end, and Coburg and Gotha were no longer our realm as the rule of the Coburgs had ceased. The monarchy's fall brought the devastating end to the only world Grandfather Coburg had ever known.

Two weeks later, Grandmother Coburg gave birth to my father. He came to this world in the peace and quiet of Schloß Callenberg and was the first Coburg born after the fall of the monarchy.

Once the political situation settled and public unrest disappeared, Grandfather Coburg and his staff began the long process of negotiating with the new governments in Coburg and Gotha what properties and artwork he was going to be able to retain. This was a very complicated negotiation since the parties involved in it had to unravel a web of property rights and ownership of priceless artwork that had been collected, and inherited, by our branch of the Wettin family for several centuries. Years were spent in reaching a negotiated settlement, much as was to be the case when I had to negotiate with the government of Thüringen for compensation for the vast forests and real estate the Communists had taken from us after 1945.

Of course, the Austrian property was private and Grandfather Coburg did not have to negotiate with the new republican government. Schloß Greinburg, Schloß Hinterriß, along with their contents and attached lands were safe, as were several hunting lodges and domains, as well as thousands of hectares in forests. However, the property spread across Thüringen was an entirely different matter. Besides tens of thousands of hectares of forests and agricultural lands, there was a long list of real estate that included everything from vast fortresses, like the Veste Coburg, and hunting lodges like the one in Oberhof. The ducal collections, for example, demanded a tireless study of every piece to find out which belonged to the state and which were private property and thus owned by Grandfather Coburg. This lengthy process, luckily, produced an advantageous outcome and by the mid-1920s all pending disputes were settled. Grandfather Coburg was allowed use of the Prince's Bastion in the Veste Coburg; Schloß Callenberg was recognized as private property, as was Schloß Reinhardsbrunn. The villa in Oberhof remained in our possession, as well as several thousand hectares of land, the revenue of which was sure to assist Grandfather Coburg rebuild and recover from the losses suffered after the end of the war. Large portions of the ducal collections were also returned to us, but they remained housed in Schloß Friedenstein and other museums, thus allowing the people access to them. In all, Grandfather Coburg remained a very wealthy landowning aristocrat.

Great-grandfather Holstein, Duke Friedrich Ferdinand.

Great-grandmother Holstein, Duchess Karoline-Mathilde.

Two very important events also took place in the 1920s. One was the separation of Coburg and Gotha into independent free states, while the second was Grandfather Coburg's wise decision to place most of the property and artwork into a family foundation (Stiftung der Herzog von Sachsen-Coburg und Gotha'schen Familie) that included family members with a stake on the legacy; these members included several non-German Coburgs as well.

The Duchies of Coburg and Gotha were created as a dual entity under the personal union of Duke Ernst I. Each had its own government, but since one duke ruled them jointly, the Imperial Diet only allocated one vote to them. There had been efforts to unify them as one political entity, but this opportunity was allowed to pass. When new house laws were passed in 1852, there was further unification and Gotha and Coburg resembled a quasi-federal state. Another attempt to attain political union failed in 1867 because Gotha's parliament did not want to assume the larger state debts of Coburg.

Nearly a year after Grandfather Coburg's abdication, Gotha had a referendum and chose to merge with the larger State of Thüringen. On May 1, 1920, Gotha ceased to exist as a Free State. Two months later, Coburg merged with the Free State of Bavaria. This decision would have deep repercussions a quarter century later when Germany, defeated and occupied, was divided between the Soviet Union and the Allies. Thüringen went to the Soviets, while Bavaria remained under Allied control. The Iron Curtain swallowed the majority of our lands, and the border was just miles from Coburg. It would take nearly half a century for us to be able to visit a free Gotha, while also beginning negotiations to regain what was taken from us.

Grandfather Coburg, who adored his mother and sister, had not seen his English relations since the outbreak of the Great War. In the meantime, his mother had aged prematurely and he wished nothing more than being able to spend time with her. Consequently, in 1921 he obtained permission to travel to England and spend time with his mother. The following year, Great-grandmother Albany traveled to the continent to visit her son at Schloß Hinterriß, a picturesque Tyrolean village. Along with their mother was Aunt Alice, who also wanted to see her sister-in-law, nephews and nieces. It was wonderful weather in the

Chapter V – Grandfather Coburg's Complicated Life

Schloß Hinterriß was one of Grandfather Coburg's favorite residences. Unfortunately, Great-grandmother Albany died there in 1922 while visiting him. Following her instructions to be laid to rest where she died, she was buried near the schloß. We sold Schloß Hinterriß many years ago.

Tyrol and the family had enjoyed a lovely time reminiscing about the past and catching up. Unfortunately, tragedy struck when on September 1, 1922, Great-grandmother Albany died of a massive heart attack.[74]

Great-grandmother Albany was deeply loved in England. Ever since marrying the Duke of Albany in 1882, she had done her utmost to become a dutiful member of the Royal Family. Her own daughter, Aunt Alice, always remembered how much her mother sacrificed of herself to aid others, all the while conveying to her children that as royalty their was a life dedicated to service and sacrifice. During the Great War, Great-grandmother Albany ceded half of Claremont House to open a convalescence home for war casualties. At one point, she sold an important piece of jewelry Queen Victoria gifted her so funds could be raised to aid one of London's poorest neighborhoods. There was nothing she would not do; there was no sacrifice too high in her efforts to give as much of herself as she humanly could share.

Following her wishes to be buried where she died, and without much fuss, her funeral took place at Hinterriß a few days later. Her remains are still buried there in a small chapel next to the castle. Schloß Hinterriß is no longer a Coburg property since we sold it many decades ago, yet it remains a place steeped in family history and the glorious days of my house. Today, we still visit the area where we own a property, Karwendel, located in a valley surrounded by the Northern

Great-grandmother Albany, Helene of Waldeck-Pyrmont.

Schloß Friedenstein was the old ducal city residence in Gotha.

Limestone Alps. I personally enjoy Karwendel very much, and many of my cousins have been guests at our hunting lodge.

Now let us return to Grandfather Coburg and the 1920s, perhaps one of the most challenging periods in his life …

War and revolution had changed his life forever. He, who had been chosen to rule, no longer was in a position to do so. While he had lost his political role, Grandfather Coburg managed to retain a considerably large portion of his property. Well, let me be honest … he managed to retain most of his property and perhaps was among the best compensated of the former ruling princes. His lifestyle, while perhaps affected by the loss of a public role, was certainly not affected much financially, and certainly not at all from a social perspective as he retained his position in society, not just in Germany, but also internationally. And yet, he longed for the old times; he longed for the period during which he had ruled the duchy and been close to the epicenter of power in Berlin; he longed for the feeling of having a purpose, a task, indeed, to make life better for his subjects in Gotha and Coburg. Much like most of his contemporaries, Grandfather Coburg reminisced about the Imperial era with a deep sense of nostalgia and pride, a time when Germany occupied an exalted position among the world's most powerful empires. The cataclysm that befell the Fatherland in 1918 had done away with the sense of security provided by the imperial structure. He felt, his social group felt, unprotected, vulnerable and filled with angst and uncertainty. They all longed for the return of the golden era that had so ingloriously disappeared!

Prince August Wilhelm of Prussia.

Grandfather Coburg seated with his mother the Duchess of Albany during her last visit to Schloß Hinterriß. She died soon after this image was taken and was buried there, as she had asked to be laid to rest where she died.

As a consequence of the Treaty of Versailles, Germany was blamed for a war which, of course, was not its fault alone. The Allies had offered peace without victors, but the fall of the Imperial government and the political weakness that ensued laid Germany powerless to resist the onerous and humiliating terms of the peace treaty. The monetary compensation imposed on Germany alone was not only crippling, but also an affront that many Germans would never forget, much less forgive. On top of these various sources of national angst, there was the national fear among the former ruling princes and aristocracy that Germany may, after all, fall prey to Communism. Hence, countless Germans from all walks of life lost faith in democracy and parliamentary government, which they blamed for being incapable of deterring the consequences of the Treaty of Versailles. Consequently, the country's economy eventually collapsed and the political situation led to extremists becoming acceptable, nay, viable options to restore national pride. None other than the Duchess of Brünswick, the Kaiser's only daughter, made one such recollection. In her memoirs she wrote: *"The struggle of millions for their daily bread led to the hitherto unknown radicalization of the masses and political strife even spread to the streets. Parliament – the Reichstag – was powerless."*[75] It was in this atmosphere of socio-economic and political unrest that extremist movements, like Hitler's National Socialists, offered *"a return to order, nationalism and patriotism."* Unrest gave them an opportunity to gain prominence. Even respectable royals and aristocrats, people who would have never before come near such brutes, convinced, themselves that *"this vulgar upstart (Herr Hitler), with his rabble-rousing tactics and his pagan, nihilist philosophy"* could possibly offer the Fatherland a roadmap to a better time.[76] Grandfather Coburg, sadly, was one the most prominent Germans who fell for the Nazi's "smoke and mirrors."

Grandfather Coburg longed for a return of Imperial times. As was the case with many of his colleagues and friends,

The Prinzenbau inside the Veste, Coburg. Grandfather Coburg was allowed to continue using it as one of his residences, during his lifetime, this part of the fortress.

Grandfather Coburg in the late 1930s.

particularly among royals, he welcomed the formation of ex-servicemen associations and groups, like the Stalhelm, whose aim was the return of public order, discipline, patriotism and nationalism, and which eventually gravitated toward the Nazis. These were seen as the panacea that would lead Germany out of its troubles and perhaps even change course to avoid the abyss of Communism. If these groups accelerated the hoped-for return to the monarchy's restoration, well, so much the better Grandfather Coburg believed. He attended large rallies and parades, and it is very likely that he also financially supported these movements, including the National Socialists. Prince August Wilhelm of Prussia, who by then had divorced his wife Alexandra Viktoria, Grandmother Coburg's sister, was also an enthusiastic Nazi supporter. Having been a close friend of my grandfather's, they both attended gatherings and parades, publicly providing these massive demonstrations with a veneer of respectability.

I don't believe it is necessary for me to provide a cover-up for my grandfather's support and enthusiasm for National Socialism. These were his mistakes and his alone, and I reject the notion that we, his descendants, should be measured by his errors, not ours. His enthusiasm for National Socialism was well known, even before Hitler assumed the chancellorship. In fact, already in October

Before the war, Prince August Wilhelm of Prussia married Grandmother Coburg's sister, Princess Alexandra Viktoria of Schleswig-Holstein. Although the marriage did not survive the war, August Wilhelm remained a good friend of Grandfather Coburg. Both were enthusiastic supporters of National Socialism. In this pre-war photo we can see them with Prince Oskar, August Wilhelm's brother, and Grandmother Coburg, who was a first cousin of the Prussian princes.

1932 at the time of Aunt Bylla's wedding, everyone knew that Grandfather Coburg was an enthusiastic supporter of the National Socialists. If anyone overlooked that fact, their naiveté must have become crystal-clear when on the night before the wedding Coburg witnessed some 4000 goose-stepping Nazis marched in a torchlight procession through the town. As if that was not questionable enough, the following day the wedding route was lined with what seemed an endless number of Brownshirts with arms extended in a solid salute. As if these demonstrations were not enough, during the wedding luncheon the newlyweds and their guests were submitted to the reading of a congratulatory message from Herr Hitler. It is no surprise that King Gustaf V, the groom's grandfather, was asked by his government not to travel to Coburg, avoiding therefore partaking in such a diplomatically risky situation. The Swedes feared, rightly so as it turned out, that *"the wedding was not improbably to be made the occasion of a Nazi demonstration,"* given the "ardent" support for the movement exhibited by Grandfather Coburg. Another notable absentee was the Prince of Wales, future King Edward VIII, who was told he could not attend by his father because *"the Duke of Saxe-Coburg and Gotha had become Hitler's henchman."*[77] In fact, in the *Eurohistory Archive*, owned by Arturo Beéche, my collaborator in this endeavor, there is a handwritten note sent by the Prince of Wales to Grandfather Coburg excusing his absence, which he blamed on the political situation in Germany. Allow me to mention also, that the *Eurohistory Archive* contains thousands of images, many of which we have used to illustrate this book. In fact, most of the photographs we used from the National Socialist era are found in Arturo Beéche's meticulously collected historical archive. Anyhow, the representation of King George V at the wedding was therefore entrusted to Uncle Alge Athlone. Also present from England was the Duke of Connaught, by then in his eighties and the last living son of Queen Victoria, who happened to be the groom's maternal grandfather!

By the time Adolf Hitler was asked to serve as Chancellor, Grandfather Coburg's allegiance to the Nazi Party was unquestionable. Once a prominent Berlin journalist, who attended a dinner party at which Grandfather Coburg was also a guest, recalled that he walked *"around with his Fascist dagger, an honor bestowed on him by Mussolini."*[78] After Hitler was in power, he appointed

Grandfather Coburg to various positions that had much public presence, but little if no influence in governmental affairs. Thus, he became commissioner for motoring and honorary leader of the Nazi Motor Corps, as well as President of the German Automobile Club. In due time he became a Major General (Gruppenführer) in the SA and in 1936 became Reichstag delegate. In late 1933, Grandfather Coburg was appointed President of the German Red Cross. By then he had also joined the Nazi Party. His enthusiasm was matched by other contemporaries. The point I am making is that his enthusiasm was not an isolated occurrence, but more a decision made by countless others of the same social milieu. In a way, all these people joined the party in order to play a role in a movement that they believed would bring Germany out of the depths of depression and poverty. Still, it is incomprehensible to me that so many members of these distinguished and historical families could have established liaisons with Hitler and his ilk.

Anti-Semitism is a pernicious societal illness. It has been present since time immemorial and I personally not only reject it, but also abhor such behavior. We live in changing times, in an era in which many minorities are finally achieving the acceptance, respect and recognition that are their due. Everyone has a right to live their own existence to the best of their abilities without fear of persecution and judgment. So to me, falling for the hateful tenets of National Socialism, its racist policies and hateful scaremongering, should have been anathema to someone with Grandfather Coburg's background. And yet, he did not shy from it, but instead fervenmtly embraced the movement. I have always wondered how could he, an English-born prince, a grandson of Queen Victoria, have allowed himself to fall for such a despicable movement …

Imperial Germany, I must say, had a far better record when it came to treatment of Jews than did other kingdoms, Russia in particular. While Jews were the objects of ethnic cleansing in Imperial Russia, particularly with government-sponsored pogroms, such was not the case in Germany. I am not naïve enough to claim that German Jews were treated as regular members of society. They were not treated in that way in any European country, not by royalty, not by the population in general. Even though Jews had been emancipated in Prussia in 1812 and recognized as citizens, the process of emancipation was not concluded until 1871. Misunderstanding and ignorance always played a malevolent role in how Europeans treated their Jewish brethren, and these were the fertile seeds of anti-Semitism. I believe that a new wave of anti-Semitism that began in the late 1870s was tied to policies espoused by Chancellor Bismarck. Not everyone welcomed Chancellor Bismarck's creation of the Second Reich. He, as talented as he may have been, was a man of indescribable ambition. Anyone who stood in his path had to be dealt with. Within Germany, the Catholic kingdoms were less than enthusiastic with the choosing of a Protestant Hohenzollern as German Emperor. The Catholic Church, as an institution, was also considerably unenthusiastic regarding Bismarck's political machinations. Bismarck, in turn, saw German Catholics as the most dangerous internal enemy of the Second Reich. In order to reduce Catholic influence in Prussia, he implemented the "Kulturkampf," a set of policies designed to attack the power of the Catholic Church.[79] Bismarck sought to appeal to liberals and Protestants (a majority of the population) by reducing the political and social influence of the Catholic Church and attempting to eliminate the Polish nationality, since a majority of Poles were Catholic.

The nightmare begins. My Coburg grandparents hosting a group of young Nazis at Schloß Callenberg.

What followed were several years of clashes between the Prussian government and the Catholic Church. Priests and bishops who resisted the "Kulturkampf" were arrested or removed from their positions. By the height of anti-Catholic legislation, *"half of the Prussian bishops were in prison or in exile, a quarter of the parishes had no priest, half the monks and nuns had left Prussia, a third of the monasteries and convents were closed, 1800 parish priests were imprisoned or exiled, and thousands of lay people were imprisoned for helping the priests.*"[80] The "Kulturkampf" eventually backfired by energizing Catholics into forming their own political party and causing a Polish revival. The "Kulturkampf" made it fine for masses of Germans to identify a minority, dehumanize it and blame it for the country's problems. This is exactly what National Socialism did to Germany's Jews. Tragically, the people fell for it!

I mention the effects of the "Kulturkampf" because I believe that the wave of anti-Semitism witnessed in late 1870s Prussia was a by-product tied to the politics of anti-Catholic hate sponsored by Bismarck. *"The Germans are not being sufficiently rebuked for their new-fangled intolerance & arrogance, & the phase of despising & denouncing all things foreign is not meeting with sufficient censure,"* Crown Princess Victoria of Prussia wrote.[81] She, and her husband equally so, was particularly troubled by *"agitation against the Jews which is currently taking place in Berlin."* The leading anti-Semite in Berlin was none other than Adolf Stoecker, a court chaplain who was close to Kaiser Wilhelm I. He was aided by the ridiculous pronouncements of one Heinrich von Treitschke, a professor of history in Berlin. He believed that there was a huge Jewish conspiracy geared toward the destruction of the Fatherland and he bemoaned it as *"dangerous …The Jews are our misfortune."* Stoecker and Treitschke invariably referred to Jews as *"leeches … parasites … an alien drop in our blood!"* This despicable race bating, tragically, took root in certain military circles in Potsdam, where the future Kaiser Wilhelm II came into contact with them. Shocked by the turn of events, Crown Princess Victoria blamed Christians, in fact, for abusing the Jews for centuries. Furthermore, she believed that this sort of agitation was not conducive to national unity – what with the "Kulturkampf" first, and then the targeting of Jews, *"chauvinistic Prussiandom"* was to be responsible for national disunity. Bismarck had sought to govern by dividing and this course of action eventually failed. Crown Prince Friedrich was equally disdainful of the anti-Semitism permeating court life and military circles, describing it both as *"disgraceful"* and a *"shameful blot on our time."*[82] However, and much as they tried to attack Stoecker and Treitschke's influence, the Prussian military was only too eager to adopt their malicious views and permeate the institution with a decidedly anti-Semitic undertone. In the meantime, many members of the Crown prince's inner circle were decidedly concerned that his eldest son was tainted by the irrational attitude toward Jews enthusiastically supported by the military clique in Potsdam.

Like thousands of other war veterans, Grandfather Coburg became an enthusiastic supporter of the Stalhelm, an organization later used by the Nazis for propaganda purposes.

I am convinced that Grandfather Coburg's impressionable years in Potsdam were tinged with the brand of anti-Semitism that Stoecker and Treitschke sponsored some two decades before. Furthermore, National Socialism, once it made its appearance in the German national scene, fit too perfectly into the Junker-inspired chauvinistic, anti-Semitic militarism that had previously infected the Prussian army. It was, one can safely argue, the same wolf, but wearing different clothes. Even so, I must point one important aspect in this discussion: there is no actual written proof that Grandfather Coburg was a virulent anti-Semite; there is also no record of what he thought of the Third Reich's "Ultimate Solution." These facts do not exempt him from blame, of course not. Was he an anti-Semite? I would argue that quite likely so, particularly influenced by the education he received in Potsdam;.Was he involved in the Nazi's extermination policies? No, he was not, in fact during his interrogation after the war he categorically denied having knowledge of these atrocities, a fact that is quite shocking in itself. Was he a public supporter of Hitler? Absolutely and he erroneously saw in Hitler a political leader who promised to lift Germany from the ashes of the Great War, but then plunged the Fatherland into an indescribable abyss of tragedy. Grandfather Coburg

German Kaiser Friedrich III.

allowed his name to be used to provide the Nazi's a much-needed veneer of respectability. Absolutely and without a doubt he deserves to be judged by history for his association with the Third Reich! I believe that enough time has passed for us to be able to discuss these topics without fear of embarrassment. My grandfather made horrible mistakes. He did, not me, and I reject to be blamed for his errors. I was a child a the time. Now as an adult, I can honestly discuss his role in those dark days. I am not afraid to do so.

The Nazis were very astute to attract prominent German people like Grandfather Coburg, to their movement. They realized that considerable benefits could be obtained from the support of the former ruling princes. This support would be easily obtained by suggesting to them that the National Socialist Party's goals included the restoration of the German Empire. For people whose entire lives had been defined by the political positions they were raised to occupy as their birthright, this was like water in the desert. The thought that a growing, vibrant political party gaining national support by the day would consider bringing back the old regime was too sweet a temptation to ignore.

It is also worth noting that Grandfather Coburg's settlement with the authorities in Gotha caused quite an uproar with the German press. Many members of the public were so incensed by the settlement of the Coburg estates, that a referendum on princely restitution was conducted. Hitler saw an opportunity to further gain the trust of the aristocracy and he declared that, *"There are no Princes, only Germans."*[83] The Kaiser had said something similar in the August 1914 declaration, *"I no longer recognize political parties, only Germans."*[84] In the end, the referendum was defeated, much to the relief of landed aristocrats like my grandfather. However, they all took notice of Hitler's public stand in their defense.

In the case of Grandfather Coburg, besides the hope that Hitler would restore the monarchy, there was his innate desire to be of service to his adopted Fatherland, thus proving to all critics that he was indeed a true German. Hence, once approached by the Nazis to become their go-between with England, he jumped at the opportunity of bringing about a rapprochement between the two countries he loved. Grandfather Coburg's connections to the Court of St. James were pristine, particularly with the Prince of Wales, who like him, wished to avoid another world war and sought to bring England closer to Germany. Besides him, Grandfather Coburg had good relations with other members of the Royal Family, as well as being well liked by other prominent Englishmen. Not only was he a first cousin of King George V, but his sister Alice was married to the Earl of Athlone, a brother of Queen Mary, King George V's consort.

These diplomatic efforts were first put into good use when in 1934 Hitler asked Grandfather Coburg to play a leading role in the launch of the Anglo-German Fellowship. Its main goal was aimed at building up friendship between the United Kingdom and Germany. It would be incorrect to think that the Anglo-German Fellowship wished to Nazify England. Together with its sister organization, the Deutsch-Englische Gesellschaft, the Fellowship would organize large dinners extolling the benefits of greater cooperation between both countries. Hopes for the prosperity of Anglo-German relations were certainly aided by a speech given by the Prince of Wales in 1935. In it, the future King Edward VIII called for a *"closer understanding of Germany in order to safeguard peace in Europe."*[85] King George V was incensed by the speech and scolded his son for interfering with Foreign Office policies. In fact, the Foreign Office saw the Anglo-German Fellowship as nothing but *"an admirable vehicle for German propaganda."*[86] The Prince of Wales, who was perceived to be pro-German, simply ignored his father and prepared to lead the charge for rapprochement with Berlin once he became king.

In search of success, Grandfather Coburg's visits to London increased. In one interview he spoke in positive terms of the *"widespread sympathy in Germany for the English people, the depths of which was not fully understood in Britain."*[87] The fact that the Prince of Wales so freely expressed his support for better relations with Germany further encouraged Hitler to continue using Grandfather Coburg's back-door diplomacy. The Prince of Wales was not alone though, for like him many prominent English aristocrats also hoped that the links between London and Berlin would be further strengthened, thus reducing the risk of both countries ending in another major war against the other. These aristocrats wanted both countries to identify Stalinism was their common enemy. That innate fear of Communism drove them toward Anglo-German cooperation, which they saw as a bullwark against Soviet expansionism. Grandfather Coburg once wrote Hitler that for Edward VIII, an Anglo-German alliance was not simply *"an urgent necessity,"*[88] but also an aspiration he hoped to achieve.

When King George V died in January 1936, Grandfather Coburg attended his state funeral. During this visit he had several private conversations with King Edward VIII and departed London very encouraged that the start of a new reign would bring success to Berlin's goals. *"For him, an urgent necessity,"* was how Grandfather Coburg described Edward VIII's hopes for an Anglo-German alliance. His report to Hitler also mentioned that Edward VIII had asked Grandfather Coburg that *"in order that confidential matters might be more speedily clarified,"* he wanted his German cousin to visit him frequently.[89]

Grandfather Coburg before the Great War.

One can but wonder how these schemes may have fared had King Edward VIII's reign been longer. Unfortunately, this falls into the realm of history's "what ifs." In December 1936, Grandfather Coburg's work was obliterated by King Edward VIII's willingness to abdicate so he could *"marry the woman I love."* From then onward, Grandfather Coburg's privileged access to the occupant of Buckingham Palace was at an end. The Anglo-German Fellowship had failed.

As President of the German Red Cross, a mostly ceremonial position, Grandfather Coburg was able to travel far and wide bringing Germany's *"message of peace"* along with him. These travels, responsible for bringing him to the USA and Japan, were goodwill missions wholeheartedly supported by Berlin. This is also one of the reasons why Grandfather Coburg began to be referred by the international press as "Hitler's Duke." He relished in the sense of importance that was gained from carrying out these "unofficial" pseudo-diplomatic missions during which he acted, frankly, as Hitler's go-between. In *The New York Times*, for example, we found a report that tied Grandfather Coburg's visit to Japan to the improvement of German-Japanese diplomatic relations and, eventually, to the Chrysanthemum Throne's alliance with the Third Reich.[90] For someone who relished the political position he had lost in 1918, this must have been a rather addictive elixir. He never realized, however, that by playing such a public part in trying to raise goodwill for the Fatherland, he was consequently tying his future even more so to the Third Reich, its policies and atrocities. I do not think that Grandfather Coburg ever realized that his association with the Nazis brought him more problems than benefits!

Meanwhile, the family had grown, in one case at least much to the chagrin of my Coburg grandparents. In the late 1920s, Uncle Leo, once he finished attending the Gymnasium Casimirianum in Coburg, left home and went to study in Brandenburg.

As President of the German Red Cross, Grandfather Coburg was tasked with several international missions. This photo was taken during a visit to Italy, where he met with Benito Mussolini. Other such journeys took him to the United Kingdom, the USA and Japan.

King George V.

Later, he went to study forestry in Bonn in preparation for the day when he would assume the administration of the family's estates and enterprises. It all seemed to be turning out rather promising for Uncle Leo that is until he became involved with a young woman whom my grandparents did not approve of due to her background. Her name was Baroness Feodora von der Horst and she was born in 1905. Her father was a member of the minor, local nobility of Rastenburg (now in Poland), while her mother was a commoner. On top of it all, Feodora had already been married once, her husband being a Baron Plerger von Perglas. How Uncle Leo and his beloved met I have never known, but what I do know is that my grandparents were most displeased with the news. Someone once told me that Feodora had informed Uncle Leo that she was pregnant with his child and thus the couple had to marry. Whether this is true, or not, they did marry in Dresden in March 1932. In punishment, Grandfather Coburg demanded that Uncle Leo renounce to his succession rights and the marriage was considered morganatic. None of the couple's children would hold dynastic rights, nor would they be part of the family foundation.

Uncle Leo had three children: Marianne (b. 1933); Ernst Leopold (1935-1996), a very difficult person who never accepted what his father had to renounced and ended committing a double suicide with his third wife; and Peter (b. 1939), who worked for several decades years with our Schleswig-Holstein cousins and eventually

Adolf Hitler used Grandfather Coburg as a go-between with anti-war elements of the English upper aristocracy and political world. My grandfather fell for Hitler's promises of an eventual restoration of the monarchy. Instead, his association with Germany's brutal dictator cost Grandfather Coburg dearly. Although he survived the war, he was a broken man whose reputation was forever shattered.

settled in Coburg, where I see him frequently. All three siblings have descendants, but none of these Coburgs are members of the dynasty or the family foundation due to Uncle Leo's renunciation.

Years later, Uncle Leo made some very disturbing and questionable mistakes that landed him in quite a bit of trouble. By then, he had divorced Feodora after thirty years of marriage. A year after his divorce, he married again a lady by the name of Maria Theresia Reindl. They lived quietly in Grein in a house provided to him by the foundation. He died there in 1972, the same year that Aunt Bylla died.

Of course Aunt Bylla's marriage to a man, who besides being delightful, was expected to become the King of Sweden, was seen by Grandfather Coburg as a great coup. Aunt Bylla and Uncle Edmund, as he was called in the family, were grandchildren of Queen Victoria's sons, the Duke of Connaught and Albany respectively. They first met at the wedding of our cousin Lady May Cambridge, the only surviving child of Aunt Alice Athlone. The wedding took place in London in 1931 and at it both Aunt Bylla and then Princess Ingrid of Sweden served as bridesmaids, while a very young Princess Elizabeth of York was one of the flower girls!

One year later, Royal Europe gathered in Coburg to celebrate the marriage of Aunt Bylla and Uncle Edmund. The wedding was described as a *"glamorous affair,"* even though it served for an uncomfortably noisy display of Nazi presence in our beloved and otherwise tranquil Coburg.[91] Aunt Bylla and her husband, a cultured man loved by all, settled in Sweden after the wedding.

King Edward VIII.

Uncle Leo.

There she carried out countless royal duties, while also providing her husband with five children: Margaretha, Birgitta, Désirée, Christina, and King Carl XVI Gustaf. I am very close to all my Swedish cousins, but particularly so to the younger ones as they are closer in age to me. Our bonds with this royal family are perhaps the closest ones we have with a ruling dynasty today. I was honored when His Majesty asked to be godfather to his youngest daughter, Princess Madeleine. We were deeply honored when Crown Princess Victoria accepted to be one of my granddaughter Katharina's godmothers. Thus continues a link between Coburg and Sweden that has existed for far more than a century, in fact since Princess Margaret, eldest daughter of the Duke of Connaught, married the future King Gustaf VI Adolf, Uncle Edmund's father.

As a young man I visited Sweden several times. Father wished that my contacts with his sister's children remained strong and steadfast. Luckily, as youngsters, we all liked each other. I like Aunt Bylla very much and I don't remember seeing in her the stern woman some historians later claimed she was. What I saw was a single mother raising five children, a widow who missed her late husband deeply. Uncle Edmund lived long enough to witness the birth of his long-awaited son in 1946. Several months later, in January 1947, Uncle Edmund went to the Netherlands to participate in a hunt hosted by Prince Bernhard. His return flight on a KLM DC-3 airplane made a scheduled stop in Copenhagen. Upon takeoff en-route to Stockholm, the airplane plummeted to the ground.

Eyewitnesses told the press that *"it made a remarkably steep ascent, at an angle of nearly 60 degrees."* The pilot *"tried to flatten out, but the plane stalled, rolled twice while falling and crashed, hitting the airfield with its left wingtip."*[92] The DC-3 exploded in a hellish fireball and those onboard never had a chance. It took the fire brigade nearly an hour to extinguish the fire and reach the remains. All bodies were still fastened to their seats. The investigation listed the cause as human error: *"Failure to remove the elevator locking pins."*[93] Along with Uncle Edmund, twenty-one other human beings lost their life in the accident. Among the casualties was Ms. Grace Moore, a world-famous opera singer.

When news of the accident reached the Haga Palace, poor Aunt Bylla is said to have "collapsed" in shock. Her step-mother-in-law, Crown Princess Louise (née Battenberg/Mountbatten), was tasked with the unenviable mission of informing the widow of her husband's untimely passing. King Gustaf V, Uncle Edmund's 88-year old grandfather, already in poor health, was also devastated by the news, just as was the Crown Prince. Reports from Stockholm that evening described a capital in a state of desolation, *"streets, restaurants and amusement places were empty … and all Sweden was in mourning."*[94]

Uncle Edmund was a great sportsman and a well-recognized shot. He was once described as *"One of Sweden's best steeplechase riders and one*

Uncle Edmund and Aunt Bylla.

*of her best fencers."*⁹⁵ He sponsored countless national organizations and royal charities, chief among them the Swedish Scouts, much as his son does today. At one point he also served as Honorary Chairman of the International Scout Federation.

Aunt Bylla was a very courageous woman. She had to be, as life dealt her a very heavy blow and she still had to raise her fatherless children. The education of my cousin, the King, was of particular importance given the future role he would play in Sweden. At the time, Sweden did not allow female succession. The Bernadotte dynasty, which at one point was flush with princes, had seen its ranks depleted by the unequal marriages entered into by most males in the generation of Uncle Edmund. In fact, out of his father's four sons he was the only one to marry royalty. Of Uncle Edmund's brothers Sigvard and Carl Johan had renounced their rights upon marrying commoners, while Bertil, who had a long-term relationship with a Welsh lady, Lilian Craig, refrained from marrying her to preserve his place in the line of succession in case my cousin Carl Gustaf did not reach the throne. Prince Bertil and Princess Lilian, who finally married in 1976, were like grandparents to King Carl XVI Gustaf's children.

Three years after the death of her husband, Aunt Bylla left Haga palace and settled in Stockholm. Her father-in-law was now King Gustaf VI

Wedding of Uncle Edmund and Aunt Bylla, Coburg, 1932.

Adolf and the royal court required her presence in the capital and, as time passed, she became very popular. Aunt Bylla was a great support to her father-in-law, particularly after Queen Louise's health kept her from going out in public. Because of her exposure, Aunt Bylla was able to show the Swedes that she was an approachable person with democratic leanings, particularly when she continued supporting the "Democratic ladies lunches," a gathering for career women designed to replace the old presentation at court ceremonies. Aunt Bylla had a great sense of humor and was particularly good at self-irony, which pleased Swedes. She was not the staunch Conservative and unbending German that an unsympathetic press believed she was.

Life ended short for Aunt Bylla when illness took her from us in November 1972. Had she lived another year, she would have witnessed not only her son's succession, but also the culmination of her efforts to educate him for the important task history had placed on his shoulders.

The wedding dinner for Aunt Bylla and Uncle Edmund. From the left: Grand Duchess Kira Kirillovna of Russia, Princess Alexandra of Hohenlohe-Langenburg, Grand Duchess Victoria Feodorovna of Russia, Grandfather Coburg, Crown Prince Gustaf Adolf of Sweden, Aunt Bylla, Uncle Edmund, Aunt Alice Athlone, Crown Princess Louise of Sweden, Aunt Helena Denmark and Grandmother Coburg.

Just as tragic for the Coburg dynasty was the untimely passing of Uncle Hubertus ("Bertel"), my grandparents' middle son. Uncle Bertel was an attractive young man – his head topped by a blonde mop of hair that was always neatly styled; his eyes a deep blue; his mouth usually sporting a wide smile. He was, quite so, both the most handsome and popular of the three Coburg brothers. He lived life to its fullest and was a magnet; his approachable personality made him noticed everywhere he went. After completing high school in Coburg's Gymnasium Casimirianum, Uncle Bertel attended university to study architecture. He was passionate about the arts and had a keen eye for structural design. Uncle Bertel also loved speeding and was happiest when zooming about in his white BMW 328 sports car. My mother always remembered him fondly and was convinced that his death was a great tragedy, as well as one from which his family never recovered.

Grandfather Coburg had grand designs for his second son, particularly after the disappointment experienced with Uncle Leo. At one point that family tried to put him on the path of none other than Princess Juliana, only daughter and heir of Queen Wilhelmina of the Netherlands, Grandfather Coburg's first cousin. However, the youngsters had other plans and Juliana fell in love with Prince Bernhard of Lippe-Biesterfeld, while Uncle Bertel continued along having as good a time as he could possibly have with his white BMW 328.

Father was very fond of his brother and I believe that his death during the Second World War affected him in particular. At the outbreak of war, Uncle Bertel joined the Luftwaffe and served as a courier pilot. He was killed in Mosty, Romania, on November 26, 1943.[96] I was just eight months' old and, of course, I have no recollection of him. I think, however, that I would have liked him very much, particularly since we both share a passion for automobiles!

Crown Prince Gustaf Adolf and Crown Princess Margaret of Sweden.

Father, some years ago, said that none of the Coburg children had a tougher time during their teenage years than Aunt Calma. She was rebellious and she was a free spirit. She was fun loving and paid little attention to caution; she was a daredevil and prone to getting herself in trouble. Their youngest daughter drove my Coburg grandparents more than a bit mad. It was not surprising then that Aunt Calma was the first of the Coburg children to marry. In December 1931, Aunt Calma married Count Friedrich-Wolfgang zu Castell-Rüdenhausen, a grandson of the first Fürst zu Castell-Rüdenhausen. In July of the following year Aunt Calma gave birth to their first child, Bertram. Two other children arrived in due time, Conradin (1933-2011) and Victoria (b. 1935).[97] By then, the marriage was already sinking as Aunt Calma's mercurial temperament easily lost interest in a relationship that given different circumstances would have probably never ended in marriage. The couple divorced in 1938 and both lost little time settling with other spouses, particularly Aunt Calma, who was pregnant by the man who would become her second husband. She married six weeks after her divorce Captain Max Schnirring, a pilot with the Luftwaffe. Five months later Aunt Calma's first child with Herr Schnirring (Calma) was born in Chile!

Uncle Edmund with Prince Bernhard of the Netherlands during his last hunt. Uncle Edmund boarded an airplane that crashed soon after take-off in Kastrup, Denmark. He, along with all the passengers and crew, died in the crash.

The Schnirrings had two more children, Dagmar and Michael, born in 1940 and 1943 respectively. Unfortunately, Aunt Calma's relative peace was destroyed on July 7, 1944, when Captain Schnirring died in a flying accident at Stralsund, Mecklenburg. Curiously, Count Friedrich-Wolfgang, who served in the Luftwaffe, also died in a flying accident over Portland, England in 1940.[98]

The post-war period was very difficult for Aunt Calma. Not surprisingly, relations with the family were also not at their best. She was a single mother with six children and very few assets. She did her best to raise them and eventually all married, except Michael Schnirring, who died in Munich in 1966 while still in his early twenties. Nothing was spared to poor Aunt Calma, who tried to find happiness yet again in 1946 by marrying a third time, but this marriage ended in divorce in 1947. She died in Erlangen in 1983 and is buried in the plot built by Grandmother Coburg overlooking Schloß Callenberg.[99]

Aunt Bylla and her children. From the left: Princess Margaretha, Princess Désirée, Princess Birgitta, Princess Christina, Prince Carl Gustaf and Aunt Bylla.

The end of the Second World War obliterated what little remained of Grandfather Coburg's dream of a strong and revitalized Germany. The country lay occupied, devastated, defeated, and hope seemed to have evaporated from the faces of most Germans. The eastern part of the country fell under the control of the Red Army, which caused the loss of all our Thüringen properties, as well as the most of the former ducal art collections. In Austria, since the Soviets were given administrative control, they also froze our properties, the Greinburg included. It was not until then that, I imagine, he began realizing the magnitude of his mistakes. If his world after 1918 had been drastically changed; the world he lived in now was absolutely foreign.

By May 1945, Germany seemed ripped to shreds. Only Coburg, occupied by the Americans, seemed to have escaped the destruction that rained over most of the country. In fact, when the Americans arrived in Coburg, Grandfather Coburg was living inside the Prince's Bastion at the Veste Coburg. General Patton, whom Grandfather Coburg had met during one of his trips to the USA, allowed my grandparents to remain at the Veste Coburg. For a few months the situation remained calm. But then, by November 1945, Patton's successor, who was not so "understanding," implemented drastic changes overnight!

Grandfather Coburg was arrested for his involvement with the Nazis. He was *"subject to several weeks of interrogations"* due to his ties to the Third Reich.[100] Initially, he was imprisoned in a camp that was previously used to house Serbian prisoners. The food was so terribly bad that prisoners were forced to *"add grass to improve the thin soup served at every meal."* Sick with arthritis, an illness that had affected him for more than a decade, the damp conditions caused him untold pain and discomfort. At one point, her husband's jailors told Grandmother Coburg that she would *"never see him alive again."*[101] It was not until Aunt Alice arrived that she, with Uncle Alge, managed *"to persuade the American, and later, the German authorities, to provide"* better quarters.[102]

Aunt Bylla.

He was placed under house arrest and ordered to move to a small cottage next to the stables at Schloß Callenberg. There my grandparents lived in strained circumstances and even obtaining food was a considerable chore. Grandmother Coburg, already in her 60s, had to walk or ride a bicycle into Coburg to buy what little food they could get. It was quite a dismal fall for a couple who had lived in castles and been surrounded by servants their entire lives. It was while living there that they received news of Uncle Edmund's tragic death. And yet, they endured!

Concerned by the living conditions of her brother, Aunt Alice Athlone finally arrived in Coburg in September 1948. With the assistance of Uncle Alge Athlone, she tried to persuade Grandfather Coburg's jailors to let him move, for it was *"all so sad and sordid,"* [103] and she feared that the living conditions suffered by my grandparents would kill her brother. *"In the long run, as Charlie was such an invalid with arthritis, he was allowed to transfer,"* Aunt Alice wrote in her memoirs.[104] Eventually, Grandfather and Grandmother Coburg were allowed to move to one of our twin residences, Elssässerstraße 10, closer to the Coburg town center. His declining health played an important role in this decision by his jailors. Once there, life began improving, even if it was for a short while since Grandfather Coburg was already ill with the cancer that would eventually kill him. Grandmother Coburg was now *"close enough to the market for catering for their bit of food."*[105]

Uncle Bertel at a hunt.

Grandfather Coburg's legal troubles took some time to solve. At one point, according to *The New York Times,* he was to face charges for being a Nazi Party member, but also for his role as Vice-President of the International Red Cross. *"He reported to that organization on the conditions in Büchenwald ... asserted that all stories of bad treatment of prisoners were nasty*

Uncle Bertel in his white BMW 328 sports car.

Uncle Leo, Father, Grandfather Coburg and Uncle Bertel.

From the left: Uncle Bertel, Aunt Calma, and my parents.

inventions," read the report.[106] It baffles the mind why he would have authored such a clearly false account. Either he did not visit the camp, or if he visited he was shown what needed to be seen for the report, or worse, he chose to participate in the cover-up that for years allowed the Nazis to carry on with their death machines. Obviously, we will never know the truth about his actions since he left us no written memoir and his interrogation transcripts, copies of some of them obtained by Arturo Beéche, my collaborator, fail to reveal much besides his support for Hitler and his role with the German Red Cross. And yet, I sit here and wonder how could such a man, who was described by all as having a soft-spoken manner, a cultured man, could have been a participant, a collaborator, in such nefarious affairs.

While I understand the fear of Communism experienced by Grandfather Coburg and his contemporaries, I cannot begin to wrap my mind around the thought that they saw in the rise of National Socialism. The Nazis were false prophets that made empty promises and used nationalism and patriotism to give achieve legitimacy. The assistance of prominent Germans, much like Grandfather Coburg, made their road to power even easier. Grandfather Coburg, in spite of being a nice man, made a terrible decision when he became involved with Hitler and his goons. This is the real tragedy of the last Duke of Saxe-Coburg and Gotha. Aunt Alice Athlone once described him as *"encompassed by the fatal hand of fortune,"* a loving sibling effort to excuse his choices. She fervently believed that her brother had been the victim of history and circumstances, for how else could she logically explain his actions.[107] Yet, victim or not, he willingly associated with the regime and supported Hitler's rise to power. There is nothing that can absolve him from having provided his support to National Socialism. for that, history has passed judgment on him.

The real tragedy must rest on the fact that Grandfather Coburg was a man who lacked the character to see that he was being used. He was born and raised in an era in which men like him were destined to rule their realms with enlightenment. When transplanted to Germany, he was an English princeling who was not yet proficient in the language of his future subjects. He had divided loyalties. That he lacked a strong character is quite obvious. In Potsdam, while

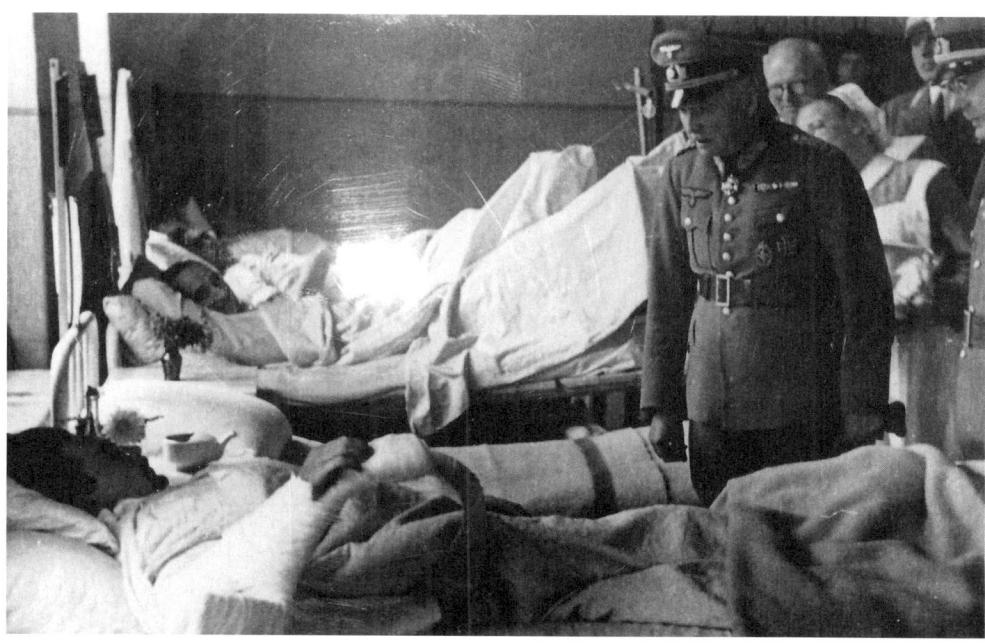

Grandfather Coburg visiting war casualties during the Second World War.

attending military school he came under the influence of ideas that in his native England would have not been tolerated. He was an English prince ruling in Germany and that forced him, to avoid criticism, to become more German than any other German. The collapse of the Second Reich left Grandfather Coburg like a rudderless ship in a turbulent sea. In England he was rejected as an enemy, while in Germany he was seen with a degree of mistrust. His support of National Socialism was an ultimately misguided effort to show Germany his absolute loyalty. He was a convert, with all its good and evils.

Grandfather and Grandmother Coburg in old age.

His failure was thinking that calm could only be attained by returning, at whatever the cost, to the safe harbor provided by Imperial times. He sought purpose, security and influence, but found none. He saw in National Socialism a false idol, one that masked its ruthlessness with a shroud of patriotism – One that covered its hatred with the type of nationalism that demanded turning a blind eye to its violence, for in the end the goal justified the means, however vicious these were.

It was during these trying times that Grandfather Coburg made the fateful decision to resign his right as main beneficiary of the Coburg Foundation, the same institution he had set up in the 1920s. By doing so, he appointed me as his successor and by doing so he avoided ruinous taxes that would have dealt our family a financial deathblow. By then, Father had left Germany and gone to Sweden, where he met his second wife, Denise de Muralt, who worked for Aunt Bylla. I had also left Germany. Mother had met her future husband and we were headed to the United States to start a new life.

The funeral of Grandfather Coburg. From the left: Herr Voights, Grandmother Coburg, Aunt Bylla. Behind them are Aunt Alice and my father, followed by Denise (Father's second wife) and Aunt Calma.

Meanwhile, an elderly and sick man who had become a recluse after the end of the war lay dying at Elssässerstraße 10. Grandfather Coburg's body, wracked by arthritis, also had to contend with an abominable cancer that grew under his right eye. It was a ghastly, festering sore that not even the best doctors accessible to him could cure. As his 70th birthday approached, so did he near the end of his long and complicated existence. Grandfather Coburg passed away at home on March 6, 1954.[108]

I was not at Grandfather Coburg's funeral since by then I was a rowdy youngster growing up in the United States. Travel being what it was then, I just could not possibly make it to Germany on time. Father and Grandmother Coburg presided over the funeral, which he later recalled as the last great gathering of the royal mob Coburg would see for many decades. Aunts Bylla and Calma also supported Grandmother Coburg. Several of my Castell-Rüdenhausen cousins were there as well. Following Grandfather Coburg to his final resting place were representatives of just about every house in the Gotha. They gathered in Coburg to render homage to someone who had meant well, but had made grave mistakes.

With his passing, it seemed that the Coburgs went into the wilderness. The family was rarely seen attending royal events. It was as if our dynasty had ceased to exist. It would take more than three decades, as well as a tremendous amount of work and effort, to remind all that we were not gone, but just not there. Reintroducing the Coburgs to the Gotha fell on my shoulders and as I look around, I can safely say that we were gone once, but we are back again!

Grandfather Coburg.

Chapter VI
Grandfather Solms and Omo

My mother at about the time of her engagement.

Throughout my younger years, due to the circumstances surrounding my parents' relationship, I was in closer contact with my Solms grandparents than with the Coburg ones. Allow me to say that whenever I think of Grandfather Solms and "Omo," as we called Grandmother Solms, I get a sense of the ambiance of peace and love that characterized their existence. They were dedicated to each other and enjoyed a long and happy marriage. They raised three children who remained very close to one another through life's many vicissitudes. Such was their devotion, that whenever possible, the children (with their spouses and own children in tow) would travel to Austria and spend long vacations with Grandfather Solms and Omo. In their presence we flourished in an atmosphere of respect and love, admiration and duty, joy and dignity. They were exemplary human beings and their memory remains alive with me, their eldest grandchild.

The Solms family is one with a very long history. The family first appears in a document from about the year 788. They were the rulers of the County of Solms, one of the countless independent states within the Holy Roman Empire. This political entity existed until Emperor Franz II dissolved the empire in 1806.

Due to the restructuring that the German states experienced during and after the Napoleonic era, the area of Solms was incorporated into the Duchy of Nassau, since the town was in Hesse, the land where most of Nassau's territories were located. Later, in 1815, Solms passed to Prussia. By then, the family had not only acquired vast territories around Germany, but also subdivided into several branches: Solms-Braunfels, Solms-Hohensolms-Lich, Solms-Baruth, Solms-Laubach, Solms-Rödelheim-Assemheim, Solms-Sonnewalde and Solms-Wildenfels. The family was mediatized at the Congress of Vienna, therefore recognizing its sovereign status, as well as its capability to marry families in the First Section of the Almanach de Gotha.

My mother's branch, Solms-Baruth, built a large estate around the town of Baruth, located in Lower Lusatia and surrounded by the Kingdom of Prussia and the Duchy of Silesia. These lands had been acquired through time and included some 15,000 hectares of agriculture and forestry land, as well as almost a dozen villages and the towns of Baruth and Casel. The family had also acquired an important estate in Klitschdorf, Silesia, which was given to the eldest son to manage. It was in Casel that both my mother and I were born, as well as the location of my parents' wedding.

The Solms-Baruth were important members of the Prussian royal court. Since their mediatization, they distinguished themselves for their service to the Hohenzollern kings, first, and later to the Kaiser, when Wilhelm I, received that title in 1871. This allegiance to the Hohenzollerns earned my great-great-grandfather, Count Friedrich Hermann (1821-1904), the

Friedrich Fürst zu Solms-Baruth.

title of "Fürst" in 1888. The elevation to the princely rank took place during the brief reign of Kaiser Friedrich III, who sadly only ruled the German Empire for 99 days. He was the father of Kaiser Wilhelm II, an impulsive man who perhaps ascended the imperial throne at too young an age.

My Solms great-grandfather, Fürst Friedrich II, succeeded his father and was Head of House until his own death in 1920. Devoted to the Hohenzollerns, he was one of the most upright members of the Berlin court. For many years he served as Lord Grand Chamberlain at the Court of Kaiser Wilhelm II. During the Great War, Friedrich II of Solms-Baruth served as Inspector of the Red Cross, a duty he took quite seriously. Through his wife, the former Countess Luise of Hochberg, Baroness zu Fürstenstein, he was connected to the very prominent Princes of Pleß, owners of vast estates in Silesia, particularly Fürstenstein and Pleß. Great-grandmother Solms, in fact, was a sister-in-law of the famed beauty, and author, Daisy Cornwallis-West, better known as Princess Daisy of Pleß. This connection to the Pleß family was later to be a considerable benefit to Grandfather Solms and Omo as it provided them a home after the loss of all Solms-Baruth properties in Lower Lusatia and Silesia (modern-day Poland).

My Solms Great-grandparents had five children, one daughter and four sons. Their eldest child, Aunt Pink (Rosa), was married to the Fürst of Salm-Horstmar. The family's four sons (Friedrich, Hermann, Hans Georg and Johann-Georg) all served in the prestigious Garde de Corps, the elite German cavalry regiment. My mother later recalled that when *"World War I broke out all of the brothers were called into my grandfather's conference room, where he told them he expected them to be an example to their troops and give their fatherland their best!"*[109] Luckily, all four Solms brothers returned home after the war, alive, if perhaps considerably aged due to the awful experiences they lived through.

Grandfather Solms, who was born at Klitschdorf in 1893, served as a Lieutenant in Belgium and France. He was later promoted to the rank of Captain and transferred to the Russian front. The war's end, with Germany's defeat, was a great disappointment for them all.

Grandfather Solms married in 1920. His bride was Princess Caroline Mathilde ("Omo") of Schleswig-Holstein-Sonderburg-Glücksburg (1894-1972). Their wedding took place at Schloß Glücksburg in May 1920, that being the same place where my Coburg grandparents had married all those years ago before the Great War.[110] Omo's older sister, Princess Adelheid, had married in August 1914 Grandfather Solms' eldest brother, Friedrich, who in 1920 succeeded as Head of House Solms-Baruth. Hence, Grandfather Solms and Omo were not strangers and had known each other for many years. It is quite likely that the war and all the chaos and suffering that came with it delayed their wedding, as it happened to countless other couples.

My mother and her beloved "Irrlicht."

My mother, Viktoria Luise, was Grandfather Solms and Omo's eldest child. Eventually two brothers, Friedrich-Hans (1923-2006) and Hubertus (1934-1991), joined her.[111] As I mentioned before, they all remained extremely close to one another and simply loved spending time with their parents. My mind is filled with happy memories of vacations and visits to the Solms relatives, particularly at Steinwändt, an estate in Austria that Grandfather Solms inherited from a Hochberg uncle.

After their wedding, Grandfather Solms and Omo settled at Schloß Casel. Both mother and Uncle Pety (Friedrich-Wilhelm) were born there. Uncle Hubertus, who was the "after-thought" child, was born in Berlin 1934, when mother was already a teenaged girl. To me, Uncle Hubertus was always more like an older brother than an uncle. He was very funny and had a dare-devilish personality. It was always great fun to be near him and enjoy his laughter. He left us too soon, as did his first wife, Elisabeth-Charlotte von Kerssenbrock, who died in 1968.[112] He remarried in 1969 Baroness Gerta Staël von Holstein (b. 1939), by whom he had one daughter,

My two grandmothers and their sister. From the left: Duchess Viktoria Adelheid of Saxe-Coburg and Gotha, Princess Alexandra Viktoria of Prussia, and Countess Caroline-Mathilde of Solms-Baruth.

my cousin Victoria Caroline, who is married to Hans Ludwig Grains. Uncle Hubertus and his first wife had three children: Rupprecht (b. 1963), who married Princess Henriette Reuß (b. 1964); Donata (b.1965), who married Baron Christian-Jasper von Brockdorff (b. 1960); and Eilika (b. 1966), who married Count Jakob Waldburg zu Wolfegg und Waldsee (b. 1957).[113] These first cousins of mine are closer in age to my own children than to me, yet we maintain good relations.

Uncle Pety played an important role in my mother's life. Unbeknownst to him, Uncle Pety was the person responsible for bringing Captain Richard Whitten into my mother's life. But I will deal with that later. Like many of the young men of his generation, Uncle Pety fought in the Second World War. He was lucky to have survived the tragedy of this war and eventually reached Steinwändt, where Grandfather Solms and Omo settled after the end of the Second World War. In 1950 Uncle Pety married Princess Oda zu Stolberg-Wernigerode (1925-1978), a wonderful woman who was the life of the party everywhere she went. They were devoted to each other and her untimely death left him very sad. Uncle Pety never remarried. Aunt Oda was simply irreplaceable. They lived for a long time in Salzburg. There, Aunt Oda gave birth to her two eldest children: Irina (b. 1953), who married Prince Hubertus zu Sayn-Wittgenstein-Berleburg; and Christian (b. 1954), who married in the United States and settled there. Uncle Pety and Aunt Oda's youngest child is my cousin Huberta (b. 1958), who is also married.[114] Aunt Oda's death was a sad loss for the family at large and Uncle Pety in particular. He outlived his wife by nearly three decades and died in 2006. I have countless wonderful memories of Uncle Pety and cared for him very much.

My Grandparents Solms led a quiet and circumspect life in Casel, where he managed the estate. Their life expanded to Austria when in 1934 Uncle Conni (Count Conrad von Hochberg, Baron zu Fürstenstein) passed away without children. A lifelong bachelor, in his will Uncle Conni left Grandfather Solms "Steinwändt," an eight-thousand acre hunting estate (with a lodge). Steinwändt is located south of Salzburg, in a valley between *"the Hagen and Tennengebirge, two mountain ranges that come together at the Pass Lueg and gradually widen into a valley divided by the River Salzach."*[115] It is connected to Salzburg by a railroad line that in due time my Solms family would use quite frequently. The lodge, built in the seventeenth century, is located on a narrow piece of land at the foot of the mountain. Bordered by the River Salzach, it is not more than a mile wide at its widest point. It is here, at Steinwändt, that I spent many of the early years of my childhood.

My great-great-grandfather, Fürst Hans Heinrich XI of Pleß, who was also titled Duke of Pleß, purchased Steinwändt, as well as other important properties in the surrounding area. Uncle Conni inherited the property at his father's death in 1907, and although not a hunter, he loved the property and spent long periods there. After his father's death, Uncle Conni erected a "marterl" (memorial crucifix) for his father. These death monuments are quite common in Austria and Southern Germany and are usually erected by the side of small walkways and country roads. It is custom for men to tip their hats when they pass by one of these memorials and for women to nod or curtsey. Grandfather Solms had a "marterl" erected for Uncle Conni near the lodge. This site became a burial place for my mother's closest family members. In fact, both mother and her second husband are buried there.

My grandfather and his brothers all refused to join the National Socialist Party. They felt that doing so was a grave mistake and did not believe any of Hitler's empty promises. Because of this quite public position, they were always under Gestapo surveillance. However, as a reservist, Grandfather Solms was asked by General Field Marshal von Bock to serve in his general staff at the outbreak of the Second World War.

During the war, many prisoners of war were sent to work in agricultural estates. By doing so, many of these men found a better solution to their imprisonment. Grandfather Solms received three such prisoners of war at Casel. My mother remembered these men fondly as they became great companions to her and her siblings. By the rules set up by the Nazis, these prisoners were not allowed many amenities, like going to the movies or attending church services. Grandfather Solms would not enforce these rules and instead the three men *"were treated as humans by us all,"* mother recalled. They were allowed to ride horses and even served as tutors to my Uncle Pety. They were given books so they could spent their leisure time reading, and, in all, they became part of the estate's extended family. Since the men were also allowed to go to the movies and go to church, my mother and Uncle Pety gave them his clothes so they would not be identified as the police. Mother later recalled that *"we took a great chance of getting caught. My parents did not know about this either; otherwise, they would have stopped us from doing it. We could have gotten ourselves"* and the men in deep trouble.[116]

Uncle Dicky Solms.

Some time after the failed assassination attempt on Hitler, the Gestapo increased its reign of repression and terror. That summer of 1944 the Gestapo arrested Uncle Dicky Solms (my grandfather's eldest brother). Grandfather Solms and his brother were at the Baruth estate offices when two Gestapo agents demanded to see Uncle Dicky. They pushed aside the servant announcing them and told Uncle Dicky that he was under arrest. Uncle Dicky had *"hated the Nazis like poison, and never made any bones about it."*[117] Exasperated by the behavior of the Gestapo agents, he demanded that they leave his office immediately. When he tried to reach for the gun he always carried, the agents wrestled him to the ground. Grandfather Solms, when he heard the commotion, came to Uncle Dicky's rescue. There was little he could do when confronted with a gun pointed at his face. Uncle Dicky told his brother that he *"was trying to get my gun out, so I could defend myself against these illegal intruders,"* he said.[118] He was handcuffed and whisked away to prison without as much as a chance to even say goodbye to his family.

Grandfather Solms, accompanied by the family's lawyer, went to Potsdam immediately. His mission was to try to secure his brother's freedom. As Uncle Dicky refused to express his support for Hitler, his jailors refused to let him go. Grandfather Solms was still in Berlin trying whatever method available to free his brother. Then, it was his turn. He was summoned to Potsdam under the excuse that Uncle Dicky wanted to see him on an urgent matter. When he did not return to his lawyer's office on the expected train, alarm invaded his representative. For some time no one knew what had happened to him: Was he imprisoned? Had someone killed him? Had he escaped? Had he died during an air raid? These must have been extremely trying times for Omo, but she bore it all with admirable integrity. Meanwhile, the Gestapo eventually visited Omo to inform her that her husband was *"in protective custody"* while being interrogated concerning his brother's arrest.

His imprisonment lasted quite some time. Omo and Mother were allowed two thirty-minute visits every week. These took place in the presence of a Gestapo officer and there was no privacy whatsoever. My mother, who visited her father many times, recalled that the room had *"a couple of pictures of Hitler, Goering and Himmler"* hanging on the wall, *"as if to let us know that we were in their fangs!"*[119] Grandfather Solms spent his time reading books Omo was able to bring him, and even though Omo brought him food, the conditions inside the prison were dire and he suffered greatly. Uncle Dicky, who was physically abused by his interrogators, had an even worse fate during this dark episode. One of the accusations lobbied by the Gestapo against the Solms brothers was that they treated the prisoners of war sent to work on their estates too humanely, thus breaking the rules.

Father, who was stationed in Denmark at the time, took leave and tried to talk to some officials into letting Grandfather Solms out of prison. Even though Grandfather Coburg was well known within the Nazi hierarchy, the Solms brothers received no special treatment. Father was unsuccessful in his endeavors and when Gestapo boss Kaltenbrunner, a nasty man mother whom described as *"rude, crude and horrible,"* told Omo that she could not gain her husband's release by begging hi: *"He is here for a good reason and will stay there until we decide to let him go!"*[120] Kaltenbrunner was extremely disrespectful to Omo, and to my mother, and there was nothing anyone could do to secure Grandfather Solms's freedom.

I can only but imagine how difficult this situation must have been for all, Coburg and Solms in particular. Grandfather Coburg's role in the Third Reich helped Grandfather Solms not one iota. Father was fighting for a country governed by a brutal regime that had imprisoned his father-in-law for no obvious crime. Uncle Pety, also serving in the Russian front, was also fighting and risking his life for a government that held his father and uncle as political prisoners. Mother later recalled this awful experience as one of the most difficult times in her long life.

The weekly trips to visit Grandfather Solms involved great risk for Omo and whoever accompanied her. On the way to Potsdam they were exposed to air raids and all sorts of danger. Then, once at the prison, Omo was humiliated constantly. And still, there were good souls who took pity on her. One time, Mother remembered one particular instance of goodwill on the part of a guard:

"He seemed to have a little compassion with us, although we did not trust him, either. He let us stay for about two hours, which was unheard of. As a matter of fact, he went out of the room for a little while to leave us alone. My father read the usual Christmas story out of the Bible, and we sang 'Silent night, Holy night' together. I cannot remember if Pety and little Hubertus were with us that night. Hubertus was then just eight years old, and I know that he had never seen his father in the prison. We had a little Christmas tree all decorated which we brought from Casel. It even had small candles on it. We also had small gifts to give to each other. My mother had brought a few little wooden boxes to my father about a month before Christmas as well as paint to decorate them with. My father was not artistically inclined like my mother, but he did remarkably well considering that fact! I still have the little box he gave me. All I can say about this Christmas Eve is that it was the most memorable one in my life. As sad as it was, we were overjoyed to be alive and together."[121]

Princess Daisy of Pleß.

Meanwhile, the situation at the front worsened. The Allies had taken Italy and landed in Normandy. The Russian Front was collapsing, laying the Fatherland open to the invading Red Army. Fearful of the worsening conditions in Casel, particularly if the Red Army reached the estate, Grandfather Solms asked Omo to move to Coburg, where at least the family would be with Grandfather and Grandmother Coburg and in Bavaria. There they would await what they all knew to be coming, the final fall of the Third Reich and its leader Adolf Hitler.

The departure from Casel was chaotic. Refugees by the thousands streamed westbound from the Eastern provinces.

The stories of abuse and terror they told concerning the actions of the Red Army chilled everyone's blood. In the midst of this commotion, Omo organized the family's retreat to Coburg as the hum of Russian canons could be heard in the east. It was a harrowing escape. Omo did her best to get everyone to bring along whatever little of value they could gather. Mother and Uncle Hubertus were forced to get on a train near Golsen, as the Nazis forbid anyone from fleeing as *"it might cause the false impression that the Russians were taking us over, which would create a panic."*[122] The departure took place in the middle of the night and the family, and many of their servants, would never see Casel again, at least not the way they remembered it. Mother described the experience as *"terribly traumatic!"*[123] While most valuables were left behind as there was no space in Omo's car, Mother did manage to bring along all her negatives, which saved us from having a great part of our private history completely erased.

From Casel they travelled to Torgau, where the refugees stayed with family friends. Grandmother Solms and Uncle Hubertus continued on their own, while Mother and I with some of the estate workers drove to Coburg. Between Torgau and Coburg, our trek was interrupted by aerial attacks, *"a frightening experience,"* Mother remembered.[124] Mother carried with her a bag that contained her jewellery, photos and negatives and whatever papers she could gather to prove who we were. During a stop, Mother left her bag in a field where we had had lunch. Later as the caravan headed to Coburg, Mother realized her mistake. Luckily, when they returned to the spot where they had stopped, the bag was found where she had left it!

Once in Coburg, we all gathered under the roof of Grandfather Coburg's home. Omo and Uncle Hubertus, Mother and me were reunited in Coburg. I have no recollection of these events, as I was barely two-years-old. My mother, who was a wonderfully accurate storyteller, told what I know of those days. In Coburg, we were all able to resume life in a manner that we were accustomed to, even though shortages were rampant and even getting the bare necessities was quite difficult. In due course we received news from Father and Uncle Pety, although Grandfather Solms remained lost to us.

Finally, with the Third Reich collapsing all around, Grandfather Solms was told he could leave the prison. From there he went to his lawyer's in Berlin. Because the Fatherland was in dire need of any available soldier, unbelievably, Grandfather Solms had to don a uniform and join the war effort. Having done otherwise would have earned him the title of traitor. Eventually, he was allowed to go to Casel, where he resumed overseeing the estate. As the war neared its end, he was forced to retreat northwesterly and reached Flensburg, near where Uncle Fritz Holstein, the brother of both my grandmothers lived. Grandfather Solms stayed at Schloß Grünholz, a Holstein property, until the situation settled. Meanwhile, in Coburg, Mother and Omo had not heard from Grandfather Solms, Father or Uncle Pety.

Fürst Hans Heinrich IX of Pleß, my great-great-grandfather.

Weeks before the end of the war, Coburg was surrounded by American forces. The town was given an ultimatum and told to surrender. From Berlin came orders to not capitulate. Hitler gave specific orders to defend Coburg and blow up the Veste Coburg if necessary. The mayor of Coburg notified Grandfather Coburg of these orders and asked him to move out of the Prince's Bastion. My mother later recalled that the destruction of the Veste Coburg was prevented by Grandmother Coburg, who *"staunch, proud and strong as she was, announced that she was not leaving and neither would the Duke!"*[125] To prevent a tragedy, Grandmother Coburg had Uncle Hubertus and me moved to a nunnery near Luetzelbuch, outside Coburg. In the end, the Veste Coburg was saved, in no small measure due to Grandmother Coburg's decision to remain there. However, after the Americans took Coburg, the nightly raids came to an end. It was as if everywhere the Allies arrived, tranquility accompanied them.

The family moved to Schloß Callenberg, where news of Hitler's suicide and Berlin's capitulation reached them. Still, no one knew the whereabouts of Grandfather Solms, Uncle Pety and Father. There were those within the family who feared the worst fate had befallen them. Meanwhile, Grandfather Coburg's mistakes came to haunt him and a he was handed serious consequences for his misguided decision to support National Socialism. He was arrested and taken to prison in Bamberg. When asked why he, a grandson of Queen Victoria and cousin of King George V, had supported Hitler and the Nazis, he replied, *"Because I thought it was the right thing for Germany and the best way for this country to get back on its feet!"*[126] This mistake haunted him the rest of his life.

Grandfather Coburg's imprisonment was very difficult for him. My mother, who in spite of his mistakes, liked him very much, knew how taxing his imprisonment was. *"Prison was physically and also mentally not easy for poor Uncle Charlie, who was not at all well and had never been a very strong-willed person,"* she wrote. Furthermore, *"He had been spoiled all his life with every comfort possible, to begin with his porridge every morning for breakfast, his special bed and all the pillows, to many more things. And now he had to sleep on a hard prison bed, and eat what everyone else had to eat. Eventually he was transferred to a prison hospital where it was found that, among other problems, he had a skin cancer between his eye and the bridge of his nose. I felt very sorry for him. Not only had his whole world fallen apart, but also he was sick and all alone in prison. I never could understand how this cultured, well-educated and gentle man could believe in an animal like Hitler and his horrific regime! I often tried to talk to him to find out what he thought about certain things that had happened, but he always put it off as advertising smears of the anti-Nazi movement. There was no convincing him that things were all wrong."*[127]

By the summer of 1945, we still had not heard any news from Grandfather Solms, Uncle Pety and Father. These were trying times as rationing was implemented and getting food was a great chore and not always possible. We, as Germans, were also restricted to a small radius, and everyone had to carry an identification card. Since we all lived in the Callenberg, our trips to Coburg in search of food required either walking or riding bicycles. Driving our cars was nearly impossible as gasoline was nowhere to be purchased. The situation did not begin to improve until the Americans implemented the Marshall Plan, but by then mother and I were readying for our departure from Europe to America, where a new life awaited us.

Uncle Hubertus Solms, Uncle Pety and Mother.

In due time, Grandfather Solms was able to depart Schloß Grünholz and make his way to Coburg. It took him quite some time to accomplish the journey given the countless obstacles a trip from northern Germany to Bavaria entailed. At times he walked; whenever possible he hitched rides on whatever transport was available, were it be a train or a military jeep. Nothing would deter him from reaching the embrace of his beloved wife and the company of his children. He knew they would be in Coburg and no doubts clouded his hopes. They had to be there, he kept telling himself, and that gave him the impetus to continue his journey. Mother was the first one to see her father, whom she recognized from behind as he rode a horse taxi headed to Schloß Callenberg, where we were all living. I was sitting on her lap while riding an American army jeep and she yelled, *"That is my father!"*[128] The jeep stopped and Mother jumped out to embrace her father, whom she had not seen for countless worrisome and difficult months. Grandfather Solms was delighted to see his eldest child and only grandchild. His possessions were reduced to what fit in a knapsack, but he could not be happier. He had finally reached his family and that more than made up for all the losses and sacrifices of the last year. When Omo saw her husband, she ran to him and both embraced for what seemed an interminable time. Mother thought that they would never let go of each other.

After a few weeks' rest, Grandfather Solms and my mother traveled with great difficulty to Austria. Their goal was to

Uncle Hubertus Solms, Mother with me, and Uncle Pety.

reach Steinwändt and examine the condition of the lodge and the estate. Omo had brought from Casel the documents that proved her husband's ownership of the estate, and, armed with these papers, he and my mother departed Coburg. They hitchhiked and even rode on American military jeeps on their trek to Salzburg, where Grandfather Solms went directly to the home of the administrator of Steinwändt. When they knocked on his door, he could not believe his eyes at the sight of my grandfather. The poor man, my mother recalled, began crying uncontrollably. It was while visiting him that he told them that Uncle Pety had reached Steinwändt some weeks before after a harrowing journey from the Russian front. Poor Omo had spent anxious months wondering what had been her eldest son's fate. Surely he must have fallen prisoner to the Russians, she believed. It was the source of untold pain to Omo and Grandfather Solms for they feared the worst.

Once at Steinwändt, Grandfather Solms was pleasantly surprised to find that the lodge and estate had gone through the war unscathed. It was, in fact, as if the war and the horrific suffering experienced by the continent had simply passed by unnoticed. The only visible sign of the conflict that had just ended was the sight of poor Uncle Pety, who looked emaciated. Inside, dangerously lodged in his lung, there was a Russian bullet that had entered his body between the collarbone and the shoulder. Miraculously, the bullet missed his heart by an inch. Because the bullet caused his lungs to bleed, the Russians thought he had tuberculosis and allowed Uncle Pety to leave the prison camp where he had spent some time. This probably saved his life. A specialist told Grandfather Solms that an operation would likely kill his son, so the effort was abandoned. Uncle Pety lived until his 80s with that Russian bullet lodged inside his lung. Once he showed my stepfather an X-ray of his chest, and in a very dramatic, yet joking way, *"unrolled it against the light saying, 'There you have the whole story: The Russian thread pointed against the heart of Europe!'"*[129]

When Grandfather Solms and Mother returned to Coburg, he began making preparations for a permanent move to Steinwändt. They were extremely grateful to the Coburgs for providing them shelter and sustenance, but the time had come to venture into the new world on their own. Omo, although she liked Steinwändt, was not looking forward to the move there. She came from Schleswig-Holstein's undulating geography, filled lakes, low-rolling hills, and open spaces surrounded by the sea. Casel reminded her somewhat of her birth home, with its open spaces and flatlands. Steinwändt, however, was a different matter. She felt as if the tall mountains surrounding the lodge would become a prison. In the end, they moved to Steinwändt and her fears abandoned her completely.

Not many aristocrats from the eastern parts of Germany were as lucky as was Grandfather Solms. All those whose property was unfortunately located behind the Iron Curtain found themselves with very little to their name. Some did manage to bring out artwork and jewels, as well as some money. But they were the minority rather than the majority of the refugees. Families like the Bavarians, Hesse, Hanover, Hohenlohe-Langenburg, Württemberg, Thurn und Taxis and Coburg opened their homes and provided shelter to cousins and friends whenever there was need. These were hard times for all and no one was unscathed by the conflict that ended days after Hitler's suicide deep down inside his bunker in Berlin. Grandfather Solms was extremely lucky not only to have inherited Steinwändt, but also to have kept it. The lodge was going to become their home until nearly the end of their long lives.

Once established at Steinwändt, Mother, with me in tow, joined her parents. These were hard years for all and Grandfather Solms and Omo were not exempted. Having lost all their German property, they survived with whatever money was produced by what little Steinwändt brought in. Yet, one would never guess that the risk of poverty was never far away. Grandfather Solms was *"a stickler when it came to keeping up the appearance of the surrounding of the house. That also was true during the summer months, when the gravel around the house was meticulously raked, and weeds and grass that dared to lift their little heads had to be taken out."* Omo, who loved decorating her house and creating a cosy atmosphere for all to feel at home, made sure that *"there were lots of flowers during the summer in front of the house, and in the little side garden, facing the south, where there was also a small plot for herbs."*[130] They did not live in abundance, but nothing ever went lacking. This is why I always thought of them as simply an exemplary couple of human beings, perhaps the best I have ever known, that is after my mother of course, who was simply irreplaceable!

Omo and my cousins Christian, Huberta and Irina Solms.

In due time, Grandfather Solms and Omo's house at Steinwändt became a bay of peace in a turbulent world outside their mountain-clad valley. We all trekked to Steinwändt for vacation and in search of peace and quiet. We would hunt and swim, walk, fish, all the while spending our time in the company of this loving and serene couple. Nearby lived Grandfather Solms' brother, Uncle Hermann Solms, whose wife Anna was also a von Hochberg, a half-sister of Uncle Conni. She also owned property nearby and since they had lost all their property in eastern Germany, the couple settled at their own estate near Steinwändt. They remained, until death, very close to my grandparents.

In due time, the happy times spent at Steinwändt came to an end. Grandfather Solms and Omo's health forced them to relocate to Salzburg, where they had better access to doctors and hospitals than in semi-isolated Steinwändt. He passed away in Salzburg in October 1971, a few months after celebrating his fifty-first wedding anniversary. Omo did not have to wait long before joining the love of her life. She died three and a half months later also at Salzburg. They both rest in eternal peace in the family plot at Steinwändt, the area's tall mountains continuing to provide them with the peace and serenity they lavished on us, their family.

Chapter VII
The War's Aftermath and Divorce

During the last few months before the end of the Second World War, the world as my parents and grandparents had known it ceased to exist. Germany unraveled and the great promises Hitler had once made, the elixir he used to gain popular support, turned into a tremendous tragedy.

On the Western Front, the Allies had been engaged in a ferocious life or death struggle since the Battle of Aachen in October 1944. By January, they scored a major victory against Germany at the Battle of the Bulge. The Third Reich was simply exhausted and lacked the forces, in men and munitions, to resist the floodgates that opened soon after. Even the Rhineland could no longer be defended and by March, 1945, the Allies seized a foothold on the eastern bank of the River Rhine and poured into Germany. By mid-April, Coburg had fallen and with that peace arrived after nearly six years of war.

The situation on the Eastern Front was no better either. After the tremendous tactical error Hitler made when invading Russia, it was just a matter of time before Germany's defeat. The Battle of Stalingrad, for example, was a blunder of hellish proportions. The Eastern Front consumed resources at a vertiginous pace, not only human (like Uncle Hubertus Coburg and so many countless others), but also in terms of munitions. The Russian winter, enemy of so many invading armies, finally achieved what the Red Army could not complete and Germany began a painful and devastating retreat. The Red Army, aided by countless Poles in search of revenge for Germany's 1939 invasion, soon enough broke German defenses and poured into Poland. Meanwhile, the defense of Hungary and Czechoslovakia collapsed, and the Red Army soon enough took Prague and Budapest. The routing of Germany's armies in the Eastern Front consumed resources that were desperately in need on the Western Front. A two front war, nemesis of so many German governments, had managed to drain the Fatherland of whatever blood and resources were left after the long conflict.

The Red Army left a path of desolation and destruction across Silesia, Czechoslovakia and Hungary. Within days of Omo and her retinue departing Casel, the area fell to the Russians. Years later we were still hearing of atrocities committed by the soldiers, who were desperate to inflict on the civilian population the same treatment the German armies had mêted out during the Russian invasion. A true sea of refugees began streaming into the western half of Germany, and many of our relations lost just about everything they had owned. It was a tragedy of cataclysmic proportions.

And yet, in quaint little Coburg, not much of this mayhem was present ...

General George Patton, an American general of great distinction, if a bit proud of his achievements, found Coburg in the path of his army. He showed considerable deference to Grandfather Coburg and initially agreed that he could remain living in the Prince's Bastion at the Veste Coburg. Later, once Patton had moved on, his successor decided that the Coburgs needed to experience a bit of suffering. This is when Grandfather Coburg was forced to abandon the Veste and seek refuge at Schloß Callenberg, before being arrested and sent to a prison for detention and interrogation. Finally, his choice to openly support Hitler came to haunt him. The experienced nearly killed him, although it zapped his spirit, and he was never the same afterward. In fact, it is quite possible that the time spent in detention played an important role in accelerating the end of his life. But actions have consequences, and like him many others now had to face their misdeeds and mistakes.

Opposite page: my beautiful Mother. She was quite distinguished and with little effort always looked splendidly.

When the Americans reached Coburg, we had no idea of the fate of Grandfather Solms, Uncle Pety or my father. We also did not know what had happened to poor Uncle Dicky Solms. All we knew was that the Solms brothers were imprisoned in Potsdam under suspicion of acting against Hitler, while my father's

The silver wedding anniversary of my Coburg grandparents provided an excellent opportunity for the Schleswig-Holstein siblings to gather. Standing in back, from left: Uncle Dicky Solms, Uncle Harald Denmark, Grandfather Solms, Uncle Bertel, Aunt Bylla, Uncle Leo, Princess Feodora of Denmark, Aunt Calma, Count Friedrich Castell-Rüdenhausen and Uncle Fritz Holstein. Seated, same order: Omo, Aunt Melita Holstein, King Ferdinand of Bulgaria, Grandmother and Grandfather Coburg, Aunt Helena Denmark, Father and Aunt Adelheid Solms.

last known whereabouts were in Denmark. Uncle Pety, who was caught in the Eastern Front, was also nowhere to be found. The angst suffered by all those living under Grandfather Coburg's roof at Callenberg was unimaginable. Mother believed that since the Americans and British had taken Northern Germany, it was quite likely that they took Father prisoner. As for the rest, their fate seemed far worse since they would have fallen prisoners to the advancing Russians, and that in many cases meant either death or being sent to prison camps out of which most did not come alive.

In the end, we were extremely lucky. As you may remember, Uncle Pety made it in one piece, although wounded, to the incredible safety provided by Steinwändt, a sea of peace in the midst of worldwide time of destruction. He was at Steinwändt when Grandfather Solms and Omo finally reached the lodge after their difficult journey from Coburg.

Mother and I remained in Coburg under the protection of Grandmother Coburg, who tried her best to support us, all the while also doing what she could to alleviate the harsh conditions under which her husband lived in prison. Grandmother Coburg worried deeply regarding the fate of Father, of whom we had not received news in quite some time. Mother continued being convinced he had survived the debacle of the last days of the Third Reich and its calamitous end. They knew his last posting was in Denmark and since that country did not fall to the Russians, it was hoped that he had at least fallen into the hands of the Allies. Grandmother Coburg, not unreasonably, worried endlessly concerning the fate of her youngest son, the one who everyone expected one day would act as Head of House Coburg.

Finally, several weeks after the Solms moved to Steinwändt, Father arrived, quite unexpectedly in Coburg. His condition was shocking, but at least he had survived the war unscathed. He was arrested by the British and placed in a prisoner of war camp, until they processed him and verified his identity. Then, realizing that he had played no role in the Nazi hierarchy, unlike his father, Father was released and in due time finished the long and arduous journey to Coburg.

Father's arrival was anticlimactic. Grandmother Coburg was, of course, delighted to embrace her youngest child. He was happy to see me. However, a rift had developed between my parents and this distance soon became a gulf. Mother felt that her feelings for him had changed and she had lost hope of making the marriage work. In the end, the hesitations she had been afraid to express before marrying Father effervesced and convinced her that they were too ill-suited to make it work. Father's reaction to his wife was also obviously worrisome. War, time and distance had cooled his initial ardor and now, with the Fatherland facing insurmountable obstacles and a long recovery, he could not fathom working hard to rebuild a relationship with his estranged wife.

I have already said that my father was a complicated man. The immediate postwar period made his shortcomings even more apparent to all who cared about him. For starters, instead of focusing his energy on us, he was more interested in fixing late Uncle Bertel's white BMW 328 convertible. Mother thought it a bit irresponsible to focus on such frivolous matters, particularly at a time when Germans were not allowed to drive and petrol was nearly impossible to obtain. However, in an effort to isolate himself from the mayhem around us all, Father just could not cope with reality. It was not to be the first time he shied away from what was expected of him in order to pursue a path of least resistance.

During the Second World War my father served with the Panzer Division.

Mother was quite shocked when some time after his return, and once he felt better, Father decided to leave Coburg. He used a visit to his brother Uncle Leo to run away from finding solutions to far more important matters. Faced with Father's decision, and much to the deep annoyance of the Coburgs (who saw me as their property), Mother made arrangements for us to depart Coburg and make our way to Steinwändt. There, she believed, she would be received with open arms and at least would count on the support of her parents given the very difficult decision she had reached: divorce.

The trek to Steinwändt took some time to complete. When we reached Munich, Gerd von Harten, an old family friend of my mother's, gave us shelter. Mother and I were lucky to get lifts on an American army jeep, the officer driving it helping with our entrance into Austria. He dropped us off at the train station in Salzburg. From there we boarded the train that would bring us to Sulzau, a station half-an hour's walk from Steinwändt. It was my first train ride and Mother later remembered the journey quite vividly, particularly my excitement. *"Every stop, of which there were many,"* she wrote, *"He looked out the window to see people getting on and off the train with their bags and packages. They were mostly country people who were taking vegetables*

This photo, taken at my baptism, is perhaps the last of my father and Uncle Bertel posing together. My uncle died in an air crash over Romania later in 1943. His remains were brought to Coburg and buried in the family plot overlooking Schloß Callenberg.

and other foods to their relatives who lived in little towns and did not have gardens … Some of the people even had live chickens in cages, and we even saw a little pig being carried on the train!"[131]

At Sulzau, Mother left our meager possessions with the stationmaster, who knew her. She carried me on her back for most of the journey that was done on foot since my Grandparents Solms had no idea that we were about to join them at Steinwändt permanently. Just across the river from the lodge, Mother finally put me on the ground and allowed me to walk up to the house. It was a steep incline, and she was nearly out of energy. I, of course, had no idea of what the journey meant and for me it was all a great adventure. She later wrote that *"I put Andreas down, and told him he now had to walk … He did not mind, running up the hill leading me on, calling 'come on Mammi!' as he had had a nice rest on my back, whereas I was totally exhausted."*[132] Only my mother and her indomitable will!

Our arrival at Steinwändt surprised everyone. Frau Brunner, the farmer's wife who was helping Omo with cooking, could not believe her eyes, *"Countess Victoria! Is it really you?"* she asked.[133] Omo gave Mother a long embrace as she suspected what had happened, but she dared not ask. Grandfather Solms and Omo were so exquisitely educated, that they hated prying into the affairs of others, their children included. Mother later recalled that her parents *"were both wonderful in the support and love they showed to my little Andreas and me."*[134] The next few years we were to spend in a little bedroom, with a living room attached, that Grandfather Solms and Omo gave to us. Again, their house, a bay of solace, peace and love where we all felt protected and at ease, became our shelter.

By summer of 1946, Mother knew that her marriage was at an end. She and Father managed to meet at the German-Austrian border and try one last time to iron out their differences. Mother brought me along so Father could spend time with me. By then, however, nothing could be done to save the marriage. Since the courts in Coburg were now open and dealing with these sorts of matters, divorce proceedings began in earnest. The biggest issue was my fate. Father vehemently believed that I belonged to the Coburgs and as the heir to my grandfather I had to be educated in Germany. When Mother realized that he had already made plans to leave Germany and settle in Sweden, she declined any compromise. *"Well, Andreas would be better off in Sweden with Sibylla and her children than with you and the unsettled conditions in Austria,"* he told Mother.[135] She was certainly not amused by the sheer notion that she would be unfit to raise me, regardless of how difficult life was in Austria.

"I was outraged to be told that Andreas would be better off in Sweden with Sibylla and her children, in a country where the language was different from the one Andreas knew and understood," my mother wrote. Furthermore, *"Quite aside from the fact that I had been with him as his mother from the beginning, and he would have missed me terribly,"* she recalled, *"he had had enough traumas in his short life! I was not going to let that happen!"*[136] And she kept her word!

In the end, Father had no other option than to agree with Mother. She promised him that the issue would be visited when I was older, but for the time being, I was to remain in Austria. *"The way I saw it,"* she later told us, *"Fritzi should have stayed in Coburg and tried to get what was left of the estate back on its feet, and helped his poor mother, who was left there by herself."* Mother, rightfully, saw Father's decision to relocate to Sweden as him abandoning *"his responsibilities … bugging out!"*[137] Father was not constant and he had trouble bringing to fruition most of the goals he set for himself. In a way, he was much like Grandfather Coburg, absent of will and considerably unwilling to deal with conflict. As he did to Mother and me, he *"bugged out"* many times in his long life and then wondered why things did not turn out the way he wanted.

A rare childhood photograph of my father and me.

As a young child and later a teenager, I do not recall my mother ever uttering a negative comment about my father. Nor would she ever say anything untoward about the Coburgs either, even when there was no assistance forthcoming to cover my expenses. Yet, she was unwilling to let me be raised in such a complicated environment as life with Father could be. She thought him to be simply incapable of setting a good example, *"this was all the more reason that I did not want Andreas to be under his father's influence."*

My parents were finally divorced in September 1946. Mother recalled the relief she felt upon opening the notification from the court, *"as if a heavy weight had been lifted from my shoulders."* Later, Mother wondered if she had done all she could to save her marriage and felt *"a kind of sadness about it all."* She felt sorry that perhaps she did not work harder to make her marriage work. However, in the end, she did what was best for us. *"I could never have bridged the difference of feelings and opinions between Fritzi and myself,"* she wrote. Then again, she believed that, *"we were just not for each other."*[138]

Chapter VIII
1946

As I reminisce about the past, it strikes me that the year 1946 was a pivotal one in my life. My earliest memory, for example, took place in that year. This memory, which I will share with you shortly, includes many of the main players and places that marked the rest of my life.

I remember being about three years old and having an exceedingly happy day. We were driving in an American Army jeep and had left Salzburg, where Mother was tending to some pressing business (later I found out that she had been dealing with the divorce from my father, a complicated situation that caused her considerable worry and concern as she was completely unwilling to have me taken from her.). Anyhow, back to my memory … we were riding on the jeep toward Steinwändt. Along for the ride were my mother and a military officer, a handsome man, who is driving us. He smiles when he looks at my mother and I think that it is obvious that he likes her.

This memory, as I mentioned earlier, contains many of the things that were important to me: Mother, Steinwändt, Austria, Dick Whitten and, of course, automobiles. Better explained, Steinwändt was our home and sanctuary of peace; I adored my mother; Austria has been a country deep in my heart, as well as the history of both my paternal and maternal families; Dick Whitten was the man who raised me; and automobiles have long been my passion of passions.

As a child, I do not think I wondered much about the whereabouts of my father. At Steinwändt I was everyone's center of attention and a wonderful world opened itself to me. The mountains and their clean Alpine air; the river meandering through the property; bicycles rides along pathways; my mother riding the bicycle as I hold on to her for dear life. Steinwändt also brings back memories of Grandfather and Grandmother Solms, their devotion for each other, their incredible inner strength when faced with a treacherous new life of sacrifice and privation. They were the pillars of our life; never crossed an untoward word between them; he focused on making life work for them with what little was left; she, along with her few staff, making sure that the house was pristinely clean, handsomely decorated, and the kitchen always busy. My uncles, loving their parents and protective of Mother and me. Uncle Hubertus, as I mentioned before, was more an older brother than an uncle; while Uncle Pety tried to be second-in-

Mother with me and her brother Hubertus.

Opposite page: My mother was a talented and passionate equestrian. My daughter Stephanie shares her love of horses.

My parents.

A rare image of my parents with me before the collapse of their marriage.

command and an asset to his family. Everyone contributed to the best of their ability, many times beyond that point, in fact, to rebuild a world lost. How could one not draw wonderful life lessons from their characters, all only too willing to provide me with the strongest foundation any child could ever have or hope for.

My mother later shared with me her reminiscences about my love for Steinwändt and country life. *"Andreas loved the freedom … he often joined the farmer Brunner* (the farmer to whom Grandfather Solms leased parts of Steinwändt) *and his family in getting the hay from the meadows into the barn,"* she wrote. I also enjoyed helping the Brunners with their cows *"when it was time to milk them."*[139] Mother recalled that the sun had roasted my skin and the suntan made me *"look like a little Indian, except for his light blond hair that looked like spun gold in the sun. He was precious!"* I tried to behave as best I could and Mother later told me, *"I was a little prejudiced, but I always got compliments about him, wherever we went!"*[140]

I remember that I particularly loved going out grocery shopping with my mother. Of course, right after the war, we were so financially strained that Grandfather Solms did not have a car. Not many people did, in fact, as this was an unimaginable luxury. The nearest little town to Steinwändt was Werfen, some six miles to the south of the estate. There we did most of our shopping *"for groceries and other necessities"* which we carried on a bicycle. Whenever a horse carriage could not be procured for our little shopping sprees, Mother rode one of the bicycles we had. She placed me inside the basket *"on the front of the bike,"* which of course I completely enjoyed because I *"loved that, and pretended that he was driving a car, initiating the sound of a motor by humming and blowing through his lips at the same time."*[141]

When I think of how much my Solms relatives lost in the final closing scenes of the Second World War, I am even more astonished when remembering life at Steinwändt. The estate was not rich. Most of it, in fact, was rather useless and unproductive from a financial standpoint. I mean, what can one grow on Alpine rocks and cliffs?

And yet, life at Steinwändt continued along the same lines that had made Schloß Casel and that estate, such a wonderful place. My Solms grandparents were excellent bosses and proprietors, hence, the inhabitants of their estates were truly devoted to them. There was an air of "old-school" Europe about them that made those in their employ be completely devoted to the family. They believed that everyone had to be treated respectfully and that they had to set an example: for how could one expect one's help to act accordingly if one did not first set and follow the rules? They did so and never expected anyone to do anything that they themselves would not do. This very important lesson I learned from them and have maintained close to my heart all throughout my long life.

Mother and me in Steinwändt.

In fact, this lesson truly has defined my life. One has to be more in the property. Have a connection to the people and not disrespect them. Treat them as normal persons. Talking to people in Coburg and Gotha or Grein and treat them as people and to not push oneself as a "big boss" – pushing your weight around is certainly not good.

Our family motto reminds us of that. We must remain true and loyal (faithful) to all those who work and help for us. If you have to conduct a negotiation, you have to be able to look at the person in the eye and be fair to both sides. You see each other two times in life … therefore you must always stick to what you have agreed. Keep your word. Do not distrust people from the beginning … do not be prejudiced of people until they prove you wrong; be open to new ideas!

The lessons from Steinwändt I guess are far deeper than initially thought!

Before discussing the entrance of Dick Whitten into our life, let me bring you up to speed with what happened with my father after 1946. All around him, in Coburg in particular, and Germany at large, there was destruction. The larger share of the family's properties, those located in Thüringen and around Gotha were lost once the Soviet Union gobbled up that important portion of Germany. The Coburgs, like the Solms and many other aristocratic families, lost considerable estates, works of arts, real estate, hunting grounds, etc …

On top of that, as you may recall, Grandfather Coburg was in detention due to his unwise meanderings into National Socialism and the reprehensible people fronting that abominable ideology. The Coburg Family Foundation was in

Aunt Bylla and Uncle Edmund leave the Moritzkirche after their wedding. Father was their train bearer.

My Coburg grandparents exit the Moritzkirche after Aunt Bylla's wedding to Prince Gustaf Adolf of Sweden.

Uncle Edmund.

dire need of guidance and action in order to achieve a sanitary rebuilding and thus guarantee that the family would not lose even more. After all, the lands in Austria, particularly the Greinburg estate, were under Russian sequestration and, for the time being, were lost to us. But my father, who seemed to avoid hard decisions and the great effort that is required of us, chose to make a quick exit rather than stay behind and help his parents.

Father had an escapist personality. He did not like confrontation, much like his own father. He avoided difficult situations and making these important decisions. He just wanted to be left alone to do as he pleased. My mother remembered this less edifying aspect of his personality and how difficult it was for her to deal with it. Like, for instance, when right after the war he was more focused on fixing his late brother Hubertus's car so he could drive along. *"I thought at the time, that this was so unimportant and a rather selfish pursuit, when other people had real problems,"* my mother later wrote.[142] Instead of worrying about the more pressing business at hand, like saving his marriage and acting as a good husband and father, as well as son, Father was unable to cope with his reality. He needed an escape and he needed it promptly. But that was my father and nothing could, or would, be done to help him find the wherewithal necessary to affect a deep personality change. Hence, with Germany in chaos, instead of helping, he bolted.

During one of Aunt Bylla's visits Father's future was discussed. Consequently, it was decided that perhaps a change of scenery would be of great help to him. This relocation would bring Father to Stockholm, where he was given a position with an important shipping company, the Johnson Line. Shipment of goods across the Atlantic Ocean was a huge business in the post-war era, particularly as the American rebuilding program, the Marshall Plan, came into full implementation. Therefore, shipping companies were the source of great income and secured countless owners, investors and employees with job security and a very good living.

In Stockholm, my father lived with Aunt Bylla and Uncle Edmund at the Haga Palace, their main residence. Aunt Bylla and Uncle Edmund formed a very united and devoted couple. They lived in a world of their own and were very protective of the children's privacy, wishing to raise their five offspring in an unaffected, loving family environment much unlike their own experience. Publicly, Aunt Bylla and Uncle Edmund were tireless in the performance of the myriad duties they had to fulfill. Both were very active members of the Royal Family and lent their

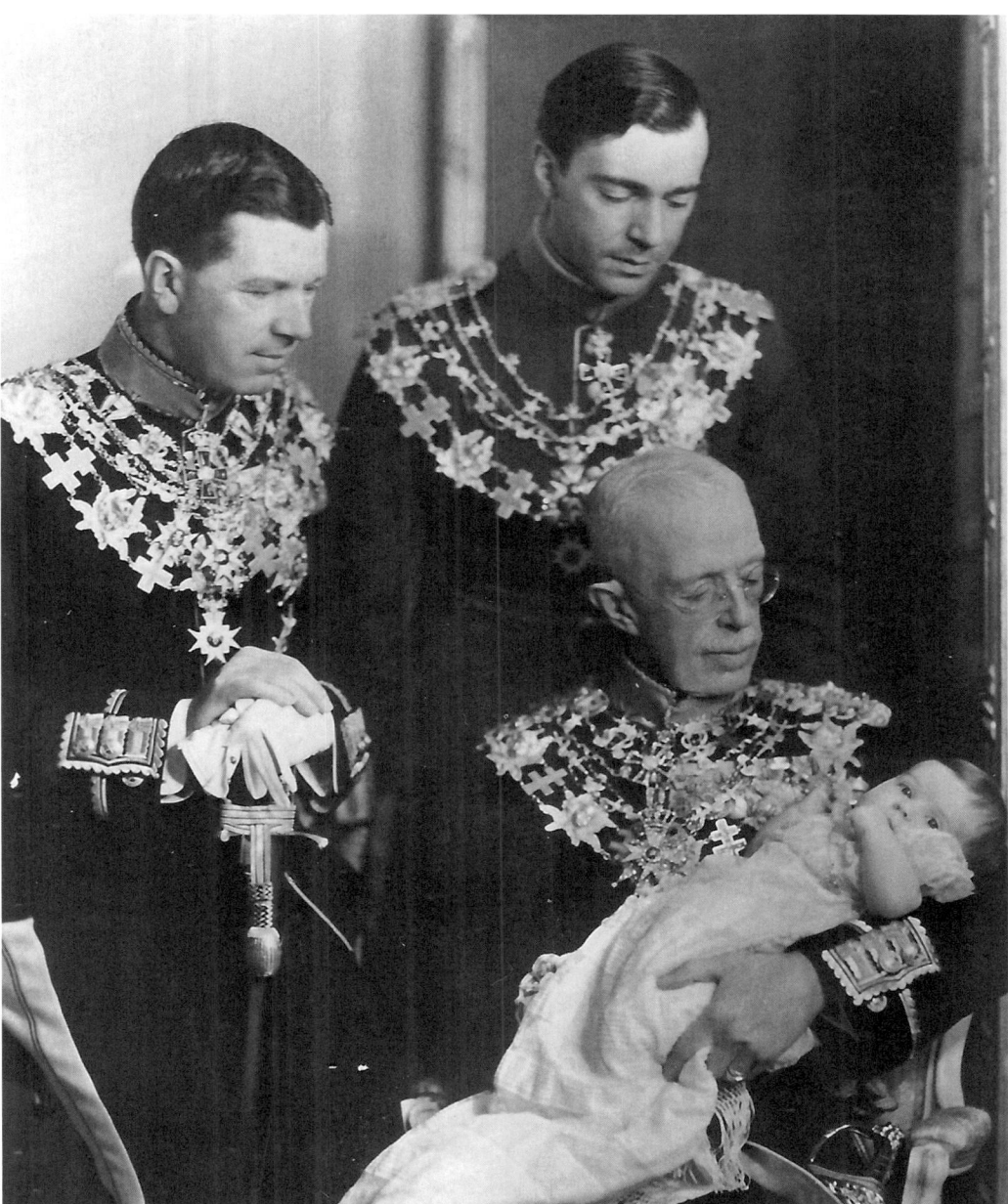

The baptism of my cousin Carl Gustaf of Sweden. Holding him is King Gustaf V, his great-grandfather. Behind them are Uncle Edmund and his father, the future King Gustaf VI Adolf.

support to countless causes from the Boy Scouts to aiding of various women's causes. Whatever little personal time they had was spent with their children in a private world in which my cousins were raised by dedicated and indulging parents who expected them to be examples for others to follow, while doing so naturally and without affectation. Needless to say, my cousins, whom the Swedish people referred to as the Haga Princesses, were exquisitely raised. Their brother, due to his late arrival, was never to remember the presence of his wonderful father. Uncle Edmund left us too early!

In January 1947, Uncle Edmund traveled to The Netherlands, where he was hosted by Prince Bernhard, who like him was a great supporter of the Scouts movement. Through Aunt Bylla, the Swedish Royal Family had become closely related to their Dutch counterparts. This common bloodline came from Great-grandmother Albany and her sister Emma of Waldeck und Pyrmont, who in the late 1870s married King Willem III of The Netherlands.

The Dutch king and his first wife, Sophie of Württemberg, had had three sons. These boys, however, had all had miserable

Queen Mother Emma, Queen Wilhelmina and Princess Juliana of The Netherlands.

Queen Juliana and Prince Bernhard of The Netherlands.

The Prince of Orange.

lives consumed by illness and vice. At one point, their eldest the Prince of Orange was suggested as a possible husband for Queen Victoria's second daughter, Alice. Diplomatically, this was an advantageous alliance for both countries. Not so, as it turned out, for the groom and his intended bride. They would have been thoroughly unhappy. Alice was an intellectual who worried about important matters and also supported women's rights, among some other socially progressive causes. Orange, who was jokingly called "Citron" (due to his weakness for very strong spirits), was an alcoholic who wasted life away and died early. His two other brothers had equally sad lives: Maurits died in childhood, while Alexander died in 1884 without living issue. By then even Queen Sophie had passed away, leaving old King Willem with a serious succession problem on his hands.

Enter the Waldeck und Pyrmont princess, Emma. She married at Schloß Arolsen, her family's seat, in 1879 the much older King Willem III, who was already in his sixties. The groom was more than forty years older than the bride. Not surprisingly, King Willem III and Queen Emma only had one child, Wilhelmina, born in 1880. This young girl became Queen of the Netherlands in 1890, upon her father's death.[143] All through her long life, she was to enjoy a close relationship with her Albany cousins, particularly Aunt Alice Athlone. Not surprisingly, the German occupation of the Netherlands inflicted a damaging blow to Grandfather Coburg's relations with his Dutch cousin. Anyhow, Queen Wilhelmina married Duke Heinrich of Mecklenburg-Schwerin. After several pregnancies and miscarriages, they finally had a daughter, Juliana, born in 1909. She in turn was a close friend of her second cousins of Athlone and Coburg, particularly Aunt Bylla. It was Juliana's husband, German-born former Prince Bernhard of Lippe-Biesterfeld, who had hosted the last hunt attended by Uncle Edmund.

The airline crash at Kastrup, Denmark, on January 26, 1947, not only killed all passengers and crew, but also made Aunt Bylla a widow.[144] Uncle Edmund was among the passengers and his death was a hugely painful blow to my dear aunt, who was left a widow with five children, the youngest barely ten months old. Father was a witness to the deep sorrow that my poor Aunt Bylla suffered. She should have found more support in him, but he was just not capable of dealing with life changing circumstances. Had Father played a different hand, he could have found a meaningful role in Sweden. Instead, he fell in love with a good woman, who happened to be the nanny of my Swedish cousins. Her name was Denise de Muralt and she was a Swiss born in 1923. I do not know if I ever discussed with Aunt Bylla her reaction to Father and Denise becoming a couple. But given how strict the Swedish Royal Court was about these matters, I am sure that old King Gustav V, a true stickler about these matters, was not amused.

Denise de Muralt, my father's second wife and mother of my Coburg siblings.

Hence, once again, a situation had arisen that required a solution to be found for my father's newest predicament. It was his employer who came through with an amenable solution: Father would be sent to the United States, San Francisco, in fact, to work at one of the regional offices. Along with him came Denise, who quit her position in the royal nursery and went to America to start a new life.

After settling in San Francisco, Father and Denise were married on February 14, 1948. Fifteen months later Denise gave birth to their first child, Maria Claudia, born in San Francisco in May 1949. Two other children eventually followed, Beatrice, born in Bern in 1951, and Adrian, born in Coburg in 1955.[145] By then however, Father had moved to South America, where he lived for more than a decade. But this period of our lives I will come to later.

Meanwhile, at Steinwändt the air of rebuilding and rebirth continued impregnating our small mountain-locked world. Uncle Pety was the first to move on. He relocated to Salzburg to work with a friend in an import-export firm. Since Uncle Pety's education had been truncated by serving in the war, he found that some schooling was needed to advance his career. Through friends he was able to attend courses in Graz and Vienna. Once he finished, Uncle Pety returned to continue working in his friend's business in Salzburg. It was while there that he met and befriended the man who would become the love of my mother's life and

Here I am visiting with Grandmother Coburg and Mother.

a stepfather to me: US Army Captain Richard Whitten, "Dick" as we all learned to call him.

When he lived in Salzburg, Uncle Pety used to come to Steinwändt on weekends. On many of these visits he would bring some of his friends and the house would come alive with noise and music, laughter and activities. My Solms grandparents thrived when the children were around them and Uncle Pety's friends only added to their joy for life. There was so much laughter all around. As for me, of course being the only child around, I surely enjoyed the attention!

The renewed social activity the family experienced was particularly beneficial to Mother. She had married too young, and I had arrived within a year of her wedding. The war, the losses experienced and the suffering had taken their toll on all. Mother was still young and as dedicated as she was to my well-being, she also longed for some fun on her own. Thus, through Uncle Pety, Mother got to meet some of his new friends in Salzburg, where she often was invited to parties and balls, particularly those held during the winter season. Mother and Uncle Pety became very popular, as their personalities were infectious and everyone always liked them. Mother always thought that *"the Austrian people were so friendly and took Pety and me in like (if) we had always belonged there."*[146] I was too young to understand how social interaction brightened my mother's face, but she certainly enjoyed having adult time with her brother and his friends.

In February 1947, Uncle Pety was invited to the birthday party of a baroness who worked for the Americans. This poor woman had barely managed to escape with her life during the last tragic days of the Second World War. In her cramped apartment, Uncle Pety met an interesting American captain who was put in charge of *"supply and distribution of food"* for the Austrians.[147] Several friends of Uncle Pety worked under Captain Whitten, and everyone liked him very much.

During the evening, Uncle Pety discovered that Captain Whitten had some pressing business in Bad Gastein, a resort town to which he needed to go as well. However, since the train service between Steinwändt and Bad Gastein did not work on weekends, Uncle Pety found it difficult to go there as his weekdays were consumed by work. Captain Whitten offered Uncle Pety a ride since Steinwändt was on the way. Plans were made and destiny took its course.

That weekend Uncle Pety had a terrible cold and he completely forgot to let us know that his new friend would be coming to Steinwändt. I, apparently, also had a cold, as Mother later told me. Along with Uncle Pety came Count Mundi Clary, who was also a friend of Mother's. That Saturday afternoon, those not afflicted with the cold went for a walk to visit our Aunt Anna Solms, who owned an estate next to Steinwändt. It was while they were out that my grandparents saw an American jeep that got stuck in the snow on our road. When he saw them walking toward him, the driver "came toward them to greet them and introduced himself." His name was Captain Richard Whitten.

He told them that he was there to "*pick up their son*."[148] Naturally, this did not sit well with my grandparents. Grandfather Solms, who did not know English, had no idea of what was being said. Grandmother Solms, however, who was fluent in English, became quite worried and wondered what sort of trouble her son had gotten into that required an American officer picking him up!

Realizing that my grandparents were suddenly afraid for their son, Captain Whitten quickly explained the situation to them and reassured them that their son had done nothing wrong. They promised to come back with help to pull the jeep out of the snow and bring it to the house. They would do so just after visiting Aunt Anna Solms, who was expecting them.

This photo of me was taken at the time of Grandfather Coburg's 60th birthday in 1944. I have always looked rather well in sunglasses!

Meanwhile, soon after Captain Whitten was left waiting by my grandparents, Mother and Count Clary, who were also out for a brisk walk in the cold, cleansing weather, ran into him. He lost little time in explaining to them, clearly, the reason behind his visit. Mother later told me that she *"found him quite charming and very attractive"* when she first met him.[149]

By the time the horses arrived to help the stranded officer, he must have been quite doubtful that they would be of much service. But these were sturdy animals and the "two-horse power" did manage to free the jeep from the snow and pull him up to the house as the good captain sat tightly inside the vehicle and steered it away from falling off the narrow road. And this is how Mother met her second husband, and Dick Whitten never made it to Bad Gastein to see his friend!

Chapter IX
An Officer and a Gentleman

The arrival of Captain Richard Whitten into my mother's life changed the course of mine. Suddenly, we had someone who quickly took over and planned a future for us. The happy days at Steinwändt were soon coming to an end, even though we did not initially realize it. A chapter was ending and an exciting one beginning. I would have to learn how to accept the presence of this military man in our midst, while also slowly realizing how happy Mother was in his company. In life, I have found that one must adapt or one becomes stuck. We adapted and eventually saw the new changes affecting our placid existence as exciting and thrilling. A new world was about to open its arms to us, and we embraced it wholeheartedly.

From this point on, I will refer to Captain Whitten as "Dick," the nickname he went by …

Dick Whitten was born in Indianapolis, Indiana, in 1910. I suppose that at some point his family relocated to the Gulf state of Louisiana, for he felt he was more Bayou than Hoosier. His parents were a great presence in his life. His mother had a predilection for big hats that always had some even bigger bird feathers as decoration. No doubt, these big hats were quite an intricate ensemble. The wearer was quite proud of them. For a boy who had never seen such a contraption, they held my undivided attention. That is why when I first met her I began calling her "Omo Birdie!"

Anyhow, let's return to the strapping Captain Whitten!

Me at around the time of Mother's second wedding.

Grandmother Solms invited Dick to join them for tea once the car had been towed out of the snow. He held sway sitting around the fireplace and telling them war stories. It also was as if Santa Claus had arrived early, for his bags were filled with goodies that survivors of wartime Europe had not seen. Herr Brunner, whose horses had pulled the jeep to the house, received some cigarettes, American cigarettes mind you, and this made his month. Others got small gifts, but the best one was a bottle of whisky he shared with my grandparents, Mother and Count Clary. They were all aghast when seeing Dick add water to a perfectly fine whisky. It must be an American custom, they thought!

I sat on Mother's lap during the tea and she knew how much I enjoyed being bounced a bit. Dick asked my mother where the father of her child was. She blushingly explained to him that she had just recently divorced. He told them that he had also divorced, so no harm there. Mother noticed a twinkle in Dick's eye, an unmistakable insight into what was running around in his brain, but would not dare say. She always saw that twinkle, and it was as if it allowed

Opposite page: Mother and Dick.

Both in Casel and Steinwändt Mother and me had our own little world.

Mother to read Dick's mind. Still, Mother later jokingly told us her first reaction to his obvious courting was, *"Brother, you are really fast on the trigger!"*

That first meeting turned into an overnight stay since the tea took rather long, and by the time Dick announced that it was time to leave, Grandmother Solms simply would not have it. Not only was Bad Gastein still an hour and a half away, but also the heavy snows that had caused his jeep to get stuck had not abated. *"The road was not easy to navigate especially with the new snow,"* and it would not be until the morning when the roads would be cleared. So no, Dick could not turn down Grandmother Solms' invitation. He stayed the night and the adults played music and talked, while continuing to enjoy the whisky, until the wee hours. Mother always remembered that first night fondly: *"We all had a wonderful time, and I think Dick felt right at home with us. We all thought that he was very funny, intelligent, and interesting, and not like a total stranger at all,"* she wrote. My mother liked strong men, and Dick, being an American officer, dressed in a nice, imposing uniform, made quite an impression.

The next day, Dick returned to Salzburg. He was visibly taken with my mother and invited her to feel free to reach him in Salzburg so they could go out to lunch at the venerable Oesterreichischer Hof, the largest hotel in town. Mother recalled that she had oftentimes stayed there with her parents. When the Americans requisitioned the hotel to be used as an officers' club, they retained most of the old staff, many of them familiar to my Solms relations. The old concierge, my mother recalled, a Herr Kreuzberger, had worked there so very long that he *"had greeted everybody from Austrian and German aristocrats, to all kinds of foreign dignitaries. Then came the Nazis, who spread themselves all over in the garish and ordinary way and had their huge swastika flag hanging over the portal of the old, dignified hotel."* To Mother's surprise, Herr Kreuzberger proved to be quite a survivor for when she returned to the hotel *"that wonderful old man"* was still there. Some things just never change.[150]

It is interesting to me that both my parents rebuilt their lives at about the same time and with non-Germans. While by this time Father was already in Sweden, where he met Denise, Mother, living in Austria, had met the American who would woo her and carry us away.

Dick's next visit was unexpected, much like his first one. Mother had gone to Salzburg but decided not to call on him so as not to seem "pushy." While she was interested in him, she also did not want to appear too eager. On top of that, Mother thought that *"frankly I was not too sure if I wanted to get involved, not only with Dick Whitten, but any man at that point."* Life was *"very tranquil, satisfying and safe."* Mother wanted to be there for me and she also felt that living at Steinwändt I was happy and in a safe, loving environment. Her ambivalence, however, was laid to rest by his persistence. Unbeknownst to Mother, Dick, however, lost no time in making arrangements to drive his jeep back to Steinwändt.

Mother was a dedicated parent who enjoyed spending time with me.

Mother was in the kitchen helping Grandmother Solms' cook prepare dinner. She heard noises in the entrance hall and opened the glass door leading there. She nearly bumped into him and blurted out, *"What are you doing here?"* Undeterred, Dick retorted, *"I came to see you!"* Along with him, Dick brought a rather large bag, the contents of which were soon to bring untold joy to the inhabitants of Steinwändt: Grandfather Solms got tobacco, which he thoroughly enjoyed as he was a pipe smoker; the rest of us shared in am ample treasure composed of cigarettes, canned ham, cheese, chocolates, a bottle of cognac and so many other goodies. For a family that had been living on a diet of potatoes and peas, followed by peas and potatoes the next night, this was an incredible vision laid in front of our magnified and incredulous eyes!

Before he left that afternoon, Dick made plans to meet my mother in Salzburg so they could go out on a date.

For the next few months, Mother's visits to Salzburg increased, as did Dick's journeys to Steinwändt. Every time he came to visit, there was a bag filled with presents, and we all grew quite fond of this tall American who had, for some reason, I thought, taken pity on us. I do not think I had an inkling about what was going on during the first few months of what was right in front of my eyes.

Mother initially thought that Dick would simply be a "flirtation." Why not, she wondered. She was single, she had never really dated – he was attractive, particularly in his pressed uniform, and seemed quite taken with her. But as the weeks passed and her trips to Salzburg increased, just as much as his visits to Steinwändt, Mother realized that this was not a "flirtation," but full-on courting. Mother later remembered: *"We always had a wonderful time together. He had introduced me to some of his fellow officers and their wives, and some of them also came to Steinwändt."*

Dick finally mustered the courage to tell Mother that he *"had fallen in love"* with her. She was not fully surprised and expected that he would open up to her any day. Still, when the question finally came, she realized that saying "yes" was not as easy as one would have thought. In fact, she later recalled that the possibility of giving Dick a yes *"frightened her."*[151] For starters there were the Solms to deal with. Even more complicated were the Coburgs, who were sure to raise objections over Mother's choice and what it could potentially mean for me: moving to the United States. Mother discussed all these matters with him, particularly raising me in a country other than Germany. But Dick was undeterred and told her, *"My mind is already made up! I want you for my wife!"*[152] Right then, Mother knew that Dick was the sort of man of never took no for an answer.

Dick Whitten.

My Grandparents Solms had many questions and hesitations about Mother marrying Dick. First, there was a considerable possibility that we would be relocating to the United States. That worried everyone since back then as transatlantic travel was not as easy as it is today. They also wanted to make sure that both Mother and I would be taken care of in a strange, faraway land. In spite of their concerns, my Grandparents Solms found Dick *"intelligent, with principles and an outlook on life that would fit in well with us."* Mother also thought that Dick was *"considerate and had a terrific sense of humor – and then that twinkle in his eye …"*

Mother and Dick became officially engaged. It all took just a few months, as it was a meteoric love-at-first-sight case. In preparation for their wedding, they began spending longer periods with each other, whether it was weekdays in Salzburg or weekends in Steinwändt. We also visited American recreation centers, spots that had been created for the families of the military personnel. These were quite a lot of fun for me as I was able to play with other children, a rarity in the adult-centric world that was the Solms household. My mother, who held her own opinions, was weary of my hanging out with some of these kids. She actually found *"American kids spoiled, undisciplined brats, and swore that ours, if we ever had any, would not be brought up that way."*[153] Sadly, I must say, I believe that both my sister Victoria and I did give Mother and Dick a run for their money!

It was during the few months before their wedding, that I nearly died. Mother and Dick had gone to a party at Schloß Bluembach, which had belonged to the arms builder Krupp family. The Americans had requisitioned the estate and turned it into an officer's recreation center. While they were away, my nanny, Elli was her name, and Grandmother Solms' maid, Mizie, had taken me to a beach on the river Salzach. As the weather was rather warm, they wanted to cool off while also letting me enjoy a dip in the river. Elli went in the water first, while Mizie held me. Tragically, Elli lost her footing and was sucked underwater by the river current. Hysterical and desperate, Mizie, who held me and did not know how to swim, could do nothing to save the life of my nanny. I witnessed the whole thing, and Mother later told me that I was terrified … no wonder!

Poor Elli's body was found down the river three days later. Mother and Dick attended the funeral, held in her home village near Salzburg. I was very shocked by it all, but Mother assured me that that Elli was fine, for *"she now was in heaven with the angels,"* and she was still watching me.

Once the shock of Elli's death subsided, life at Steinwändt returned to its meandering course. Mother and Dick were frightfully busy with all the preparations around their wedding.

As he, an American officer, would be marrying a citizen from a former enemy country, an endless array of paperwork had to be presented to the authorities. They, in turn, could not believe that someone with Mother's background had not belonged to any of myriad Nazi organizations. Of course, these investigators had no idea of what poor Grandfather Solms had experienced at the hands of the Gestapo. Anyhow, the investigators even interrogated Grandfather Solms, who having had plenty of experience with interrogations during his time in prison at the end of the Hitler era easily fielded all their inquiries. Hence, once the investigators were satisfied, Mother and Dick were granted permission to marry.

Mother had lived in such strained circumstances since the departure from Casel that her wardrobe was in dire need of replenishment. Dick helped her quite a bit by purchasing clothes for her in the Military Commissary. It was a special exception because she was marrying. *"I was able to buy some lovely brown tweed for a suit and a few other things, including a pair of shoes,"* items she badly needed, Mother later told me.[154] This fabric she took to a tailor, and he made her the suit she wore to the civil ceremony, held in Salzburg on November 5.

That morning, Mother recalled, *"I put on my pretty new suit, and Dick in his uniform looked so handsome."*[155] Her parents did not attend the civil ceremony, as it was a formality. A small champagne luncheon at the famed Oesterreichischer Hof followed before they returned to Steinwändt to prepare for the religious wedding ceremony, scheduled there for the next day.

Dr. Entz, the head of the Lutheran Church in Austria, an acquaintance of Grandfather Solms, agreed to officiate at Mother and Dick's wedding. I wanted to make sure that I would be part of the wedding festivities. Mother reassured me that late afternoon when she and Dick returned from Salzburg, already husband and wife in the eyes of the law.

The wedding ceremony was not attended by a large number of guests. Of course, all the estate workers, including the farmer Brunner and their spouses, were invited. Also present were Grandfather and Grandmother Solms, as well as Uncle Pety and Uncle Hubertus. I sat with them and tried to behave as well as possible. It was, in fact, an exciting day for me as with Dick marrying Mother I was sure to gain a father. Mother later remembered that *"the wedding ceremony was beautiful, and the whole surrounding in which it was performed was absolutely perfect … It had to be a good omen for a wonderful life ahead of us!"*[156]

Mother after we settled in the United States.

Chapter X
Mother's Second Marriage

Up until Mother's wedding to Dick, I had basically grown up without a father. Hence, a few months short of turning five-years-old, I had gained a father the same day Mother gained a husband. One of the biggest concerns everyone had was how Dick was going to manage raising me. This was a very important task as I was destined to inherit the Coburg legacy, being the eldest son of my father, who in turn was the only eligible son left to Grandfather Coburg. Both the Solms and Coburg families were sincerely concerned about this matter, but everyone was reassured in the end because Dick was an upstanding, honest and committed man. I personally think he did a fine job and treated me just as if I had been his son.

He was, perhaps, a little indulgent with my sister Vickie, but she was an adorable, fun-loving child that no one could resist. Dick was quite taken with Vickie and since he was never close to the son he had had with his first wife, my sister was the apple of his eye. Later on, I must admit, Vickie gave our parents a run for their money, even more than I did. She was irrepressible and more than a bit mischievous, and continues to have the sort of personality that simply wins you over, even when she is being bad. Oh, and Vickie can be really bad ... but who can say no to her? She remains a great companion and I enjoy her visits very much. I love my sister, I truly do, even when she drives me crazy ... but I guess that is what sisters do!

Anyhow, let's return to the story we left off in the last chapter ... the arrival of Dick Whitten into our lives!

Mother and Dick went on a short honeymoon in Berchtesgaden, the beautiful Alpine resort that had been the realm of the Bavarian Royal Family until Hitler decided to move in and nearly ruined the place. In their absence, I remained at Steinwändt with my new nanny, Fraulein Maria Wimmer, and my Grandparents Solms. I do not remember much of the time I spent without Mother. Memories come and go, but I do remember the excitement that followed their return, since it meant we were leaving Steinwändt for city life in Salzburg.

Initially, Mother and Dick settled at the Oesterreichischer Hof, at least until a suitable apartment was found for them. This first home was

Here I am with my baby sister Vickie.

Opposite page: Here I am at about 3 years old.

at Münchener Fahrstaße 22 and it was in a quiet neighborhood on the outskirts of Salzburg. Mother particularly liked the place because, as she said, *"it was like living in the country."*[157] Next door, I remember there was a vegetable garden that was diligently maintained by an older couple, with the help of their son, daughter-in-law and grandchildren. They grew delicious vegetables, which they sold in the Salzburg marketplace. Mother used to buy from them and our kitchen was always nicely filled with fresh food. The years of privation and potatoes and peas and peas and potatoes now seemed but a faint memory.

The house had three bedrooms and several other rooms. One of the bedrooms was for Fraulein Wimmer and me, while Mother and Dick slept in another bedroom. The third one was kept ready for guests. As my Grandparents Solms had no furniture to spare, since everything was lost in Casel, Mother had to rely on acquiring furniture from a warehouse that the Military Government kept to supply the needs of couples like them. Mother

Here I am visiting with Grandmother Coburg.

always remembered this, our first home, quite fondly and she thought it was a *"comfortable and homely"* little nest.[158]

It was while we lived there that Dick insisted that I attend an American kindergarten. Having been a single child for a very long time, as well as the center of everyone's attention, I am sure I was in desperate need of contact with other kids. This meant that I could have friends that I could visit. Furthermore, attending this school would allow me to be familiarized with English. I initially hated it and cried every morning before the bus picked me up. I am sure Mother felt quite guilty and I did not feel like helping her feel any better. Some of the kids there were rather nasty and teased me mercilessly because I did not know English very well. And yet, as I have always done, I soon adapted and became more confident. As my knowledge of the English language increased, the teasing decreased. The kids there called me "Andy," and this nickname, used by family and friends, has stuck with me my entire life.

We also had a huge Great Dane named Bob. That dog was my shadow and wherever I went, there was Bob keeping a watchful, protective eye over me. I was fascinated by dogs and have always had one at home. However, at the beginning I had no idea that there were dogs and bitches. One time, while we lived in Salzburg, I was horrified when I saw little dogs crawling out of a friend of "Bob's" – "*Mammi, Mammi,*" I yelled at my mother, "*look at the little dogs … they all crept out of him!*"[159] Obviously, I had no knowledge whatsoever of anything concerning the birds and the bees, and by then the old curse "*beware of the roving Coburg eye*" had not yet visited me. I think Mother was quite relieved that my astonishment at what I witnessed did not lead into a detailed explanation of how "things" worked between females and males. The fact that Mother soon enough became pregnant confused me even more. That conversation, much to her utter relief, was one that we would not have for years!

By the summer of 1948, it was quite visible that my mother was pregnant. Earlier that summer, I was sent to Murnau, in Bavaria, to

Grandfather Solms and Omo remained at Steinwändt for many years.

spend a vacation with my Grandparents Coburg. They had rented a house there and hoped that the fresh air would help improve Grandfather Coburg's health, which was giving everyone much concern. Not only had he suffered considerable privation during the time spent in prison after the end of the war, but also he was battling a tumor that had grown directly under his right eye and had slowly grown disproportionately in size. This ailment, in fact, not only disfigured him, but also was the main cause of his death.

By the time Dick brought me back from Coburg, where I had accompanied my grandparents at the end of their vacation, there was little time before the arrival of my mother's second child. Unfortunately, I was not much of a witness to all those happy moments since I was dreadfully ill myself at the same time Mother went into labor. One day I came home quite sick from kindergarten. As it turned out, I had the mumps and quickly gave them to my pregnancy-exhausted mother. I was so sick that I ended in hospital for some time and was still there when my Mother was brought in to give birth to my sister

This is a photo of me at about the time we left Germany to settle in America.

Victoria, known to us as "Vickie." Although she was a small baby, weighing some five-and-a-half pounds, she was very healthy and soon became the object of Dick's undivided attention. She was a cute baby and Dick was quite proud of little Vickie, whom he thought *"looked like a Whitten."*[160] My mother, far less emotional about those matters and always extremely matter of fact, did not wish to burst her husband's bubble, although she was quite convinced that *"Newborns all look alike, but I was not going to say that!"*[161]

Meanwhile, I was still hospitalized and kept from my mother. She remembered that even though I was in a different wing, she *"could sometimes hear my screaming"* when the nurse came in to give me penicillin injections. *"Poor little boy,"* Mother said, *"His little bottom looked like a pin cushion."*[162]

Finally, nearly a week after my sister's birth, they were all allowed to go home, much to everyone's relief and joy. I, however, still recovering from my illness, was not released from hospital until some days later. Grandparents Solms were delighted with Vickie, although Grandmother Solms was quite annoyed that the baby had come so quickly, thus robbing her of the opportunity to be with Mother during the entire ordeal. But even then, my dear sister arrived when she wanted to, not when she was expected!

Once I rejoined the family, Mother was very concerned as to how I would react to my sister. For nearly five-and-a-half years I had been the only child in the family. Now, not only did I have to share everyone's love and attention with a new baby, but also a girl! Mother later remembered that her initial concerns were put to rest when she noticed that I *"seemed to be very proud"* of my little sister and when she cried, *"always went to the crib and patted her gently."*[163] I guess, to this day, I remain very protective of my sister and even though separated by a continent, I still Skype with her almost every day. Although I no longer visit Louisiana, where she and her children live, Vickie visits me in Coburg almost every year, particularly around the holiday season.

Everyone worried about Bob though. How would this huge Great Dane react to the new addition to the family? He was very protective of me, that was clear. But would he be as protective of my sister, we wondered. To be safe, Mother and Dick kept him from my sister's room. Then, one day Grandmother Solms came to visit. She was one of Bob's favorites and was always very happy to see her. Mother and Grandmother Solms went into Vickie's room. Bob nudged the door open and *"came in, he gently took Grandmother Solms' hand in his huge mouth and with a low, but friendly growl led her out of the room, as if to tell her, that she was not allowed to touch the baby."* Mother and Grandmother laughed about it, but from that day on Bob was allowed to go into the room. Mother remembered: *"He sometimes put his big head over the crib as if to check on the baby, and* *then lied down next to it to guard her."*¹⁶⁴ He was a great dog, our Bob. Mother and Dick, myself and Nanny Wimmer would be welcomed by him with a wagging tail and a big smile; *"everyone else got a deep growl as a reception!"*¹⁶⁵

My sister's christening was celebrated at Steinwändt, and I was allowed to play an important part in the proceedings. Superintendent Entz, who had married Mother and Dick, came from Vienna to officiate. After Herr Entz pronounced her names, "Victoria Astrid Solms," Mother placed her in my arms and I kneeled before the altar with her to be blessed. Mother later remembered: *"It was a lovely ceremony in the confines of the closest family and in the wonderful old house,"* that she loved so much.¹⁶⁶

Grandmother Solms, a talented hostess like few others, arranged for a nice buffet to follow the ceremony. By the time we finished our meal, little Victoria had had enough of pleasantries for a day and accordingly notified us all that she was more than ready to head home.

I have already mentioned that to us all, Victoria has always

I was not destined to be a great equestrian, although I tried my best.

been "Vickie." Grandmother Solms always used nicknames for everyone in the family. Mother was "Toria." Her brother Friedrich Hans had been known as "Pety" forever. Her youngest brother was called "Huber," while I had become "Andy." These nicknames, a sign of affection, remain so to this day!

Chapter XI

An American Life

The time we spent in Salzburg was very pleasant for our young family. Vickie kept growing and our nannie was quite busy with the two of us. Mother and Dick were a very popular couple and their life was consumed by our needs, their social obligations and many weekend visits to Steinwändt. Mother made a great effort to be the best wife she could possibly be for her husband, who in return visibly cared deeply for her. Our English, Mother's and mine, greatly improved and soon enough she began copying Dick's unmistakable Southern accent, quite different from the British accent with which she had spoken the language until she married him.

In life, I have always believed, we have to adapt to the circumstances surrounding our present … we either adapt, or we are left behind. Hence, we adapted and began becoming more American, less European!

Grandmother Solms was not amused by many of these changes, in fact. Several years later, during one of our visits to Austria, she bitterly complained that Mother and I spoke "slang," as she called American English. Mother, never one to keep quiet, respectfully tried to explain to Grandmother Solms that *"She had to realize that I had lived in America and not in England, and that it was like Austria and Germany, where everybody talks German, but the accent is entirely different in both countries."*[167] Well, truth be told, even within each of these countries accents can be quite different from one region to the next!

By the time I was six years old, I was quite fluent in both languages, German and English. These two are the two most prevalent languages spoken by descendants of Queen Victoria, for it seems that everyone in the family was basically born bilingual!

My sister Vickie and Jolly.

Anyhow, some time later, after we settled in the United States, bilingualism became an issue, a serious one in fact. When Dick was present, since his German was, well, not there, Mother always spoke to us in English. However, when he was not present, Mother always used German with us and she wanted to make sure that Vickie and I would grow up completely bilingual. This was quite smart of her, of course, as I was expected one day in the future to inherit the Coburg legacy and for that I was surely to need fluency in German almost as a prerequisite to fulfilling my duty and obligations. Bilingualism worked fine while we lived in Austria, but when we eventually relocated to the United States, as mentioned before, it became a major problem. When school friends and classmates, for example, realized that I spoke German, they started calling me *"Kraut!"* – *"You are a Kraut,"* some of these bullies would yell at me.[168] Hence, much to our detriment, we began phasing out German and we reached a point when most of the German I had known was lost. In fact, by the time I returned permanently to Germany in the early 1960s, I basically had to learn German from scratch. Can you, dear reader, imagine what it was like for me, the heir to Coburg and

*Opposite page:
At an apple eating competition.*

My mother in the 1950s.

Gotha, successor of the last reigning Duke Carl Eduard, to arrive in my birth country not knowing its language? I felt, at times, that I shared an incredible array of similarities with Grandfather Coburg, a young man who arrived in a foreign country whose language and culture he had to learn in order to blend in!

Another important thing that we had to learn in our new life as a young American family was budgeting! Mother had little concept of money. Actually, many aristocrats of her generation had a minimal idea of the value of money, much less how to manage it. Those in her milieu lived off the proceeds of the lands, and many had professionals managing their estates. Hence, the value of money was not really something they were explained, ever. Mother went through a culture shock once we settled in Salzburg and she had access to the commissary, where she found an unimaginable array of products that she had never seen before. She was like a kid in a candy store, but one who had been handed a blank check. Mother simply had to sign her name on each bill and these would then be sent to Dick once a month. Boy, did Dick get a shock after he opened the first bill – Dick walked in our home nearly dying from an apoplectic attack!

Poor Mother, she could not help herself. She had been living under rationing for nearly a decade, at least since war ignited when Germany invaded Poland in September 1939. She had no idea of what it meant to work within a budget. In fact, she had no idea of how to shop for a family, much less run a household. So, to avoid having poor Dick die from shock every time the commissary bill arrived, my poor mother had to teach herself how to live within a budget and, as she later recalled, she *"was learning fast and, after a couple of months, I* [was] *considered to be pretty much an expert shopper!"*

And still, life continued in spite of these "oops" moments. Soon enough, the extra room in our house became the one used by visitors from Steinwändt. Grandmother Solms came to Salzburg frequently, sometimes to have lunch with Mother and do some shopping, other times to spend the night and be with us children. Uncle Pety and Uncle Huber also became frequent visitors in Salzburg. In fact, Mother and Dick's house saw guests more often than not, a custom that continued in the United States, once they relocated. They were always happy with people visiting, particularly Mother when the visitors were members of her adored family. Again, the bonds that united Mother and her siblings and parents were unbreakable, and they formed one of the tightest family groups I have ever seen.

Then, just as we were getting used to our life in Salzburg, Dick received notice of his relocation back to the United States. This news immediately sent our small family into turmoil since the paperwork required seemed insurmountable. Mother being an Austrian, while I still had German citizenship, this meant that poor Dick had to do twice the paperwork required. Since my father was already in San Francisco, even he had to sign off permission for me to leave for the United States. In fact, even Mother, with whom I was traveling, had to sign paperwork saying that she was fine with me traveling to the United States with her – bureaucracy at its best!

After painful goodbyes to family and friends, we traveled from Salzburg to Bremerhaven, where we boarded the *USS General Darby*, a US Navy transport liner that later saw service in Vietnam. We left Germany on December 13, 1948, sailing across the Atlantic Ocean toward New York City, where we arrived a few days before Christmas. Mother remembered the sea voyage in far less glowing terms than I did. For me, being on such a large ship as we sailed to a new country, it was perhaps the most exciting experience I had ever had. Not for Mother, who spent quite a bit of the sailing suffering from the ravages of motion sickness. In fact, even once we landed in New York, she continued to suffer it for several days.

We stayed in New York City shortly after the authorities processed us. Dick, meanwhile, had arranged for us to board a train to New Orleans, from where we would continue to his mother's home. The train journey was quite long. in fact, as it took us two days and one night. I remember that our compartment was very comfortable and even had its own private

Mother with Vickie and me.

little bathroom. At night the porter came in and converted the seats into beds and *"covered them with snow-white sheets and fluffy blankets."*[169] In the morning, while we were at breakfast, the porter once again came to our compartment and arranged everything so that when we returned, the bed had magically disappeared. As a child, I remember how exciting this all was, even though at times the long stretches of railroad track bored me to near despondency. Mother and Dick tried their best to keep me occupied, but I am sure I was nearly a pest!

It was when we arrived in New Orleans that I was confronted by the indomitable woman we learned to love, Omo Birdie. She had not seen her son for several years and now he was returning home with a new wife and two children. She seemed to take to Mother immediately and made her feel right at home. Her home was in the Garden District, not far away from famed St. Charles Avenue, and a nice old Black lady, by the name of Miss Emma, assisted her. She was completely dedicated to Omo Birdie and when told that I was a great-great-grandson of Queen Victoria, she replied, *"Oh, I remember Queen Victoria. We should put him under a bell jar and set him on the mantelpiece!"*[170]

I did it my way ...

Chapter XII

Our First American Christmas

If I thought that New Orleans was going to be our home, I was to be sadly disappointed for during our first few years in the United States we moved about a fair deal. We had traveled from Austria through Germany, across the Atlantic, landed in New York and railroaded to Louisiana. Our life had seen plenty of upheaval in the last month of 1948. However, the trekking was not yet at an end for El Paso, Texas, was our final destination, at least for the time being.

Meanwhile, since we had been traveling for the last three weeks, by the time we settled at Omo Birdie's, Christmas had come and gone. I remember feeling more than a little desolate since the Christ-Child (Father Christmas) seemed to have forgotten about me. Mother knew how disappointed I felt, and as always, she set about making it alright – What a wonderfully splendid woman she was!

Firstly, she told that since we had moved so much, the poor, dear Christ-Child was at a loss as to where to leave our presents. This, she reassured me, would be solved that very day when she and Dick made sure that He knew where we were. A decorated tree would be set near a window and this would serve as guide so He knew we had stopped moving. So, on the afternoon of Boxing Day, we left the house and went to buy a tree and Christmas decorations, finally settling on one that seemed to still have a little life left in it. Then, unbeknownst to me, and while Vickie and I took a nap, Mother and Dick left again and found a few toys to place under the tree. By the time I woke up, the Christ-Child had magically found us; perhaps the electric lights that illuminated the tree (the first time Mother and I saw such a contraption) had done the deed. I was ecstatic and exceedingly happy for even Sister Vickie got a new stroller, as Mother was in dire need of one – that Christ-Child somehow always knew what Vickie and I needed!

Playing in our yard with sister Vickie.

That first Christmas in America brought us many other new things, some incredible, others not so much. First of all, Mother could not believe how humid New Orleans was. Up until then she had always celebrated Christmas under heaps of snow, whether it was at Casel, Coburg or Steinwändt. Now, however, there was not a snow flake in sight and, in fact, Mother realized her clothes were all wrong and she needed to acquire some lighter garments. In order to do so, Dick took her to a department store. We were left with Omo Birdie, who as the assistant manager of a theater mainly worked evenings.

As it was common to do then, Mother and Dick boarded a streetcar to go to downtown. While Dick paid the amazing fare of $0.07 per person, Mother walked past the conductor and toward the rear of the streetcar where she saw many empty seats.[171] Since all the front seats were taken, she did not think about it twice. A seat was a seat!

Just as Mother was about to sit down on one of the empty rear seats, Dick grabbed her arm and pulled her up. *"You can't sit here,"* he

Opposite page: A visit with Santa Claus!

Vickie with the lady who helped Mother with household chores.

whispered.[172] Mother was perplexed as to why she could not sit in the empty seats, *"Why not"* she asked? Dick gently told her, *"They are reserved for the Negroes, because they are not allowed to sit in the front seats."*[173] Mother was not only speechless, but she never forgot that blatant example of what she believed was un-American behavior. She could not possibly understand why if there were no empty seats in one section, she was forbidden to take one of the empty ones in another section. But this was the South in 1949, and Jim Crow laws were fully in place. It would take nearly another two decades and the death of countless good people to bring the beginning of full desegregation to a much-needed start. In the meantime, Mother raised us to believe that every human being, in spite of different racial, ethnic and socio-economic backgrounds, was worthy of success and deserved our respect. She never truly accepted that dark aspect of Southern society and culture.

We spent about a month in New Orleans, a time that, besides the streetcar incident, Mother thoroughly enjoyed, as it was like a second honeymoon for her and Dick. Omo Birdie had some lodgers in her house to supplement her income, since she had been divorced from Dick's father for many years. These people quickly became friends of my mother's and she, being as gregarious as ever, quickly became everyone's favorite. Mother had an amazing gift to make every feel at home in her presence!

As Mother never liked idleness, even though we were not staying in New Orleans for long, she lost little time in enrolling me in a local kindergarten, the same where Dick had attended dancing lessons oh so many years ago. They were set on helping me have as American life as possible for they both, Mother and Dick, fervently believed that it would make me a well-rounded person. They were right, of course.

It was also at this time that we met Dick's sister Jean and her husband Mr. Philip Hardy, who apparently was rather well off. Mother always considered her a bit spoiled and hoped against all hope that Mr. Hardy would be able to set her straight. He never did, of course, and Jean always got to do what she wanted. Sixteen years Dick's junior, Jean was also a social butterfly and one who seemed consumed by gaining social position. I do not think Mother ever warmed up to her. She did, however, feel very comfortable in the presence of Dick's father and his wife Kay. Of him, Mother said, *"He was a handsome man with impeccable manners,"* while his wife she described as *"a sweet, gentle lady,"* of whom Mother and Dick became quite fond.[174]

Also when we were living in New Orleans, we became aware of a frightful pest, the flying cockroach. These flying cockroaches petrified Mother, while I shrieked in horror every time one of those beasts decided to pay us an unwelcome visit. I believe that is one dislike we both shared. I think that when we finally left New Orleans we were both quite relieved to leave them behind

One of the most impressive geographical aspects of the United States is the great expanse of territory that separates big cities and states. To this day, it feels as if the country goes on forever. When we boarded the Sunset Limited train on our way to El Paso, the scenery we could absorb outside the window, particularly as the bayou disappeared and was replaced by the dry land that covers such an important portion of the gigantic state of Texas, fascinated me. I will never forget that train ride, as I became an honorary porter. Our porter was a thoroughly nice man who must have taken pity on Mother, traveling by herself with two children, one of them just a few months old. So, to help Mother out, the porter asked her if he could rely on my assistance to go about checking everyone's papers and tickets, while also helping set up the beds for that evening. It was my first important job and I loved it!

Chapter XII – Our First American Christmas

From the left: Me, Mother, Grandfather Whitten, Aunt Kay (Grandfather Whitten's wife), Dick and Vickie.

Once we settled in El Paso, an interesting city surrounded by desert and with very little vegetation, I became enthralled by cowboy culture. Mother and Dick began taking us to rodeos, and these gatherings seemed magical to me. It was then and there that I told Mother that I had decided what I was to become when older: a cowboy! I can only but imagine what fun they must have had listening to my childlike fascination with this important historical aspect of the American West. Anyhow, I was so serious about becoming a cowboy that Mother remembered that my *"biggest wish was a pair of cowboy boots, a gun and holster and a hat."*[175] Once put together I was quite a sight. *"I do not think that a day went by that Andy did not wear the boots and the hat, and with his bare little torso all suntanned and his shorts, he had that holster with the gun strapped around him like a professional,"* Mother later said.[176] I was so proud of being a cowboy that one time when Dick showed me a *Life Magazine* article about my cousin Carl Gustaf of Sweden *"who would one day be king,"* I replied to Dick, *"What a shame, he can never be a cowboy!"*[177]

Mother also recalled that the weather in El Paso suitet us extremely well. She always believed that Vickie and I had never been as healthy as when we were breathing in that dry desert air that characterizes El Paso. By then, not only heat, however, was a concern, but also rambunctious little sister Vickie, who made sure she kept everyone occupied. She was "full of spunk" and crawling everywhere. In fact, if we paid no attention to her, Vickie would sneakily crawl out of the house and into the yard, causing us all considerable worry. As her diapers were made of cloth, she was able to withstand the considerable thump she received on her bottom every time the screen door slammed on her.

Mother being as industrious as ever, also decided that investing in a Singer sewing machine would save the family considerable resources. In due time, Mother learned to be quite a professional women's wear designer and she and Vickie were the models for many of her creations. Well, I must say, none of us escaped 100% having to wear some of Mother's rather intricate ensembles. At least, they were nicely looking and nothing like Omo Birdie's hats.

Then, just like that, our El Paso days came to a quick end when Dick received orders to relocate once again. This was to be our third relocation in less than a year. Dick was offered a higher position in Washington, D.C and he could not turn it down. Off to the East Coat we went!

Chapter XIII

Army Life Across the USA

When we left El Paso, we drove the car Dick had bought to Lincoln, Nebraska. There we met Omo Birdie, who was babysitting Dick's nephew, Calvert Hardy, Jean's son. We did not get to stay long because when Jean found out we were there, she called from Rome, where she and her husband were on vacation, and asked that we leave immediately. Apparently, she was concerned that we might be bringing the poliovirus into her house. There was a polio epidemic at the time and if affected many children. Still, Mother believed it was *"far-fetched and ridiculous"* of Jean to say these things.[178] But it was her house and her call put an end to our visit.

From Nebraska we continued to Indianapolis, where Dick was born. Mother could never grasp how large the United States is and she was always truly astonished by the size of each state and by the geographical changes one could see from one region to the next. Mother was very inquisitive and she noticed everything around her. Anyhow, after spending two days with Dick's family in Indiana, we continued to Washington DC, where Dick was to be stationed for the time being.

After an exhaustive search around the capital, Mother and Dick found a small house in Falls Church, VA, a suburb of Washington DC. The neighborhood was popular with young military families and because many of them purchased their homes, Mother was happy knowing that it was not a transient community, but instead one in which we would be able to make friends. The house Mother described as *"A brand-new little brick house with a full cellar and a screened porch, living room, kitchen, bath and two bedrooms."*[179] Indeed, a far cry from the sort of homes Mother had once lived in. Yet, she loved it.

A nice photo of Dick and me.

I also enjoyed living there and soon enough made friends with children from the other military families living in the neighborhood. Some of these families Mother had already met in Austria, so it was as if an old chapter was reopened. Vickie, however, was still too young to go about the neighborhood as I did. In fact, she was at home with Mother, but was growing each and every day. She was also developing quite a personality, that Vickie, and this got her in trouble very often. One night Mother and Dick wanted to have half an hour to themselves before dinner. Dick was exhausted from his work and Mother wanted to be with her husband. We were told to find something to do and leave them alone. Oh, dear Vickie ... she just would not have it. Instead of leaving our parents alone, she kept going about and running like a weasel. One way or another, she was going to make them pay attention to her. Dick, hoping to get her to stop, *"tried to put her in a chair, she made herself stiff as a board, and there was no way, short of hurting her seriously, to get her to sit in that chair,"* Mother recalled and added, *"We finally took her, screaming and kicking, to her room, telling her that she could let us know when she was ready to say that she was sorry and was able to behave herself."*[180] They even had to lock the door since Vickie would just not stay in the room otherwise. That Vickie, boy, does she have a will, my sister!

Opposite page: Mother with our beloved and terrible Jolly.

Having breakfast with Vickie.

Even though we moved around quite some, it always amazed me that Mother was so easily able to settle down and build herself a nice niche. She was very good at making people feel at ease around her and she was a wonderful hostess. She also became a good cook and would always quickly find where the best places for shopping were, whether it was groceries or clothes. She continued making a lot of her own clothes and many of ours, and one time she left me in the car for about three hours while she went shopping for sewing patterns. I was not very happy with her, I must confess, but she had had a great time looking for the materials needed for her next creations.

I remember that when we lived in Falls Church, we would drive around a lot on weekends. Mother loved driving and so did Dick. We took long journeys in their car and made stops here and there. During these outings we also visited the countryside, and Mother was quite taken with "*its wonderful horse farms and lovely big old houses, usually on a hill overlooking the meadows delineated by white wooden fences. It was both peaceful and beautiful.*"[181] We got to see many battlefields of the Civil War, and also visited the historic homes of Presidents Washington and Jefferson, Mount Vernon and Monticello. I may not have enjoyed myself as much as I should have, and Mother worried that we were too young to benefit from this cultural experience. Yet, I remember these visits quite vividly today, so more than she expected must have stayed with me.

It was in the fall of 1949, and while we were living in Falls Church, that I started first grade. Mother was concerned that other kids at school would catch my accent and tease me for being German. Luckily, none of her worse fears materialized and I had a great time there.

With sister Vickie.

With Dick and our family car, which took us to so many places around the United States.

We lived in Falls Church when we took in that infamous scoundrel of a dog, Jolly, a wire-haired fox terrier that was our best friend ever. Mother found that there was a kennel in Lower Marlboro, Maryland, that had several dogs for adoption. It was there that we first met Jolly, who was all of eight weeks old. Mother always thought that the name fit Jolly splendidly, but she also grew to think of him as another "Dennis the Menace!" One time, while he was still a puppy, we went to a museum and left Jolly at home. Upon our return, Mother discovered that little, sweet Jolly had vandalized our home, and he *"had torn down every curtain in the house and was sitting by the door wagging his little short tail greeting us with a big smile! And to finish the job, he had unrolled the roll of bathroom tissue and pulled it into the hallway!"*[182] How could we get mad at him? Still, from then on, every time we left the house, Jolly was left inside the bathroom, oh, and the bathroom tissue roll was put away!

We were still living in Falls Church when Mother adopted a street cat. Poor Dick nearly had a conniption when he returned home from work to find a cat had joined the family. Mother named him Tommy, and she quickly went about getting him cleaned and ready to live with us. He fit in almost immediately and truly appreciated Mother for giving him a home. Vickie took quite a liking to Tommy and he basically allowed my sister free reign over his daily destiny. Tommy weighed nearly 18 lbs and dear Vickie would lift him without any fear. She could do to him whatever she wanted and he would just let it happen. He was the cat that naughty Vickie tried to flush down the toilet. Mother found poor Tommy after his ordeal as he shook his feet and desperately tried drying his face. Vickie described what she had done as *"just trying to give him a bath!"*[183] Vickie was also notorious for bringing lizards and toads home. Unfortunately, Mother would not have it, and Vickie lost her new pets. I was not as exotic in my pet selection for dogs, cats, and parakeets were enough for me.

Just another "American" family: Mother and Dick with Vickie and me.

We lived in Falls Church for a little over one year. Our stay there came to an end in the fall of 1950, when Dick received orders to ship out to Korea. Mother had been fearful that our contented existence in Falls Church would not last and she was therefore not surprised when the Korea news arrived. She decided, however, that after driving Dick across the United States to San Francisco, from where he was scheduled to depart, we would settle in Louisiana so we could be close to Omo Birdie and Dick's father.

Mother was sincerely worried about the future. The time spent in Falls Church had been a happy one for us, and also for the very first time we had been able to live as a regular family. But now, with Dick shipping off to war in a faraway land, Mother was beside herself. Little did we know at the beginning of this difficult time that she was suffering from hyperthyroidism, an illness that later on caused her much pain and considerable suffering.

Jolly, Mother, Vickie and Dick.

Mother with Vickie and me.

We left Falls Church in January 1951 and reached Omo Birdie's home a few days later. While we were there, Mother and Dick found a home where we would live while he was in Korea and to add to their troubles, a new school had to be found for me as well. Mother decided that since they did not know how long Dick's deployment would be, it would be best if I was instructed at home, thus minimizing the trauma of me making friends only to lose them soon after. Hence, a lady by the name of Ms. De la Houssy was hired to be my instructor. Mother remembered her as *"a lovely elderly lady, who knew just how to handle little boys like Andy, being not too overly interested in studies."*[184]

Finding a place in New Orleans proved too costly. So, instead, Mother and Dick found a home in Waveland, Mississippi. *"It had two bedrooms, a glassed-in gallery, a large living room, 1 ½ baths and a beautiful kitchen. Across the front of the house was a screened-in porch which we used as a dining area almost all through the year,"* Mother remembered.[185] The house also had a nice yard with lush plants and lovely rose bushes, and this suited Vickie and me just fine, as it would give us ample space for our cavorting about. There was a garage with an apartment on top. Mother eventually rented the apartment to a nice man, whose presence on the property gave her a sense of security since most of our neighbors were there only on weekends. However, since the house had some renters living in it, we could not move in until June 1951; meanwhile, we stayed in New Orleans with Omo Birdie.

At some point, Mother and Dick decided that we would drive him to California. Omo Birdie came along on the road trip, which was a grand experience for Vickie and me. Dick had to be dropped off at Camp Stoneman Personnel Center, in Pittsburg, California, a town located on the Sacramento River delta. Since we had until late February, they decided that we would make this a big road trip. I wonder how many women in 1950s United States actually drove across the country. Mother, a daredevil on top of everything else, did not think about it twice. She was simply delighted with the opportunity to see more of the country she had adopted.

Prince August Wilhelm of Prussia and Princess Alexandra Viktoria of Schleswig-Holstein.

From New Orleans we headed west, making a stop at New Braunfels, Texas. This is a colony founded in March 1845 by a Prince of Solms-Braunfels. Along with him had come *"two hundred Germans to make Texas their new home."*[186] Mother was quite taken with New Braunfels and she *"was amazed how the German culture had been preserved throughout that long period of time and several generations."*[187] Interestingly, most people still spoke German there, particularly the elderly. There were German signs on the store fronts and the restaurants specialized in German food. To make matters even more interesting for Mother, *"On the way out of New Braunfels we ran across the little village of Solms!"*[188] She remembered this being more a hamlet than anything else as it was composed of three houses, *"five chickens and a lot of tumbleweed."*[189] I think Mother was the first Solms to visit New Braunfels in many a generation!

The next big stop was Palm Springs. Coincidentally, while there we visited with Aunt Aly Holstein (Alexandra Victoria), one of the sisters of Grandmother Coburg and Omo. She had been married quite unhappily to Prince August Wilhelm of Prussia, another infamous Hitler supporter. "Auwi," as he was called within the family circle, was an early supporter of National Socialism and throughout Hitler's reign of terror never wavered in his support for the dictator. Even Auwi's father, Kaiser Wilhelm II, was quite livid with his son for being such an outspoken Nazi. Grandfather Coburg and Prince Auwi were in close contact since his Potsdam days. As the Kaiser and Kaiserin welcomed his English cousin into their home, their children became close friends of Grandfather Coburg. It was not surprising, then, that the Kaiserin played such an important role in assisting Grandfather Coburg's path eventually crossing that of her niece Princess Viktoria Adelheid of Schleswig-Holstein-Sonderburg-Glücksburg.

Anyhow, Aunt Aly was in Palm Springs as a guest of some wealthy friends of hers. She was a very talented painter and after her divorce from Auwi Prussia she subsidized her meager income with the sale of her paintings. In Palm Springs she painted many desert scenes and also managed to annoy her guests. Aunt Aly *"was an artist ... and was like most artists very temperamental."*[190] Aunt Aly was also quite eccentric and she loved living in a trailer. Even when her brother, the Duke of Schleswig-Holstein, offered her rooms at Schloß Grünholz, Aly turned him down and opted for a trailer. It was as if she refused to grow roots anywhere. Well, even in Palm Springs she convinced her hosts to find her a trailer and park it in their front yard. Years later I remember her visiting Grandmother Coburg, while still spending considerable effort on her various paintings. I own several of them and when I see these paintings, Aunt Aly always comes to mind.

From Palm Springs, where we finally managed to escape Aunt Aly's embrace, we headed to Yosemite National Park. *"What an awesome experience for all of us,"* Mother described it.[191] We admired the tall trees and *"the grandiose landscape with its waterfalls rolling over the tops of the mountains falling into the deep valley below in a giant cloud of spray."*[192] I had never seen the type of rainbows I saw in Yosemite and I was truly fascinated by this incredible place.

From Yosemite we drove the large stretch into San Francisco, where we did a lot of sightseeing and took full advantage of the city's rich cuisine. We found San Francisco a most fascinating city. Chinatown was particularly incredible for us due to its customs, businesses, culture and food. The mixture of rich sounds, smells and tastes made Chinatown become an icon in my mind and once we left, I longed to return. Perhaps these memories played important roles in my future visits to San Francisco, once when my wife and I brought our children, and lastly when I spent two weeks at Arturo Beéche's home while we worked on this book.

Aunt Aly Holstein in her mobile home.

Chapter XIV
A Time for Difficult Truths

It would take forever for me to give a detailed accounting of the 1950s and what I did on a regular basis. Besides, I also think that you, dear readers, would become thoroughly bored with some of these minutiae. Suffice to say that I led a very conventional life, one quite similar to that experienced by most US Army brats.

First, I must say that even though we, my father and I, lived in the USA at the same time, we never saw each other. It is very simple … my father was an extremely complicated man!

At one point, we returned to Europe as Dick was stationed in France after his return from Korea. It must have been around 1952-53. During that time I did visit Coburg to spend time with my grandparents. Grandfather Coburg was already very sick and the cancer on his face was quite visible. He was feeble, hunched over because of arthritis and one knew that he had little time left. I remember that during that visit he gifted me a beautiful antique knife that he had possessed for a very long time. He was particularly kind to me, as I would one day inherit his estates. Due to taxation issues, and surely also because of my father's questionable behavior, like leaving when he should have stayed and helped rebuild, Grandfather Coburg made me his heir. As a child, I received nothing from the Coburgs, and Dick paid for my upbringing. He had assumed that responsibility when he asked Mother to marry him and he never complained or regretted doing so. In fact, many years later my father said, *"It is funny, to have a grown up son without having had to raise him."* He wanted me as a friend, not a son … he did not want to be a father as that required involvement, dedication, a lot of work, and, above all, selflessness. I wanted a father, not a friend.

Mother with Vickie and me on our way to Europe.

Anyhow, once I left Coburg I never saw my grandfather alive again. He died at home in Coburg on March 6, 1954. His funeral was attended by his surviving children, as well as a bevy of royal relations, and many decades would go by before Coburg again witnessed such a large royal gathering.

Grandfather Coburg's passing also deepened the rift already in existence between Father and the team of people his father had put in place to run the Coburg Family Foundation. Father's nemesis was Herr Voights, a trusted advisor of both my Coburg grandparents. Father and this gentleman never saw eye to eye and distrusted each other intensely. Given Father's behavior since departing Coburg after divorcing my mother, Grandmother Coburg and her team quite likely thought he was too immature and self-centered to

Opposite page: As American as James Dean!

Denise and my father after they married.

be trusted with running the family's financial affairs. Hence, if Father thought that after Grandfather Coburg's death he would gain control of the Coburg Family Foundation, he was sorely disappointed. Grandmother Coburg and Herr Voights kept an extremely tight leash on it all.

Anyhow, in the United States we moved about quite a bit due to Dick's army obligations. One time, we lived in Staten Island and Brooklyn when he was stationed in New Jersey. Because of this, I graduated from a high school in New Jersey, Red Bank High School. I used to drive my stepfather's car with friends to New York. We could buy beer there at eighteen, while in New Jersey you had to be twenty-one!

In my mind, countless episodes of a mostly happy time dance about disjointedly when I think of all those bygone days in America. In Louisiana, I remember walking to school barefoot because it was so hot. Then I would sneak to the seashore and try catching crabs. It was quite a unique upbringing for a German child. My sister and I loved taking our shoes off and walking into the muddy puddles of brackish water. It really was such a different life from that experienced by the overwhelming majority of my Gotha relations across Europe.

I remember that we always had pets since Mother loved them. She longed for the horses she had lost in Europe, so I guess she replaced them with dogs. Of course, we had that funny Fox terrier Jolly, as you will remember. Oh he loved chasing other dogs that Jolly. One time he needed to pee so badly, he jumped out of the car. He was a bit crazy and liked to run after iron birds that neighbors displayed on their lawns. He simply hated birds and once chased a prized cock of Omo Birdie's. Grandfather Whitten was so upset with Jolly that he shot at him and the bullet landed between his legs. He was scared, well just a bit, because soon enough he was running after the chickens again. He was an incorrgible dog that Jolly. He also had an intense dislike of cats. One time our cat gave birth and Jolly killed the poor kitty cats. Nevertheless, Jolly was quite good at protecting us. He kept us safe. One time a child pushed me out of the school bus, Jolly saw him and jumped on the boy. After that, how could we not take that dog everywhere!

In Mississippi, we went to catch crabs, I stuck my toe into a bucket filled with crabs and one would not let go of my toe. We laughed and laughed. Another time my mother dropped a bucket of crabs on the kitchen floor and they all ran around snapping their claws and trying to get her feet, she was barefoot and we all did a funny dance to avoid stepping on the crabs and more so getting our toes snapped by them.

I became a hunter at an early age.

I think that if anyone had seen us from the outside, they might have thought that we were a family of crazies. Well, maybe we were a bit different!

Whenever we visited Omo Birdie, because she worked at a theater as I mentioned before, we would get to go to the cinema often. It was a great treat for us and we were able to see the best movies as we were seated next to her. A definite plus was that she liked giving us candy bars!

Vickie and I were mischievous children. Perhaps because of this, Mother had to counterbalance and not lose her temper, for otherwise we would have driven her mad. My sister Vickie got drunk at the age of three. She was seated on a high chair. There was a pitcher of beer near her. As the night went on, there was less and less beer, but Vickie's eyes kept getting bigger and bigger. By the time they realized what was going so, she had drank much of the pitcher of beer. That was her introduction to the effects of too much drinking!

Another time, we gave Mother's dog garlic to make him stop begging at the table … then we locked the dog in her room and the dog kept farting. Mother and Dick's bedroom had quite an awful smell when she went in it and was quite upset that the dog had been locked in there. Oh, but when she found out it was us, who not only gave the poor dog garlic, but also locked him on her room, she came out running after us with her silver riding crop. We ran for our lives!

Denise and my brother Adrian.

In Argentina with my little brother Adrian.

Mother was quite relaxed, but she also expected us to behave in particular ways. She always expected us to know our place. One time, I said something I should not have said to her, I was nearly forty, and she turned around so quickly and slapped me on the face and told me *"don't you ever forget that you owe respect to your mother!"* And just like that, I was out in my place.

As the end of the 1950s approached, I was sent to Argentina, where Father had moved with his family, now consisting of Denise, his wife, and three children. Beatrice, who was born in Bern, joined Claudia in the nursery. Then in 1955, Denise gave birth to my half-brother Adrian, a nice boy who was destined to have an extremely complicated relationship with our father.

After arriving in Argentina, where Father awaited me at the airport in Buenos Aires, we went to his home, a large building with a fantastic swimming pool. Denise and the children were there and the children were very curious about their much older half-brother. One time, I found them peeking at me while I was sleeping. They always wanted to have an older brother. I remember

My love affair with automobiles began early in life. This is one of my favorite photos and I chose it for the cover of this book!

we had a very good time during my visit.

Toward the end of the trip, I had an accident when playing with firecrackers. A cocker spaniel distracted me while lighting them and one of the rockets exploded in my hand. By the time I reached New York my hand was still bandaged and my mother nearly fainted when she saw what I had done to myself. She was not happy!

I next saw my father in Coburg, probably in the early 1960s. In 1961, after finishing school, I spent the summer with him in Argentina. I was there about three months. Soon after my arrival, Denise flew back to Switzerland with the children and on that day Katrin Bremme (Katja), my father's new friend, moved in. She was more than twenty-years my father's junior and in due time she became his prized possession. I was unpleasantly surprised. I wrote to my mother and told her that Katja had moved in, and she wrote to Aunt Bylla in Sweden and the secret was out. You see, I was raised to respect my father and what I witnessed him doing troubled me deeply. Neither my mother nor Dick ever said anything bad about him. They wanted me to get to know him, and I did. However, I was also raised with very strong foundations instilled in me by

With Father when I visited him in Argentina.

Mother and Dick and I knew right from wrong. I could not compromise my moral principles just to gain Father's approval. And I did not!

Katja had worked in Berlin as a ticket salesgirl and went to Argentina seeking a new life. It was there that she met my father and began a relationship with him. Eventually, she became his Pygmalion. Katja was not a bad person, but she forgot her place and actively worked to ease Denise out of Father's life. He, of course, was not innocent in this matter either. I can only imagine what pain poor Denise felt when she discovered the betrayal. I am sure it was also quite difficult for my siblings, particularly the girls as they were older. Adrian, surely, was deeply affected by the collapse of his parents' marriage. I think our father was very lucky, for in the end we all tried our best to have our individual relationship wih him work. Mother had no issues with either one of her ex-husband's wives. As for Denise, well, I never really discussed

Father and Denise with my half-siblings: Claudia, Beatrice and Adrian.

these matters with her. However, whenever she had to be with us for important family events, like Beatrice's wedding, she made the best of it and comported herself with admirable poise. Denise was a nice woman and her children adored her.

At the end of my stay in Argentina, we sailed on a Johnson steamer and landed in Antwerp. Katja sailed with us to Europe. During the night Father would slip out of the room and go sleep with her. He convinced himself that I did not know what was going on, but for me it was terribly disappointing to see my father behaving in this manner. It was also very confusing for me. In Antwerp he had a new Mercedes coupé waiting for us…ivory white with red seats, and I was impressed. I was not raised in the United States in any sort of wealth. Dick made a good living from his Army job, but we did not live in abundance. We had enough to be happy and rarely did we know that our parents were not as wealthy as some other kids' parents.

From Antwerp, we traveled to Greinburg, but by the time we reached Salzburg the snow made it impossible to continue. We had to finish our journey to Grein by taking a train. Coincidentally, once our visit to Greinburg was at an end, from there we

During my visit to Argentina I got to meet my Coburg siblings for the first time. From the left: Claudia, me, Adrian and Beatrice.

Uncle Friedrich Holstein.

traveled to Hannover and could not reach Hamburg because of the great floods of 1962.

By that time, the matter of my education was of great concern to all involved: Coburgs, Voights, Mother and Dick. Already in the early 1950s, they had discussed the possibility of me staying in Europe to attend a boarding school. But my mother would not have it and she said no. With my father in Argentina, Grandmother Coburg in Grein, and my mother in the United States ... she was not willing to leave me all alone in Germany. And when Mother said no, there was no point in arguing. No meant no!

During our long European vacation, Father and I visited many relatives, many of whom I was meeting for the first time. We visited the Duke of Schleswig-Holstein, brother of both my grandmothers. Friedrich Holstein suggested that the Coburgs had to find a way to tie me to the property, since after all I was going to inherit everything. As a large landowner, he believed that success in management of one's land was only possible when the owner felt one with his property. I think, nowadays, that he was quite a sage. Perhaps I listened, after all, for I always felt close to our property and treated its care as a sacred stewardship placed on me by destiny. I know that I tried my best and I believe that my descendants will prosper for years to come because of my management of our legacy.

Toward the end of our visit, we went to visit my godmother Aunt Bylla and I first met my Swedish cousins. While in Sweden, I remember going to visit the Vasa, the old ship that was raised from the bottom of the Baltic Sea. I went to see this relic with Uncle Gusty, the old King Gustaf VI Adolf. He lived at Drottningholm Slot with Aunt Louise, his Battenberg wife. This was a huge palace for just two elderly people. He was a great smoker and played tennis. His shirts all had a "G" engraved in them. He was a very educated man, an amateur archaeologist, and quite erudite. She was very English, one of the last Battenbergs. She was very quiet and reserved.

Margaretha, my cousin, took me around Stockholm and we had a great time together. Christina, her sister, is my age, and since then a special bond has existed between us. We are Princess Madeleine's godparents, to boot, and at her wedding a few years ago we had place of honor. My cousin, King Carl XVI Gustaf is a little younger, by some three years. But from this visit developed the close ties that I have always had with the Swedish royals, my cousins. At that time, my cousin Birgitta was already married to Hansi Hohenzollern and they were much in love. One did not get to see them much.

From Stockholm I went to Coburg and stayed there for some time. It then became apparent to me that there were deeper problems within the family than I had previously thought or known. My father once came to me and asked: *"Which side are you on? Mine or your grandmother's?"* I was not on anyone's side…I was on the side of our family.

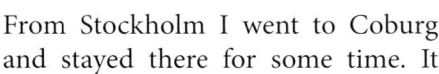

A visit to Grandfather Solms. At front, from the left: Vickie, Uncle Pety with Irina, and me. Behind are Aunt Oda, Grandfather Solms, Uncle Hubertus Solms and Mother.

In Coburg, I lived with my Grandmother Coburg. She was very possessive and quite strict. Nonsense did not amuse her whatsoever. A few years earlier in 1959, when I had visited Coburg, I befriended a boy by the name of Christoph von Knobelsdorff. But he liked to sit and read the Bible…no wonder my grandmother wanted him to become my close friend. Later, I met his brother Hanko, who became a fast friend with whom I usually snuck out, got in trouble and had lots of fun. Today, he is the Chairman of the Board of the Coburg Family Foundation. Anyhow, Hanko and I were terrible and we really did get into a lot of trouble. Father gifted me a little Karmann Ghia. We had befriended a Swedish exchange student named Anita. We were both in love with Anita, but I had a car, and he did not. To this day he teases me about winning Anita's attention!

Christoph von Knobelsdorf became a close friend during the time I stayed in Coburg with my grandmother. More than five decades later, we remain very good friends and now he is the chairman of the Coburg Family Foundation.

Steinwändt, Grandfather Solms and Omo's home.

We also went to Würzburg, where I had an American girlfriend. We had plenty of fun, perhaps a tad too much though. Well, I gave her strawberry wine, but it did not sit too well with her, or she had just too much. The poor girl got so drunk that she had an accident in her pants…and on the copilot seat in my car…*"it served me right!"*

One time we went to a little bar in Coburg, opposite the Ehrenburg. This was the sort of dive that parents did not like very much. To us, it held an interesting and tempting allure and, of course, since it was forbidden, a magnet attracted us to it. Anyhow, that night at the "Bar Rohmann" there was a party for an American soldier who was redeploying back to the United States. We snuck into the party and Hanko and I drank, to our heart's content, all the beer and vodka cherry that we could lay our hands on. I could not even drive my car so I walked all the way to the house. I snuck in, but just as I reached the top step, which was loose, I lost my footing and fell to the bottom of the stairs. Of course the barking of Grandmother Coburg's wretched dogs awakened everyone and the awful raucous caused by my falling down he stairs. My grandmother was furious; my stepmother Denise took one look at me and said: *"It serves you right!"* Waking up the next morning was, well, beyond difficult!

My grandmother had two dachshunds that she loved intensely. They were a couple…one was old and blind and barked and growled every time you got near him. I was a naughty boy. I found a shop in Coburg that sold materials for practical jokes. One of them was a plastic vomit. The cook at my grandmother's was such a clean freak that I decided to play a joke on her. I laid the fake vomit on the floor and she thought it was one of the dogs. She nearly had a heart attack when she saw it, yelling and screaming at the poor dogs. She was in such a state that I had to tell her it was a joke.

I had already done something similar to my mother some time before. But I scared her pale with a fake spider, a huge black one that I hung on the wall. I nearly gave her a heart attack.

Here I am with Mother's Dachshunds, Kathi and Lisa.

My poor siblings were also not spared. I used to love to play terrible pranks on my poor sisters. Once, I scared my sister Beatrice while we were in Grein…her poor hair nearly stood from fright after I scared her while we were watching a terror movie!

I was a terrible prankster … but I do think I have become a nicer one now!

Chapter XV
The 1960s, College, and Return to Germany

For me, the decade of the 1960s was one fraught with uncertainty and complications. I was expected to find a solid footing, but all around me the only place where I found grounding was with Mother and Dick. Unfortunately, I just could not stay there in a state of vegetative suspension while outside a world raged and beckoned my participation, whether I wanted to join in or not.

This time was also one during which I learned a lot about my father, much of it aspects of his personality that I questioned and sincerely disliked. Let me say one thing, before continuing. I was not raised by Mother to hate my father. If I said otherwise, I would be doing a tremendous disservice to both her and Dick Whitten. I would never, ever, disrespect them so!

Dick paid for my upbringing. My father never, if rarely, sent Mother any money. It was not until I was older than they started sending my mother money to contribute to my expenses. In fact, although Dick raised me, and I believe he did a fine job doing so, my father never met him. That, now, I find not only incredible, but also very telling of how difficult and complicated Father could be to those around him.

That having been said, I cannot avoid the fact that Father was a very complicated human being, as I have stated before. This I first began to realize when I went to Buenos Aires to visit him, a story I shared with you in a previous chapter. I do remember the excitement of air travel. I took an Aerolíneas Argentinas flight that had a stop in Bogotá, Colombia. I was wearing a suit, as one did back in those days when air travel was elegant and people took care of themselves. Today one sees people in shorts and sandals, jump suits and even pajamas. Well, not in those days as I do not think they would have allowed to you board the airplane to begin with. Anyhow, my first shock was when we deplaned in Bogotá: the heat – I nearly passed out from it!

Riding in the countryside during my visit to Argentina.

Opposite page: With my mother at Fort Hancock, in Sandy Hook.

At Schloß Greinburg with the first new car I ever owned. It was a present from Father.

With my mother in the early 1960s.

The second shock I received was something Father said to me soon after I arrived: *"It is funny, to have a grown up son without having to have raised him."* I suspect that this disappointed me quite so as I expected, hoped perhaps, that I would begin building bonds with this faraway father about whom I knew so little. Sadly, he he had other ideas in mind… he did not want to be a father, just a friend. I guess it was his way to eventually convince me to join him when he unsuccessfully attempted to take over the Coburg Family Foundation. With my father a lot of his problems in life emanated from his approach to everything: with me or against me!

In 1961, when we traveled across Europe, I was able to buy my first car. I have always had a true passion for automobiles and everyone who knows me, knows that I simply love cars and have had quite a few prized ones, like the Bentleys I have now, which are incredible machines. Anyhow, back then my meager budget allowed for a VW Karman Ghia, a beloved car that I brought back to the United States at the end of the European journey. It was my first car and I loved it. The car had a particular horn and the dogs always went crazy when they heard it. It was also the car in which I had my first accident, one of a very few number of collisions I have had because although I love speeding, I consider myself an excellent driver. Well, with the Karman Ghia, I once got distracted and rammed into the back of someone's car.

Finally, in 1963 I went off to university, Louisiana State University (LSU) in Baton Rouge. While at LSU, I tried my best to be very active and involved in campus life. I was in the Reserve Officer Training Crops (ROTC). Then, I founded the fraternity Delta Tau Delta…at the time it was a colony. Twenty-five years later I returned to LSU, and they made me an honorary member.

Allow me to state something very clearly: I was not a good student. My mother thought I should get an education, but I felt I was not made for that sort of life. I more preferred the practical implementation of business than the theory. I think that my son Alexander is wired the same way! My grades were barely average and I barely managed to stay afloat. I am sure that I was quite a source of worry for my elders. My son Hubertus was a far, far better student than I ever was.

When I went to LSU, I liked going to the French Quarter, as it was a lot of fun. We drank French coffee and ate donuts. We partied a lot and got away with even more. We were go-lucky youngsters, typical

During a visit to Grandfather Solms. After living for years at Steinwändt, my Solms grandparents moved to Salzburg.

of that period in one's life, focused on one thing only: fun. We were so crazy…one time I went to the French Quarter with my college friends and we got so drunk I had to get my sister, who was 13, to drive us. She did not have a driver's license. Goodness were Mother and Dick furious with me. I am sure that Vickie loved the experience, but I got in a lot of trouble for that stunt. I was so drunk and felt awful, and my mother, who was furious at me said, *"IT SERVES YOU RIGHT!"*

I remember lying on the bed, it was so hot, taking a shower in the middle of the night, and the sheets were always wet.

I have to be completely honest and say that my best subject in college was GIRLS! Again, I was a terrible student…so of course, after a while, I had to get out of college and take time to find my bearings. College was a good time though!

Because my grades were so lackluster, I had to get out of school for a semester… I was just not made for it. Hence, going to Europe seemed the best option available for the time being. I went to Coburg to stay with my grandmother for some time. I hoped that while I was there, I could figure out what I wanted to do with my life. Besides, I

With Dick in Austria.

With Sandy Spence, my first serious girlfriend.

was in my early twenties and it was about time I began developing links to our heritage and land. Remember what Uncle Friedrich Holstein had said, *"chain him to the property."*

In the United States, I had a girlfriend, Sandra Spence, "Sandy." I liked her very much, but I also knew she would not be able to fulfill the life I was destined to. I feared the cultural differences would be too much and perhaps her heart would not in it. Her mother was a nice Colombian lady, while her father worked for the United Fruit Company (UFCO). This was a huge conglomerate with extensive dealings and plantations in many of the countries with coastline on the Caribbean Sea. At some point in history UFCO was so powerful that it played a role in who was to be president of several of those Latin American countries. Anyhow, her father got Sandy a new car, a baby blue Mustang and I was in the cabal for it…oh she was beside herself. It was great. I hated saying goodbye to her, in fact, I hate goodbyes at the airport, to this is day I hate them.

By the time I returned to the United States again, Mother and Dick were once again living in New Orleans at 1528 Eighth Street. Unfortunately, soon after I arrived, we discovered that I was going to be drafted and sent to fight a useless and unnecessary war in Vietnam. Faraway Vietnam was not my business. I was not in agreement with what was being done there, either. On the other side, at some point I returned to Germany to begin preparation for taking up the inheritance that awaited me. Therefore with deep regret, but much conviction, I returned to Germany and joined the German military. I was up for the draft in both countries. But at least Germany was not involved in any war!

I renounced my American citizenship in Vienna. I wrote a letter to the State Department and I said that I had to take over the family business in Germany and Austria, and I was choosing my German heritage. I wanted to be sure that the government knew I was not anti-American. I enjoyed my many years in the United States very much and forever will have fond memories of the time I spent there. America welcomed us after the war, it provided me with many opportunities and memories, but it was time to start a new chapter in life.

I left the United States in around 1965 and was to remain away for the next twenty years.

A rare photo with Grandmother Coburg and Grandfather Solms.

I did it my way ...

Chapter XVI

A German Life

By the time I arrived in Germany, to begin a new chapter, Father had divorced Denise. She returned to Switzerland to be close to her family and she raised Claudia, Beatrice and Adrian there. My half-siblings were to have very shallow Coburg roots due to the break-up of their parents' marriage. In fact, I think that of them Adrian suffered the most from the disintegration of their family unit. From then on, he was to have a very hard time getting along with Father and this marked them both. I missed my brother and two sisters and did not get to see them often due to the unique circumstances affecting us all. Later in life, we all grew closer and each one, in their way, learned how to cope with the failings of our father. Well, at least Claudia, Beatrice and I. Poor Adrian could never truly forgive Father and his distant and complicated relationship to his offspring.

Father's personality affected us all. It is undeniable and to ignore it serves no purpose. For example, one time Katja, who liked rock music, and I were listening to some records and dancing to American rock. It was an innocent moment shared with a stepmother who was about my same age. Father was not the sort of husband who would take Katja dancing or anything like that. She and I liked many of the same rock musicians of the time and we started dancing. When Father entered the room to see what was making so much noise, he found us dancing. It was as if he had found us in a compromising entanglement. He was furious and lost his temper like I had not seen him do before. Was he jealous … did he think that I was flirting with my stepmother … why would he think that of us … was his own conscience clean?

Denise and my brother Adrian.

I have a forgiving personality. I give people second chances because I know that everyone makes mistakes and deserves an opportunity for redemption. I do not think my brother Adrian was like that. He never forgave Father and in turn my father did not know how to confront the damage he had inflicted on my brother. It was a very toxic situation and one that perhaps our father, as the head of the family, should have had the gumption to fix. But Father hated confrontation and it was simpler for him to find refuge in his own little world in Greinburg than reaching out and correcting a situation that he created. Consequently, Adrian drifted away from

Opposite page: My father, who was an talented photographer, took this photo of mein the early 1960s.

In Argentina with Father and my brother Adrian.

Grandmother Coburg and Aunt Bylla.

us and we all missed him. It was very sad for us all to witness, but there was almost nothing we could do to prevent it.

I guess all of us, as everyone else does, wanted a loving, caring father – someone who would be supportive and a source of strength. I have tried my best to be that to my own children. I had it in Dick Whitten, even with his peculiarities, but I never got that from my own father. Father lacked that source of depth and dedication; he was incapable of giving of himself to us. Again, this is just to explain how his character affected everyone around him.

When I arrived in Germany, Father and Katja were living in Hamburg, where he continued to work for the Johnson shipping line. By then, Father had made several grave mistakes that were to affect the remainder of his life. His second divorce was not well received by both family and business associates, as everyone knew the story behind Katja. When he presented her to Grandmother Coburg, she looked at Katja and asked, *"You are not going to be divorced, are you?"* They never were, but she became my father's obsession.

When he came back to Coburg after divorcing Denise, he never really wanted to run the business. He always called it *"counting the trees."* He wanted the benefits while not having to do the work it seemed to those in charge of the Coburg Family Foundation. By then Herr Voights was succeeded by Baron Hans Max v.u.z. Aufsess, as General Director. Rüdiger von Pezold succeeded Aufsess, and then Count Carl Gustaf Wachtmeister, who came from Sweden, succeeded as President of the Board. He was followed as President of the Board by my friend Hanko von Knobelsdorff, who served one period and retired.

Anyhow, the Coburg children hated Voights with a passion and this contributed to the malaise that the family lived in. It was a difficult situation. He was very close to Grandmother Coburg, who trusted him blindly. I think he did take advantage of her and when she died we found in her will the list of all the things she had already handed over to him during her lifetime. It was quite shocking.

By the fall of 1970, my Grandmother Coburg's life was coming to an end. She died in Grein, Austria, on October 5.[193] I traveled to be at her funeral. Her remains were brought back to Coburg and laid to rest in the burial plot built by my grandfather on that hill behind Schloß Callenberg. Already buried there, waiting for her, were her husband and their middle son Hubertus.

By then my father was finally free, or so he thought. The Coburg Family Foundation had been set up that so that no one person would have complete control of it, thus further protecting the family's wealth from mismanagement. The long struggle to gain control of the Coburg Family Foundation began in earnest after the death of my grandmother. Father put up a good fight, but he was unsuccessful. By 1996, however, it was time for me to take control and I organized the ouster of von Pezold. I felt that the Coburg Family Foundation needed to be managed by the family, and from then on everything changed and we have prospered beyond our wildest dreams.

Katja, as it turned out, was Father's greatest problem. His downfall began when he became obfuscated with Katja! Everyone was quite upset about his relationship with her. Aunt Bylla particularly was as she thought it was reprehensible what he had done to Denise. He was in the Johnson Line's Hamburg office, where he seemed to get stuck. His relationship with Katja was also not well received at work. It made the company directors pass him over for promotions. Johnson Line was a very conservative enterprise and they just simply could not overlook Father's problem: Katja.

As if this was not already difficult enough for him, he also got in trouble in some business dealings. He became involved in a consortium that wanted to buy woods in Austria, near Vienna, to make veneer. They built a factory that never produced a sellable item. The money was spent and my father was left with the debts. He had bank guarantees and the business partners ran with the money and he had to declare bankruptcy. These were very hard years for him, as it seemed that nothing he tried worked.

Eventually, he moved to Grein. While there he tried to gain control of the Coburg Family Foundation, but the Board resisted his efforts. He lived in a golden exile in Grein. The Foundation, in fact, had to find a way to keep his creditors away, while also helping him have a decent life. He was a really tragic figure…he was not only the absent "duke," but also the handicapped one, his ailment being his obsession with Katja!

He spent the remainder of his life away from the public eye, secluded in Grein in the company of his beloved Katja, who became a little prized possession for him. Someone who dressed like he wanted, did what he wanted, and kept him happy. Quite sad really!

Father and Katja at home in Greinburg.

Katja had two thoughts in her brain: Her and Father. When I took over, he had gone to Austria, which was against the Coburg Family Foundation laws. I went to Hinterriß to discuss matters with them. It was a very difficult situation. During that conversation, Katja told me that I lacked authority to tell them what to do. In her eyes, I was not the real head of the family, only on paper. However, in spite of our differences, I compensated them financially and made sure that they did not lack anything. I think that Father was confounded by me; I was everything that he was not.

He made an absolute mess out of his life. He was always too careless and inconsistent. He avoided his duty, lived for himself, and lost everything in the process. Well, he did get to keep his beloved Katja.

Father died in Grein in January 1998.[194] Katja remained living in their apartment and also died in Grein. She passed away in July 2011.[195] In later years we always included her in family gatherings and she frequently joined us. I must say that she behaved nicely and then, when done, returned to Grein.

Now, let me return to my arrival in Germany, now some fifty years ago!

After entering the German military, I was stationed in Eutin,

Throughout all these years I have remained in close contact with my Leiningen cousins. Here I am talking to Aunt Eilika Leiningen while attending a party in Langenburg.

During the time that I worked for the Japanese firm MITSUI.

in the Reconnaissance Battalion 6. I was there for two years, but initially had quite a bit of trouble adjusting. Firstly, I had to basically learn German again since Mother and us children had not spoken much in it for many, many years. At times I was so confused that I had no idea what my superior officers were asking me to do. I can only imagine what they thought about this German-born kid, raised by an American military officer in the United States, who was now back in Germany trying to learn how to be a good, patriotic German! Does it sound familiar, perhaps?

While I was living in Northern Germany, Sandy came to visit me in Hamburg. It was a nice visit, but I was convinced that it would be too difficult for us to settle down and get married given our cultural differences. Sadly, I had to close that very important chapter of my life, never to visit it again. I did not keep in contact with Sandy, so I do not know what became of her.

After the fulfilling of my military service, it was time for me to learn the family trade: timber and forestry management. For a half year I went to Castell to learn how to trade timber at Markt Bibart. This is a town near Rüdenhausen. Then I went to Leiningen to work at a sawmill. I lived with the Leiningens, family relations who also have a long history with Coburg. In fact, Queen Victoria's mother, the Duchess of Kent, was firstly married to the Fürst of Leiningen. The only daughter of this coupling, Feodora, was Queen Victoria's only sister. Feodora Leiningen married the Fürst of Hohenlohe-Langenburg, another family with deep connections to Coburg. Both Grandmother Coburg and Grandmother Solms were granddaughters of one of Feodora Leiningen's daughters. While living with the Leiningens, their mother Fürstin Eilika (née Oldenburg) thought that I would make a good match for her daughter Melita, but I did not want to. She later called me a bad boy because she wished I would date her daughter, but I was already engaged to Carin Dabelstein, the woman who became my wife.

After working for the Leiningens, I

went to Rosenheim for half a year. Then in 1969 I did an apprenticeship with Müller & Sohn, importers of foreign wood. I went to trade school there and worked for two years.

After that I went to work for the Japanese firm MITSUI…but by then I had married.

When I arrived in Germany, I had little contact with any of the other royal and princely families. In fact, I knew very few people. I had been away for nearly two decades and had not grown up in close contact with any of these people. Hence, when I settled in Hamburg, I had to make my own friends.

Although Grandmother Coburg expected us to marry into other Gotha families, her wishes went unfulfilled. Father had already broken bounds when he married Denise de Muralt, who would have never qualified as an equal marriage under the old rules governing the families that composed the famed Almanach de Gotha. Grandfather Coburg allowed the marriage surely because I was just a child and Father was their last viable son. Having Father produce a spare would guarantee the family of another generation of Coburgs. Therefore, the marriage was not prevented and Father and Denise married and went on to have their children.

Years later, when Father divorced Denise to marry Katja, as he was head of house, he approved his own marriage. Thus, with what moral authority could he force me to marry "equally?" Of course he would not force me to do so, therefore leaving me to my own devices.

For a short time, I was engaged to Heike Diesbrück, a girlfriend of my stepmother Katja, but we didn't marry. One evening we invited some people over to my father's. Count Friedrich Castell-Rüdenhausen asked me when I was getting married, but I never answered the question. A few days later we knew there was no point in continuing a relationship that was destined to fail and put a quick end to it. At least, I had enough sense in me not to embark on a ship that was headed for the rocks.

Enter Carin Dabelstein, my wife!

I was alone in Hamburg and did not have a large group of friends. I longed for company. I was young, could afford a good life and wanted to have someone to share good times with. A friend of mine, who was dating Carin's sister, arranged for a double date. It was a blind date. I liked what she was wearing and I felt very attracted to her. We started a relationship in 1966. She was working for a Japanese company in Hamburg, where she was born. Her father had a small printing shop and the girls were raised in Hamburg. I went out on a double date. I got engaged to her at some point, but I could not make up my mind. For several years we continued our relationship, but we were both too busy to settle down.

My wife, when we were dating.

At one point, I introduced Carin to Grandmother Coburg, who seemed pleased with my choice. By then my grandmother had seen it all. She met Carin and liked her. Was she a choice she would have approved under different circumstances, no … but after everything she lived through, she was willing to accept it. The line had to continue. She had lost a son during the war. Her eldest son had had a miserable life. He renounced membership in the family. His wife tricked him into marriage and eventually their marriage was a mess and collapsed. He made mistakes that paled in comparison to my father's. So, Grandmother Coburg had lived through it all. So why not look positively to

Carin and me with her sister, Inge, and their mother, Frau Dabelstein.

a new beginning with Carin and me…

Carin and I married civilly in Hamburg on June 18, 1971.[196] Our religious wedding was some six weeks later and it was also celebrated in Hamburg. Not surprisingly, when I informed Father of my decision to marry Carin, he approved my choice, but still complained bitterly that the dates chosen by us did not fit his schedule. Consequently, Father and Katja did not attend our wedding. Mother, Dick and Uncle Hubertus Solms where the only family from my side who were present. It was a small wedding without much fanfare. Neither Carin nor I wished to have a huge wedding as it did not really fit our personalities; besides, I did not know many members of the Gotha and I guess quite a few of the ones I knew were not happy with my choice. Funny, as if their opinion would have mattered a pfennig to us. However, these issues, and others not worth getting into provided the scenario for a rocky start to our marriage.

I must say, however, that Carin's introduction into the rarefied world of German royal and princely families was not easy. She always felt that several of them were a bit cold toward her. In turn, she was cold back. So for years to come she would not look forward to attending many of the events to which we would be invited. Many times, I just chose not to attend, as I did not want to be there without my wife. Sadly, it was, again, as if the Coburgs had disappeared from the Gotha scene. It was not until many years later that I decided that if she did not want to come along, I would go anyhow. Many times I brought one or more of my children, particularly Hubertus, who as my successor would need to establish good connections with the other royal and princely families of Germany and beyond. He always made a good presence and was liked by everyone, and this made me exceedingly happy. In the meantime, Carin stayed at home involved in her own projects and chose not to accompany me to anything other than some events hosted by our closest family members. Unfortunately, in due time this situation led to distance between us. We had trouble agreeing and faced the regular issues couples have. I think that our marriage could have collapsed completely at one point. But, I realized that I would be taking my father's path, one that I always told myself I was not going to follow.

Our first child, Stephanie was born in late January 1972. We were then

Our wedding.

Chapter XVI – A German Life

Carin and me followed by her parents and Inge. Behind them is my mother, who came from America with Dick to attend our wedding.

living in Hamburg, where Carin's mother and sister were of great help to us. Stephanie, in due, time grew very close to Carin's only sister and this special connection has continued to this day. Later that year the Coburg family suffered two losses. Uncle Leo died in Grein in May after a life thrown away without having achieved much to call a success.[197] A few months later we lost Aunt Bylla, who passed away in Stockholm on November 28.[198] Her passing, a great loss to us all, not only orphaned my Swedish cousins, but also left the Royal Family without a "first lady."

Other family members had also began building lives of their own. A few months before my wedding, my sister Claudia married Gion Schäfer, a promising young lawyer from Switzerland. Their wedding took place in Bern and they eventually had two daughters, my nieces Christina and Gianetta. Both married and had children, giving Gion and Claudia five grandchildren.

Three years after the birth of our first child, we had our first son, Hubertus, who shares the name of two of my uncles, Hubertus Coburg

With our daughter Stephanie on her first Christmas.

Sister Claudia and her ex-husband, Gion Schäfer. They had two daughters, Christina and Gianetta

and Hubertus Solms. He was born in Hamburg in mid-September 1975 and from an early age showed to be a promising child from whom much could be expected. As a proud father, I must say that Hubertus has achieved all the goals that were set for him and he has given us much pride and joy.

In 1977, Coburg witnessed two of our family's celebrations. On May 4, we welcomed our son Alexander into our lives. He was the first Coburg prince born in our proud town since my brother Adrian's birth in 1955. In fact, Alexander is the last Saxe-Coburg and Gotha to be born in Coburg since both my grandchildren were born in Munich.

Some five weeks after Alexander's birth, we witnessed the last alliance between two members of the Wettin dynasty. This unique event took place on June 12, when my sister Beatrice married Prince Friedrich (Fried) of Saxe-Meiningen, a nephew of Archduchess Regina of Austria, consort of the eminent late Crown Prince Otto, eldest son of Emperor Karl and Empress Zita.[199] Beatrice and Fried, as we called him, had two children: Maria-Alexandra, born in 1978, and Friedrich-Constantin, born in Heilbronn two years later.

We all got together every once in a while in Grein, where Father and Katja lived most of the year. Father was always very close to Claudia and Beatrice; in fact, far closer than he ever was to our brother Adrian or me. It was during one of these visits that Father and our brother had a terrible row. It made Adrian reach deep inside and confront Father with his actions. Father, as can be imagined, did not like to have a mirror placed in front of him. The truth would hurt too much and Father had hurt Adrian far more than any of us realized. From that day onward, he wanted nothing to do with Father and the Coburg name. He refused to be addressed by his title and any mail we sent to him addressed in that manner, he would return unopened. It was a very messy situation and neither handled it correctly, unfortunately for us all.

Sister Beatrice, with Denise, at the time of her engagement to Fried Meiningen.

It is worth mentioning that an important

chapter in our family's history was closed in early January 1981 when we received news of the death of my Aunt Princess Alice, Countess of Athlone. Born in 1883, she was Grandfather Coburg's only sibling and biggest supporter. For Aunt Alice, there was little that her brother would do that she could not find a way to protect him from the consequences. True devotion united these two siblings, and the love she felt for her brother extended to her nephews and nieces, particularly Aunt Bylla, whom Aunt Alice visited in Sweden. Her disappearance truly severed the last living link we had with our English cousins and these bonds no longer are as strong as they once were, much to my chagrin.

Lastly, Aunt Calma died in September 1983, leaving my father as the last surviving offspring of the last Duke of Saxe-Coburg and Gotha. Aunt Calma, much like her siblings, could not wait a minute before running away from her parents. The combination of Grandmother Coburg's iron will and Grandfather Coburg's absentee parenting style affected their children deeply. My grandfather was a weak man. But his wife was a very strong woman. She basically ran the show. She had her opinions and she did not like to be challenged or questioned. Perhaps this is why life proved to be so difficult for her. Grandfather was always away, particularly during the National Socialist years doing his own things. The children were left under the care of nannies and they were under the strict guidance of Grandmother Coburg, who also basically ran the Coburg Family Foundation with the aid of the infamous Mr. Voights, who was the true 'éminence grise' within the Coburg family.

Contact with Aunt Calma's children has not always been frequent. My cousin Count Bertram Castell-Rüdenhausen, a painter, lives in Vienna with his wife. His sister Victoria lives in the United Kingdom. I like Victoria very much and although we have not always seen eye to eye. Their brother Conradin, who settled in Finland, was very nice and I saw him several times. Sadly, he died a few years ago. Their Schnirring siblings (Calma and Dagmar) I have had almost no contact with. I suppose we have become too large a family and with too many branches links become stretched and eventually break off. I guess it is the cycle of life ...

Aunt Bylla and King Gustaf VI Adolf, her father-in-law.

Aunt Alice Athlone.

Chapter XVII

The Fall of the Berlin Wall and the Quest for Fair Restitution

Little did we know that an irreversible process of change, with deep political consequences, was to be the most lasting effect of the election of a new pope in the fall of 1978. At the time, relations between the Soviet Union and the Western democracies were at a very low ebb. Leonid Brezhnev, the Soviet dictator, held sway over Russia and its Eastern European satellites with an iron fist. In the West, Europe tried to find its footing as many of the continent's leading democracies joined in an effort to create a political entity similar to the United States, a united Europe with shared goals that went beyond the free movement of goods across borders. The United States, still reeling from the crisis caused by the impeachment of President Nixon, wondered if it was in its best interest to play a larger international role in a world that seemed to resent its geopolitical power. Meanwhile, at the Vatican Pope Paul VI died in early summer, only to be followed by the very brief pontificate of Pope John Paul I. John Paul II, the former Cardinal Archbishop Karol Wojtila, whose power base was centered in Cracow, Poland's second largest city, in turn succeeded him.

Carin and Alexander on our first visit to Schloß Friedenstein in 1990.

The election of a non-Italian to succeed to the chair of St Peter had, as it turned out, deep repercussions. Not only was John Paul II the first non-Italian to occupy the Holy See in more than four centuries, but also he came from a country behind the Iron Curtain. Poland, in spite of Communist efforts to stamp out Catholicism, had remained deeply religious and Cardinal Archbishop Wojtila had stood for years as a beacon of hope for an oppressed country. His election as Pope was a direct challenge to the Soviet Union's reign of terror over the countries that had remained behind the Iron Curtain after the end of the Second World War.

Shipyard workers led by a popular labor union activist by the name of Lech Walesa organized the first public demonstration of this challenge. He was the leader of a labor union called Solidarnosk (Solidarity) that flat out questioned the Polish government's unfair treatment of factory workers. Solidarity organized protests in the port city of Gdansk (Danzig) and these caught the Polish Communist government off guard, particularly when Pope John Paul II publicly expressed his support for the demands presented by the workers. Strikes spread across Poland and the situation became untenable for the government, which in turn reacted violently in its efforts to not only destroy Solidarity, but also eliminate its political leadership. Mr. Walesa, a true patriot, was imprisoned along with many of his comrades. The world's

Opposite page: My wife Carin and me in the 1980s.

I did it my way ...

The Coburgs in the late 1970s. Seated from the left: My wife, Claudia Schäfer, Katja, Father, Adrian, Beatrice and Fried Meiningen. Standing: Gion Schäfer and me.

Schloß Reinhardsbrunn, 1990.

outrage knew no bounds and in the end the Polish government was forced to release its political prisoners. Leading the international influence from behind closed curtains was none other than Pope John Paul II.

It was obvious to us all, that the unthinkable could actually happen: the fall of Communism. The following ten years witnessed a further erosion of the Soviet Union's grip on the countries behind the Iron Curtain. Matters finally came to a boil in the summer of 1989, when even students in Beijing, China, of all places, dared to stand valiantly against the oppressive rule of Communism.

The revolution that eventually toppled the Polish Communists lasted ten years. Their fall from power set off a domino effect across Eastern Europe: after some ten months of protests and political upheaval, the government of the German Democratic Republic fell, followed in ten weeks by that of Czechoslovakia, which in turn was followed in ten days by the fall of one of Europe's most vicious dictators, Nicolae Ceausescu of Romania. Bulgaria and Yugoslavia soon followed.

Chapter XVII – The Fall of the Berlin Wall and the Quest for Fair Restitution

At home with our children: Hubertus, Stephanie and Alexander.

The Berlin Wall, that symbol of political oppression that had failingly attempted to cut off part of Germany from foreign influence, fell on November 9, 1989. At the time I was hunting at Karwendel, a beautiful property we own in the Austrian Tyrol. I first heard of the fall of the Berlin Wall as I drove from Karwendel to Coburg, where when we arrived there were some 70,000 Eastern Germans who had basically invaded the town. I remember watching events on television, feeling flabbergasted and awaiting at any moment a major reactionary effort coming from either the Soviet Union or the dying government of the crumbling German People's Democratic Republic. Neither, much to our relief, happened. What did happen was that in the face of overwhelming pressure, the Hungarian Communist government simply threw its hands up in the air and stopped preventing vacationing Germans from crossing the border into Austria, something that could not have happened before the fateful summer of 1989. Thousands of Eastern Germans packed their government-issued Travant (Travys) cars with whatever they could, headed to Hungary and then made a sharp turn toward the Austro-Hungarian border. Many of them were allowed to cross into the West with their ramshackle automobiles; others simply abandoned their fume-spewing Travys at the border and walked into Austria. No one stopped them and the border guards, overwhelmed by the sea of humanity flowing under their machine guns, opted not to stop the unstoppable.

Overwhelmed by the flood of people escaping from inside the Iron Curtain, the Austrian government, with assistance from the United Nations and other Western democracies, set up camps to receive these refugees. In Budapest, the Communist government succumbed to political reality and refused to place roadblocks to prevent East German, Czechoslovakians, Poles, Romanians, Yugoslavs and Bulgarians from leaving their countries. It was as if a house of cards simply tumbled to the ground after someone blew a light breeze on it.

Coburg was just kilometers away from the border with East Germany. I remember driving around town during those heady days of change and being unable to move much. All of a sudden it was as if we were swimming in a sea of Travys. They were everywhere. Eastern Germans had not had access to Western goods and they flocked to our shops and markets, buying everything that they could lay their hands on. I clearly remember walking into a supermarket only to find the shelves

Spending time with my mother and Dick. Throughout the years, they visited us in Europe and I traveled several times to America to visit them.

With my father.

completely empty. It was simply unbelievable.

As you may recall, the bulk of our properties and real estate were located in Thüringen. At the end of the Second World War, that part of Germany was given to the Soviet Union. Gotha, therefore, fell under Russian control. Once the Russians arrived, Grandfather Coburg and his advisors knew that there was nothing they could do to salvage the ducal collections, housed at Schloß Friedenstein in Gotha, much less any of our many other estates, like Reinhardsbrunn and Oberhof in the Thüringer Wald. Everything, from forests and agricultural lands, to castles and hunting lodges, along with priceless artwork was lost to us. The only properties left to the Coburg Family Foundation were what we had in Coburg and Callenberg, as well as the Austrian holdings. However, since Austria had been placed under Russian oversight, even Greinburg and the thousands of hectares we owned there were, for a time, lost to us.

These were very difficult times for our family. Financially we faced ruin. Politically, we were smack in the middle of a major mess caused by Grandfather Coburg's outright support and cavorting with National Socialism. Rebuilding the family's future was, at times, an insurmountable task, but one that Grandmother Coburg, Herr Voights and other employees of the Coburg Family Foundation began in earnest. This, unfortunately for him, was the task that Father refused to undertake when he packed his bags and left Coburg to go start life in Stockholm. The rebuilding

With my friend Archduke Michael Salvator of Austria-Tuscany, who has visited Coburg frequently. His family owns a property near Grein.

took place without him and those responsible for it never forgave him for leaving at the hardest possible time for my grandparents. He had demonstrated that he was incapable of showing the consistency required to rescue the family and build a lasting legacy for generations to come.

At the end of June 1990, the governments of the Federal Republic of Germany and the DDR finally signed an agreement allowing for the free movement all Germans. Now, we could finally enter the DDR without fear of arrest or reprisal. In Neustadt, near Coburg, I remember that there was a ceremony presided by the Secretaries of State, Ministers Stoiber (for Germany) and Diestel (for DDR). There were military bands of the border control patrols of both the Federal Republic and the DDR. It was a very festive and congenial ceremony. They played national anthems, signed documents and the long process to erase the border between both countries was started.

As soon as I could safely cross into the DDR, I drove all the roads around our old property. I wanted to see with my own eyes what had happened to our real estate, properties, hunting grounds, forests, lodges and castles. I was very careful not to

Schloß Reinhardsbrunn.

An abandoned watchtower at the former East German border in Eisfeld. Notice the broken glass on every window. There were countless such structures to keep citizens inside East Germany. The watchtowers were manned by armed guards!

In 1998 I again visited Schloß Reinhardsbrunn which was then in ruins.

upset anyone, while also making an inventory of what was left so we could prepare for when the issue of restitution was finally raised.

In the meantime, in 1993 my mother and I returned to Casel for the first time since we left before the arrival of the dreaded Red Army. She had a visa to enter the DDR, but at the border there was no one. All the buildings were abandoned; it was like a ghost town. By then, little remained of the old government of the DDR that had kept such close watch on the movements of its citizens.

It was a very emotional journey for us, but particularly for Mother. In Casel she met some of the old estate people that she had once known so well, but had been unable to escape to the West. The house was in a bad state. The Russians had burned the furniture and even used the toilets to wash their potatoes. What valuables had been left behind when the Solms departed were now all gone, perhaps hidden somewhere in Russia? We visited the house and even the church where I was baptized and my parents married. My mother was also baptized there. For my mother, it was coming full circle from departure to an unknown future to returning now as an American married to a former army officer.

My mother went into the house and she knew exactly what each room was used for. Then we went to Baruth and had coffee with the Protestant minister.

Our Solms cousins received land back, but they sold it to the government. The family was disseminated over three continents and many of them had built lives away from Germany. Managing a landed estate under those conditions would have been simply a formidable task that none of them wished to undertake. My objective, however, was for us to gain the most land possible and I set about trying to achieve my goals. One can invest liquid assets, but land always gains solid value and, if managed well, can also provide enough revenue to sustain a very good living. So no, the Coburgs would ask for land, not cash!

My father had attended school near Reinhardsbrunn. Since I had always heard of these properties and their

Chapter XVII – The Fall of the Berlin Wall and the Quest for Fair Restitution

This is what the East German border posts looked when we went to visit our former properties. It was as if the entire governmental structure had evaporated.

importance in our family's history, I wanted to see them with my own eyes. I went to visit Schloß Reinhardsbrunn, but it was sadly in quite a state of disrepair. Father was never able to come to see the East. By then he was wheelchair-bound and he could no longer travel. For me, it was a great sense of satisfaction to be able to recover as much as we did, even though it was only 40% of what we had lost.

Now, how we went about it was a mix of luck and savvy. Because the Coburg Family Foundation was a de-facto international group, it placed us in a better position to negotiate. When Grandfather Coburg transferred all our property to the Coburg Family Foundation back in the 1920s, several shareholders were Coburgs who lived outside Germany. This fact, luckily, made it easier for us to demand restitution.

At stake were two major issues: our land and the artistic-cultural legacy, including the ducal collections and various castles and palaces. I initially sought compensation for both. I prepared with a team of lawyers and did our due diligence. Herr von Pezold, who then still served as head of the Board of Directors of the Foundation, arranged for investigations to be conducted in the state archives. While conducting our searches there, which I knew would be necessary to gain a solid footing when negotiating with the government, I struck it lucky. An old man informed us that there was an old Russian order stating that confiscation of international property would not be allowed. Since the Coburg Family Foundation was considered to be such an institution, I knew I was on good footing. At the same time, I knew I had to negotiate and avoid at all costs becoming cocky and upsetting the authorities. If I treated them with respect, I believed they would treat me in like manner.

Of course, when I presented our case for the restitution of our land, I asked for everything I could. Early on, during the lengthy negotiations, I realized that I would have to be flexible as it would have been simply impossible for the government to hand back to us every hectare of land and every piece of real estate that Grandfather Coburg lost. My idea was to get my foot in the door with the authorities. Let them get to know us; do not come across as hungry absentee landowners; let them know I intended to stay and keep the forestry enterprise going; all the while keeping people employed. It worked!

At the time, I was negotiating with the both the state government of Thüringen and the Federal authorities in Bonn. We agreed on a price. The Federal Government eventually restituted 6200 hectares to us. The State of Thüringen restituted 800 hectares for buildings and real estate that the state kept.

When I hired foresters, I tried to find capable people who wanted work and wished to stay there. They were happy to be able to stay on the land, but under new management. Funnily enough, they also liked to drink schnapps a lot.

I thought we should have a person at the property. I called the former forester and asked him to aid us. He had been trained by Grandfather Coburg and wound-up at the end of his career working for me, another full circle. He worked for several years for me until his wife was sick and he had to resign. They could not tend to her in Friedrichroda and we helped him to have her moved to a better clinic in Wiesbaden. They were shocked, as they never expected that we would do this for them. I bought a big house that was built by a forester who worked for my grandfather in the early 1920s. So we bought it and fixed it. I was making a statement, I was back and I was not going to be an absentee landlord. I was investing in them, so they would invest in me.

We rearranged the property to make it more efficient to manage. We had to modernize and change many things to make more money and become more competitive. At the same time, we were forced to recognize some rights several people had acquired during the Communist years. For example, there was a Russian man; his name was Igor, who had a hunting right in one of our properties. He shot anything that moved. Whether we liked it or not, we had to tolerate these small details, while keeping in mind our larger goal, which was the acquisition of forests.

In the meantime, I knew that the administration of the Foundation had to be modernized. I needed people working for me who were willing and eager to support my vision and those who feared risk and action, sadly, had to go. In 1997, I decided to take over the property, not the Coburg Family Foundation. Herr von Pezold was not happy with my decision and he quit. He was a good man, but his vision no longer met the needs of the times. The evening before our board meeting, Count Wachtmeister was asked if he would become the new head of the Coburg Family Foundation Board of Directors. After half an hour, he came back and told me, *"I will do it."* The majority of the Foundation board had to be German; the minority can be from other countries.

Father and me hosting King Carl XVI Gustaf of Sweden.

Once the Board of Directors agreed, we then decided to take back our legal case regarding the ducal art collections. In doing so, I demonstrated goodwill. The government did not expect us to take this course of action and they were completely surprised. But this decision, ultimately, changed their approach to us.

I got a right of passage to the Ducal Palace in Gotha. And I demanded that they always mention the provenance of each piece, thus future generations would always know where the artwork came from. We also received a permanent seat on the board of the new organism under which the art collections were placed: Schloß Friedenstein Foundation. At one point, during our negotiations, I reminded them that the castle alone was of great value. Doctor Jürgen Aretz, Cultural State Secretary for Thüringen, looked at me and said, *"I will wrap a bow around the castle and gladly give it back to you."* Of course I said no … Schloß Friedenstein would cost millions to repair and run, and I did not want that onerous expense. So, the best course

Chapter XVII – The Fall of the Berlin Wall and the Quest for Fair Restitution

After we settled with the authorities, my son Hubertus and I surveyed our new properties. To do so we took helicopter trips over Thüringen. Here we are joined by our lawyer Herr Behn and by Herr Wachtmeister, one-time director of the Coburg Family Foundation.

of action was to stop the lawsuit to recover the artwork, while focusing on receiving restitution for the real estate that was confiscated from us by the Communists. Herr Aretz, although he represented the state of Thüringen, and I became good friends, two gentlemen who could negotiate fairly. We learned to trust each other and that was very important during the process of restitution. We felt we were fair to each other and all, in the end, benefitted from it. We have one seat on the new Art Foundation and 75% is owned by the city of Gotha, while the rest by the state of Thüringen.

Hence, during my leadership, we managed to regain a large forest in Thüringen. All in all, I would consider this a great achievement. These lands, added to what we own in Austria and elsewhere, mean that the Coburg Family Foundation now owns large of forests, agricultural lands and hunting grounds. Not too shabby, I would argue!

The Foundation had to finance itself and not depend on banks. I always managed to keep the Coburg Family Foundation debt-free and this has allowed us incredible freedom of action in investment. So, all excess profits were set aside for a rainy day fund.

Frankly, when I look at what we have achieved in the four decades during which I worked for my family, I can sit back and smile. While history will be the judge of my tenure as Head of the House of Saxe-Coburg and Gotha, I am convinced that I did not disappoint either my family nor our legacy!

I did it my way ...

Chapter XVIII
Happy Hour ...

This is one of my favorite photos of dear Carin.

As I approach the end of our time together, I look around and take notice of all those who have played role in my life. In spite of how difficult life was as times, I think that in the end I have been blessed with a very good life. Surely, there are some things that I should have done differently, others I should not have done at all. But there is no point in philosophizing about spilled milk. What is done is so, and there is nothing we can do to change the course of what we have already lived. Now it is time to relax, enjoy and treat each day as a "happy hour" surrounded by loved ones and friends!

First and foremost, I must say that I appreciate the sacrifices my wife Carin made. She hesitated to move to Coburg for she feared that she would not adapt to life in a small town after having lived in Hamburg since birth. Truth be told, I do not think that she was ever truly happy in Coburg. Yet, she made the best of it and we moved on … we always moved on … and did not allow ourselves to be overpowered by our choices, personalities and issues. We did what we thought was best and lived with the consequences.

Sadly, at a time when we ought to be spending our twilight years traveling and keeping each other company, my wife is consumed by a debilitating and terrible illness. I am at least able to provide her with the best care possible and she is well taken care of here at home. She is never alone and the nursing staff helping us take care of her are marvelous and deeply dedicated to making her as comfortable as possible.

As for our children, they have all now settled into their own very busy lives.

I see our daughter Stephanie quite often when we are in Coburg. She stops by the house several times every day and, although at times we argue, she is a great companion and a loving daughter. I have always liked the name and my cousin Stephanie Leiningen had it. There was also another Stephanie in the Coburg family, Crown Princess Stephanie of Austria, from the Belgian branch of the Coburg dynasty. She married very early Crown Prince

Opposite page: A time for reflection before my happy hour.

Rudolf of Austria, the only son of Emperor Franz Joseph. We also gave our daughter the name Sibylla in honor of my Swedish Aunt. As a token of goodwill, we asked Katja to be one of her godparents.

Stephanie attended school in Coburg, grammar and middle school. After high school, she chose not to attend university. Instead, she did an apprenticeship in business administration. After that she was employed by the Coburg Family Foundation and worked with me for many years. Once I retired, Stephanie dedicates most of her time and efforts to her beloved horses. She is an excellent equestrian and has a marvelous touch with horses. She rides nearly every day!

She spends her time working at Schloß Callenberg, where she now lives in a house previously used by Grandfather Coburg. She also has some business interests dealing with equestrian matters. She is absolutely passionate about horses. Our dogs Bonni and Balou are her guardians.

She is very sweet, very princess-like. Stephanie had a difficult time with her mother and always got along better with Carin's sister. Stephanie, who is very conscious of what our family represents, always wanted the "lady of the house" to be outgoing, active in family matters and a fitful companion for her father. This, Carin just did not like doing. She preferred to stay home lost in her own world, rather than joining me and fulfilling

Our daughter, Princess Stephanie, with our dogs Bonnie and Balou.

the role I had hoped she would. But that was just not my wife's personality and how could anyone expect her to be something that she was not. Stephanie wishes that the Coburgs remain active and present in the world into which we were born; she wants the Coburgs to be out and in public playing the role that our old family legacy has bestowed to us not only in Coburg and Grein, but also in Gotha. She is very interested in the family's history and her passion can be witnessed in several rooms she has arranged at the museum in Schloß Callenberg. She also truly enjoys spending time with her niece and nephew.

Our son Hubertus was born the same year we moved to Coburg, where I began the long process of taking over the Coburg Family Foundation.

Opposite page: Our daughter Stephanie.

He was a sweet little boy. Hubertus was a very good student – learning came very easily to him. He did military service for two

Stephanie on her horse Ronchamps.

I did it my way ...

Carin, the children and I at Karwendel, where we usually spend the month of August.

years, something Alex, our youngest, did not have to do as by then obligatory military service was abolished. Hubertus studied law at the University of Würzburg. He then worked in Louisiana for a law firm. After his first stint in the United States, he attended the London School of Economics, followed by another two years at the Maximilian University in Munich. Everywhere he went, his grades always made us very proud, as he was a very distinguished student. He went to New York to work for the Deustche Bank for six months and then was offered a position that kept him there for five years. He only returned to Germany when I decided to retire and he accepted to work for the Coburg Family Foundation.

Opposite page: Hubertus and Kelly on their wedding day.

It was while living in New York that he met Kelly Rondestvedt, the American woman he was to marry in 2009. Their wedding, a new gathering of the royal mob, the likes of which Coburg had not seen in decades, was a grand affair. The local newspapers called it: "our royal wedding." Thousands of people took to the streets to partake in the celebrations, while more than one hundred royals traveled to Coburg to witness the ceremony. Among the guests were two Kings (Carl XVI Gustaf of Sweden and Simeon of Bulgaria) with their consorts (Silvia and Margarita). The guest list included a veritable "who's who" of the German Gotha, as well as representatives

Hereditary Prince Hubertus and Princess Kelly on their wedding day. Surrounding them are King Carl XVI Gustaf and Queen Silvia of Sweden, and King Simeon and Queen Margarita of Bulgaria.

My son Hubertus and his wife Kelly in Sweden.

from royal families from across Europe. It was as if the Coburgs reminded royal Europe that we may have gone for a bit, but we had certainly returned to stay.

After their honeymoon, Hubertus and his wife returned to New York City, where Kelly also worked for an important banking institution. During his stay in New York, I visited our son many times. Then when illness began affecting my health, I once again flew to New York to have a serious discussion about his future. I wanted him to return to Germany and take the mantle from me. I agreed to retire if he returned. He, and his wife, returned to Coburg and have now settled here. Hubertus manages our family's interests and he is doing a fantastic job doing so. He brings a new approach, with different ideas and is well-prepared to be a success in today's different environment.

Hubertus and Kelly now have two children, Katharina and Philipp. I was overjoyed with the arrival of the new generation and was particularly proud to see that they were baptized at Schoß Callenberg, a place with such a long tradition in our family history. I enjoy seeing them when I can and hope to be around many more years to see them grow.

Our sweet son Alexander had a difficult birth and was very overdue. He was very a very tall baby, and had long hands and fingers and we called him "Spiderman." He was not a bad a student, but school was challenging for

With our son Alexander, who is quite fond of all his pets.

Alex. It took him a while to find his footing. He was always a free spirit, but needed structure. For a time, he went to a boarding school, but his educational foundation was not strong enough. Always, with structure, he gets done what needs to get done. But he is easily distracted by his surroundings. He is dyslexic, and that hindered his education. In the end, we decided that university was not going to be the correct route for him. Instead, we felt that best for him would be to learn forestry. He did not want to attend forestry school, so all his knowledge, and he has gained quite a bit of it, is empiric, passed to him by our forestry staff that has taught him everything he knows. Alex lives in Grein, where he is in charge, under the guidance of our Forestry Directors, of the forests we own there. He likes modern music and loves fast cars. He has a fascination with spiders and knows so very much about them.

Alex is a very loving son. He is very nice to me, really. He gets along with everyone and is always a joy. I love all my children dearly, but the one who has the softest touch is Alex. He is a gentle soul and that makes me very happy. I hope he finds a wife one day and he gets to be as happy as he makes me.

As for my four siblings, only three remain now. Sadly, Adrian left us some years ago, when to our utter shock we were notified via email that he had committed assisted suicide. His sons knew of their father's plans and were sent on vacation so as to not be there when doctors helped Adrian bring his life to an early end. It was all far too clinical for my own taste, but that was what he chose. He suffered from an illness that hindered his hearing and as a musician it was as if that loss took away his will to live. Quite sad indeed.

Alexander dressed in costume for Mardi Gras.

I did not really know my brother, as I did not see Adrian often, particularly after his fallout with our father. We got closer in the last few years before he died. However, it was not long enough, at least not as much time as I wish we had had together. I also wish I had had the opportunity to bid goodbye to him.

When in October 1984 Adrian married Lea Rinderknecht, he did not bother asking Father for permission. Consequently, for succession purposes, the marriage was morganatic, not that it mattered to Adrian one bit. I met his first wife once. They had two sons, Simon and Daniel, and then separated and eventually divorced in 1993. Simon is studying marine biology in Scotland. Daniel lives in Switzerland, where he continues his father's musical legacy.

He rebuilt his life with Gertrud Krieg (b. 1958), known to us as "Trudi." For a few years they lived

Our son Alexander with cousin Ferdinand Württemberg.

Our son Alexander driving. Like me, Alexander is a car enthusiast.

together and then he married her in 1997. She had two children from a previous marriage. They lived in Switzerland, but Adrian's passion for Afro-Cuban music took him often to Cuba. He was, without a doubt, a very talented musician. Adrian worked and performed with musicians, theatre groups and artists since 1984. In Bern, Switzerland, he established his own music school, "Percusión Afro-Cubana," where he taught Rhythmic Solfeggio and Afro-Cuban percussion. He was the leader of his own musical group Okantomi, which performed traditional Afro-Cuban drum melodies, songs and dances for many years. Alongside his engagement in Afro-Cuban percussion, he played as a drummer and guitarist in several music groups.

From 1987 onward, he spent considerable time in Cuba studying and researching Afro-Cuban percussion and Afro-Cuban music. He was trained by some of the most prominent and recognized master drummers and singers. Adrian further developed his knowledge through the study and transcription of percussion and songs from records. In 1996 the Conjunto Folklórico Nacional de Cuba authorized him to teach Afro-Cuban percussion.

My brother, as it turned out, had found his calling. Since 1994 he studied Bata drumming and Songs of the Yoruba, an ethnic group from Nigeria. One of the greatest Yoruban singers and Bata master drummers of Cuba trained him. As a highly respected Santero, a priest in that unique religion practiced in the Caribbean, *"he preserves and transmits the*

Opposite page: Our son Alex with one of our dogs.

My brother Adrian.

sacred songs and Bata drum melodies of Yoruban culture in Cuba." Due to his prowess and knowledge, he was elected to play, sing and document the complete anthology of the Oru Seco, Oru Cantado, Rezos and Cantos y Toques especiales. In 1999 Adrian received the "Juramento" as tamborero (drum player) in Havana, Cuba.

Sadly, Adrian's passion for Afro-Cuban music and drumming caused him hearing problems. He was completely frustrated by a buzzing he heard inside his head and no doctor could bring him relief. This hindered his ability to play and brought him great frustration. Also, this was the reason behind his decision to terminate his life early. My brother felt that he could not possibly continue living if he could not hear and thus play his music. It was very sad for me, his older brother, not to be able to properly say goodbye to him.

In her widowhood, Trudi has increased contact with us. She has visited me in Coburg and Grein, and I have enjoyed these visits immensely. It is as if in my older years the women of Coburg surround me: my sisters Vickie and Beatrice, my daughter Stephanie and my sister-in-law Trudi!

Sister Claudia with our cousin Hansi Hohenzollern.

I first met all three of my father's children with Denise when I visited Argentina. Claudia had a special place in our father's heart and he called her his "gold pheasant." As I mentioned before, she was born in the United States. When Denise left Argentina, at the time that her marriage to our father was irretrievably damaged, she took the children with her to Switzerland. This is why my Coburg siblings were raised in that country. With Gion Schäfer Claudia had two daughters: Christina and Gianetta. Christina is an emergency nurse and Gianetta, a psychologist.

Claudia was very creative and artistic; a great painter. She also loved having a good time and has always had a carefree spirit. Her ex-husband is an excellent lawyer and a judge, as well as a notary. He always wanted Claudia to use her abilities, but she would not. I suppose she always doubted her talent.

Unfortunately, with time Claudia and Gion's marriage did not work. They divorced and she moved to Chile. It was a considerable shock to us all and Gion never remarried. He was a good husband, I believe, and worked hard to provide his family with a very good life. Gion is a man of great integrity and I am proud to be his friend.

Life, however, has not been kind to poor Claudia. She had cancer and the treatment was initially successful. However, her illness has returned and as I write these lines, my sister is not well.

My niece Maria-Alexandra Meiningen and sisters Beatrice and Claudia in the Hall of Giants, Schloß Ehrenburg, Coburg.

As for our sister Beatrice, I also met her in Argentina. Later, I saw her frequently in Euope, particularly when we would all visit our father at

Opposite page: From the left: Katja, Father, Denise, Beatrice and Fried Meiningen.

My late brother-in-law Fried Meiningen.

My sister Beatrice.

Gion Schäfer, Fried Meininge, my nephew Friedrich-Constantin Meiningen and my sister Beatrice at a family event in Greinburg.

Greinburg. She married Prince Friedrich of Saxe-Meiningen (Fried) in 1997, theirs providing the last marriage, to date, between lines of the Wettin family. He was the only son of Prince Bernhard of Saxe-Meiningen (1901-1984) and his first, and morganatic, wife Margot Grössler. Bernhard later divorced his wife and in 1948 married Baroness Vera Schaffer von Bernstein, by whom he had another three children, among them Prince Konrad, present Head of House Saxe-Meiningen. Perhaps my brother-in-law's difficulties came from the fact that Fried, although the eldest son, was not the heir given the status of his parents' marriage. This issue continues to plague that branch of the Wettin family as Konrad has not married and has no direct heir. The last male heir of marriageable age is my nephew Friedrich Constantin, but his own uncle refuses to recognize him as such.

Anyhow, Fried was a difficult man. Before his marriage to Beatrice, Fried surprised us by asking that Beatrice be granted a dowry, which left Father a bit stunned. Of course his request was politely declined. Fried had a very high concept of his own importance and that made life difficult for him and my sister, who was not raised to be that way. He even criticized the wine we used at a party I gave for them before their wedding. I was perplexed. It was very strange!

Fried was involved in hotel management and owned an antique business. He also had a company refurbishing machines to resell them. The business ended badly and he, unfortunately, went bankrupt. Beatrice ended having to face the debts contracted by her husband.

Beatrice wanted to be a librarian. Later she studied natural medicine, which she continues to practice. They had two children. Her daughter, Maria-Alexandra, is a very successful lawyer. Their son, Friedrich Constantin, has a deep interest in the culture and religions of India. He works for a large company in Switzerland. Maria-Alexandra was married briefly; Friedrich-Constantin remains unmarried.

Vickie, my American sister, married Jack Taubin, a Coast Guard officer, and had two sons. When they were married, Vickie was very young and Dick and Mother were concerned about the future of the marriage. After the birth of my nephews Keith and Todd, Vickie and her husband divorced. She later met her second husband, Michael Beveridge, with whom she had a daughter, my niece Victoria Beveridge. Michael was a man of all trades. In fact, he was a very sweet man … I enjoyed him. He always said, *"Do you know what I mean,"* to which I replied, *"No, Michael, I don't!"* He was always puzzled by my reply … it was very funny!

My nephews Simon and Daniel, Adrian's sons.

Vickie lives in Louisiana in the home our mother owned. When mother died, I renounced my share and gave it to Vickie. She comes to Germany nearly every year, usually around the holidays. I like her company very much, even when we bicker as siblings do. At home, one of the ladies who helps us explains Vickie's American custom of drinking cold water with ice as "Vickie water." There is no doubt that it is nice to have

This photo was taken outside my apartment at Schloß Greinburg. From the left: Alexander and Stephanie, Trudi, me, Beatrice, Daniel and Claudia.

Vickie and me with Dick. This photo was taken at Fort Handcock, Sandy Hook, New Jersey.

Vickie around and I always look forward to her company!

Vickie has three children, her middle son, Todd, has been a frequent visitor to us. He has helped me with our website and always has good input. Todd, with Arturo's agreement, designed the cover of this book. For that I am extremely thankful as I think it looks quite nice. There is no doubt that he is very talented.

I must admit that Vickie and I had a wonderful mother. She had a great sense of humor ... everywhere she went she was the center of attention. She never made any fuss. She knew how to do everything; she taught herself; she made everything homely; even when we slept in army cots, she always made everything homely. Mother was very independent, a straight shooter who had an endless well of drive, energy and initiative.

I always visited her in the USA ... she made me go to the supermarket and made me do things that in Germany I did not have to do. She always wanted us to remain humble and grounded, unaffected and simple. The end of the Second World War was the end of her world. Instead of wilting and letting this great tragedy rule the rest of her life, Mother saw an opportunity to build a new life for herself and went ahead and did it quite successfully.

Opposite page: Trudi, Vickie and Beatrice.

Between 1965-1985, I did not come to the United States. Instead, Mother and Dick came to Europe often. We saw them in

My mother and Dick in their later years.

My sisters visit us in Coburg frequently, particularly Vickie and Beatrice. This image of us three was taken in a local Coburg restaurant.

Coburg and Salzburg, they visited Greinburg … in fact, they lived in Salzburg after Dick's retirement. However, Dick did not like living there because it was too cold. They returned to Louisiana and settled there permanently.

Dick Whitten was a good man. He raised me, when he had no obligation to do so. He promised Mother, before they were married, that he would be a father to me, and he did not disappoint either one of us. I am, and will always be, thankful to him for having taken care of us. We had very different personalities, Dick and I. Many times I wanted to give him a piece of my mind, particularly as in his later years he could be unkind. The one time I lost my cool and we had a serious argument, Mother defused it. She knew her husband's ways; she was aware of his failings; she loved him nonetheless. That, I admit, I have always respected.

My stepfather left us in October 2001. By then, Mother had been dealing with her own ailments for some time. I visited her often and tried to be very supportive of Vickie's efforts to care for our mother. She passed away in March 2003. Her death was a deep loss to us all for she was, simply, irreplaceable.

It was their wish that both be cremated and their ashes brought to that magical place where their love story began, Steinwändt. Although my grandparents sold the estate many years ago, the family did keep a small burial plot near the house that had provided them with an opportunity to rebuild their lives after the Second World War. Mother and Dick rest now next to her parents. Grandfather Solms was laid to rest there in October

Mother was never happier than when her dogs surrounded her.

Chapter XVIII – Happy Hour ...

My sister Vickie with Hubertus Sayn-Wittgenstein-Berleburg and Irina Solms and one of their daughter Marie. Also in the picture is our cousin Count Julian Solms.

Mother and Uncle Pety dancing.

1971; Omo followed him just a few months later. She wished to join him. They were married for fifty-one years and were devoted to the other. It was as if without him, there was no need to hang around.

As for my uncles, Pety and Hubertus, both are now deceased. Uncle Pety died while away in Africa in 2006. He had been a widower for a long time as his wife, Aunt Oda (née Stolberg-Wernigerode), had predeceased him in 1978. Uncle Hubertus died too soon. He passed away in October 1991 while still in his mid-fifties. Gerta, his second wife, survives him.

Of all my Solms cousins, I am closest to Irina, Uncle Pety's eldest child. She was born in 1953 and twenty years later married Prince Hubertus zu Sayn-Wittgenstein-Berleburg (b. 1948). They had seven children, but later in life made the decision to separate. Hubertus became a Roman Catholic and I wonder how much that decision contributed to their distance. Anyhow, I like Irina very much and she is always invited to all our events, both in Coburg and Grein. Hubertus, her husband, is also very nice.

Irina's brother, Christian, married an American, Melissa Butler, and settled in the United States. She died last year just weeks short of her sixtieth birthday. They had several children, but I don't have much contact with them. Also, Uncle Pety and Aunt Oda's daughter, Huberta, married an Israeli and they have three children.

As many of you may remember, the King of Sweden, Carl XVI

I did it my way ...

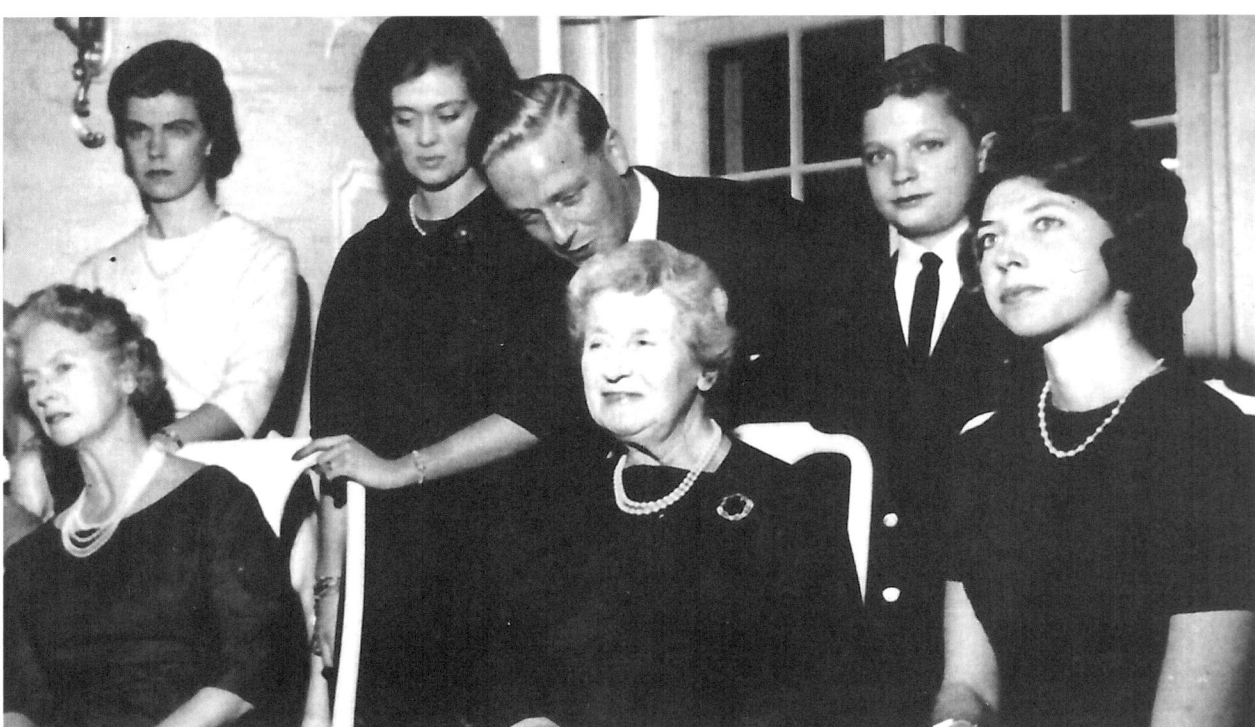

Standing in back, from the left: Princess Margaretha, Princess Birgitta, Prince Hansi Hohenzollern, future King Carl Gustaf of Sweden. Seated, same order: Aunt Bylla, Grandmother Coburg and Princess Désirée.

Gustaf, is my first cousin. I first met him when Father and I visited Stockholm in the early 1960s. Since then, I have remained close to my Swedish cousins, particularly Princess Christina and the King, as they are the two closest in age to me. I also keep in close contact with Prince Johann Georg (Hansi) of Hohenzollern, the estranged husband of my cousin Princess Birgitta. She lives most of the time in Spain, while he resides in Munich. Interestingly, Hansi is a Coburg descendant since his ancestors include Queen Maria II of Portugal and her second husband, Prince Ferdinand of Saxe-Coburg and Gotha.

The King of Sweden is prone to pranks just as much as am I. One time, for example, I believe it was in the late 1960s, we put a lot of firecrackers inside my boots. The resulting effect was that as the explosives ignited, the poor boots went up in the air and round and round. I imagine the palace guards were not amused. We laughed until our stomachs ached ... silly boys!

I have always enjoyed visiting Sweden, a beautiful country with stunning geography. The King and I once saw the mid-summer moon from a boat. It was an amazing sight and one that I will never forget.

Both the King and Queen have frequently visited Coburg, Greinburg and several of our other properties. They love nature and also enjoy walking in the mountains. They were in Greinburg for my sixtieth birthday and the King gave the toast of honor. He had us all in stitches as King

King Carl XVI Gustaf and Queen Silvia.

Chapter XVIII – Happy Hour ...

My goddaughter Princess Madeleine of Sweden. This photo was taken at her father's fortieth birthday in 1986.

My cousin Princess Christina and her niece Princess Madeleine.

King Carl XVI Gutaf and Queen Silvia attended my sixtieth birthday party at Schloß Greinburg.

Carl XVI Gustaf has a keen sense of humor. For Queen Silvia's fiftieth birthday, where the Swedish custom of dancing around a maypole was introduced to us all, I played quite a prank with the King. We were terrible to my a friend. We gave him one shot of schnapps after another, toasted and toasted, all while we, myself and other conspirators, drank a less toxic mix of beer and wine. Naturally, we got our poor unsuspecting friend completely drunk. *"Serves him right,"* Grandmother Coburg would have said had she seen us!

In all seriousness, though, I think the world of the King and Queen of Sweden. We have remained close throughout all these years and much to our delight, our children are also close friends. Carl XVI Gustaf and Silvia honored me when they chose me as one of the godparents of their second daughter, Princess Madeleine, whose wedding I attended in 2013. My son Hubertus and Crown Princess Victoria are also very good

Crown Princess Victoria of Sweden talking with Alexander, Stephanie and me at Greinburg.

With King Carl XVI Gustaf and Queen Silvia in 2009.

friends and she is the godmother of his eldest child, my granddaughter Katharina.

Of the King's four sisters, as I mentioned in an earlier chapter, the one I am closest to is Princess Christina. My cousin married Mr. Tord Magnuson (b. 1941) in 1974. They had known each other for a long time, but their relationship was not widely known to the Swedish public. Due to the strict law that then governed the marriages of the Swedish Royal Family, their union was considered unequal and Christina lost her style of "Royal Highness." Her brother granted Christina the courtesy title of "Princess Christina, Mrs. Magnuson." Tord and Christina, and I like them both very much, have three sons, all with children now. Interestingly, between the death of Aunt Bylla and the marriage of the King, Princess Christina served as Sweden's "first lady," since she was the only royal princess left living in the country. She remains an active member of the King's family and occasionally performs engagements of an official nature, attending events such as the Nobel Prize ceremonies. She also served as Chairman of the Swedish Red Cross for nearly a decade.

Like her sisters, my cousin Princess Margaretha was educated at home in the Haga Palace. She later attended a dressmaking school in Stockholm. She met her husband, Mr. John Ambler, while visiting the United Kingdom. They married in 1964 and settled in Oxfordshire. Due to her entering an unequal marriage, she received the courtesy title of "Princess Margaretha, Mrs. Ambler." They had three children; all married with children of their own. Although John and Margaretha separated in 1994, they never divorced. John died in 2008. Margaretha visits Sweden frequently, particularly for family gatherings.

Opposite page: King Carl XVI Gustaf and Queen Silvia at our son Hubertus' wedding.

My Swedish cousins at the wedding of their nephew Prince Carl Philip. From the left: Princess Christina and Mr. Tord Magnuson; Princess Désirée and Baron Nils Silfverschiöld; Princess Birgitta of Hohenzollern; and Princess Margaretha.

Princess Birgitta was born at the Haga Palace in 1937. Of my Swedish cousins she was the only one to marry a member of the Gotha. She met Prince Johann Georg of Hohenzollern in 1959 and they were married in 1961. "Hansi," as we know my cousin's husband, and Birgitta settled in Munich, where he has lived for many years. They had three children, two sons and a daughter. However, in 1990 Hansi and Birgitta decided to separate. She is a great golfer and lives in Mallorca; Hansi lives in Munich and is now retired. He is an avid hunter and visits us in Coburg.

My cousin Désirée, born in 1938, married a Swedish nobleman, Baron Nils August Silfverschiöld, born four years earlier. Upon her marriage, she was granted the courtesy title of "Princess Désirée, Baroness Silfverschiöld." They had three children, a son and two daughters. The couple lives in Sweden, where Baron Silfverschiöld owns estates.

With my friend Hansi Hohenzollern.

Of course there are countless other members of the Gotha to whom I am very close. One of them is Prince Leopold of Bavaria ("Poldi Bayern"), who also happens to be a close friend to the King of Sweden. For decades "Poldi Bayern" worked for BMW. He is an excellent driver and has incredible experience in racing. He shares this passion for speedways and races with my cousin then King of Sweden, who is also an excellent driver. One time, I think it was in 1980, the King invited us to a shoot

Chapter XVIII – Happy Hour ...

With my friend Poldi Bayern.

In Sweden with Fürstin Benedikte zu Sayn-Wittgenstein-Berleburg.

in Sweden. The husband of a friend of the Queen offered us a free flight in his airplane, but to do so we had to get to Düsseldorf in record time. Poldi drove us from Nüremberg to Düssseldorf in about two hours, a record no doubt. He was driving a special Mercedes Benz. I guess that the police light Poldi placed on the roof of the car helped us in never getting stopped by the unsuspecting autobahn polizei!

King Simeon and Queen Margarita of Bulgaria, as well as his sister Princess Marie Louise and her husband Bronislaw Chrobok, besides family relations, are also very good friends. King Simeon, who also sees me as the Head of House Coburg, has visited our town many times. He has also been to Greinburg and to our hunting lodges in the Tyrol.

I have always have the greatest respect for him, for I consider my cousin Simeon a man of great integrity and someone who would give it all for his country. Simeon lost his father the same year I was born. Three years later, Communists who in their haste to rid themselves of the Bulgarian Royal Family did not bother to have the child king sign an abdication ousted the nine-year old King Simeon. Along with his mother and sister, Simeon departed Bulgaria with what little they were allowed to carry.

Our cousins King Simeon and Queen Margarita of Bulgaria.

For some time they lived in Egypt along with Queen Mother Giovanna's parents, King Vittorio Emanuele III and Queen Elena. Later, Giovanna settled in Estoril, a beautiful seaside resort on the coast north of Lisbon. That area eventually became a refuge for many royals, among them: the Count and Countess of Barcelona and their children; the Count and Countess of Paris, and their large brood of children; King Carol II of Romania; Archduke Josef of Austria and his family, and the family of the Dukes of Braganza. In fact, some time ago, our cousin Duarte, Duke of Braganza, invited me to visit Portugal. I accepted his kind invitation and while there was treated with near royal status since the last King of Portugal, Manoel II, had been a Coburg!

In due time, Simeon found a wife in Spain, Margarita Gómez-Acebo. She had also lost her parents at an early age when Spanish Communists assassinated them during that country's terrible civil war. She is very nice and I have enjoyed our friendship for many decades. Simeon and Margarita married in Vevey, Switzerland, but settled in Madrid, where their five children were born. All have visited Coburg and I personally find them delightful. I think that both Simeon and Margarita who, in spite of their position, have experienced a lot of tragic moments, are among the strongest and most devoted couples that I know. I always enjoy having them visit us in Coburg and the times we have spent together have been very special.

Another set of cousins who are frequent visitors and guests are the Württembergs: Ferdinand, Eugen, Alexander, and Sophie. They are the children of Princess Nadejda of Bulgaria, King Simeon's aunt, and of her husband Duke Albrecht Eugen of Württemberg, who like his wife was a Coburg descendant. All are exquisitely educated

Opposite page: King Simeon and Queen Margarita of Bulgaria

Simeon and Margarita with their children. Kardam, Kyrill, Kubrat, Konstantin and Kalina.

Carin with King Simeon and our cousin Johannes Heinrich of Saxe-Coburg and Gotha.

Chapter XVIII – As I Approach the Winter of My Life ...

The wedding of our son Hubertus was attended by many royals from across Europe. Among them were King Carl XVI Gustaf and Queen Silvia of Sweden, King Simeon and Queen Margarita of Bulgaria, and also Prince Georg Friedrich of Prussia.

With my cousin Sophie Württemberg.

and talented people, as well as a joy to visit with. While the brothers live in Germany, their sister Sophie lives in Paris, where she is well known in the highest circles.

Closer to Coburg, I have always enjoyed close connections to my cousins of Hohenlohe-Langenburg. The late Fürst Kraft visited us often. He was among the descendants of Queen Victoria who attended an exhibition I organized at Schloß Callenberg to commemorate the centennial of her death in 2001. Kraft, however, died a few years later and not until lately have I reestablished contact with his son, Fürst Philipp, who was among the relatives who attended the launch of Arturo Beéche's opus book on our family, *The Coburgs of Europe*. I have been in contact, though, with Philipp's uncle Andreas and his nice wife Luise, who live in Munich. We not only are related as descendants of Queen Victoria, but also share many of the same friends.

As for our English cousins, establishing links with them has been a bit more complicated. Three of The Queen's children (the Prince of Wales, the Duke of York and the Earl of Wessex) have been our guests in Coburg. They all accepted our invitations to attend opening ceremonies to various exhibitions, while also touring the birthplace of the Prince Consort, our closest Coburg common ancestor. I met the Duke of Edinburgh several times, once in Langenburg, where we attended Kraft's funeral, and then I have met him in Sweden. I have not met The Queen yet, but would like to one day. Other English cousins who have visited us include Prince Michael of Kent and his nephew Lord Nicholas Windsor, who was here with his wife Paola for Hubertus' wedding. Prince Michael was our guest of honor at the Queen Victoria Exhibition in 2001. He brought with him a piece loaned to the exhibition by The Queen.

A few years ago, I received an invitation to come to Buckingham Palace. Hubertus and Kelly accompanied me. It was both interesting and very exciting. While there, the Prince of Wales welcomed us and introduced us as his cousins from Germany. Everyone was quite polite and welcoming. It was a wonderful experience to have shared with my son and his wife. I think that our branch of the family had not been invited to Buckingham Palace since Grandfather Coburg attended the funeral of his first cousin King George V in 1936. I sincerely hope that our links to the British cousins continue strengthening in the future as our shared Coburg legacy is historically important.

We do have a close relationship with our Belgian cousins. King Baudouin and Queen Fabiola, King Albert II and Queen Paola, and their sister Josephine-Charlotte with her husband Grand Duke Jean of Luxembourg, have visited us several times. Albert II and Paola's children are also in close contact with us. We had a strong Belgian presence at Hubertus' wedding and I know that my son will maintain this important link to the Belgian Royal Family.

In 1995, with Carin, I attended the sixtieth birthday of my cousin Kraft Hohenlohe-Langenburg.

Our English cousin Prince Michael of Kent came to the opening of the Queen Victoria Exhibition in 2001.

A visit from my cousin Peter and his family. From the left: Stephanie; Johanna and Peter Jr.; their daughter Louisa; Peter; and Malte, Peter Jr.'s son from his first marriage.

At the presentation of Arturo Beéche's book The Coburgs of Europe. *Front row, from the right: Peter Prinz von Coburg, me, Hubertus, Stephanie, Alexander and Mr. David Higdon. In the following row, are: Louise and Andreas of Hohenlohe-Langenburg, their nephew Fürst Philipp, and Prince Clemens of Saxony.*

As Head of House Saxe-Coburg and Gotha I have always been open to meeting members of our extended family. Some have been more amenable to receive our hospitality, others, well, not so much. My Uncle Leo's children are a perfect example. Uncle Leo and his first wife were the parents of three children: Marianne, Ernst Leopold and Peter. While I have had a very good relationship with Peter, a retired educator who now lives in Coburg, that was not the case with his brother Ernst Leopold. Peter worked for many years for a private school, Louisenlund, located in Northern Germany. He and his late wife Roswitha settled in Coburg after he retired. They had two sons, Peter and Malte. Both sons have given Peter grandchildren Roswitha's time in Coburg was short, sadly, as she died in 2013. Peter visits me nearly every week and we often have lunch together.

Ernst Leopold, Peter's older brother, was a complicated man. I always felt that he blamed the family

Opposite page: At Buckingham Palace Hubertus, Kelly and me were received by the Prince of Wales.

King Ferdinand of Bulgaria, who lived in Coburg, with Father and Grandmother Coburg.

for his father's decision to renounce his rights to marry his first wife in 1932. I had nothing to do with that matter, but rules are rules. Uncle Leo knew what the rules were and still he chose to marry in contravention of House Law. This decision was the reason why Uncle Bertel was the next heir until his death in 1943. Then, my father became heir and I followed. Ernst Leopold had a hard time accepting that, although a Coburg by birth, he was not a dynast and thus did not have access to the Coburg Family Foundation.

He firstly married in 1961 a lady by the name of Ingeborg Henig, by whom he had a son: Hubertus, born in 1961. Two years later, Ernst Leopold divorced his wife and quickly married Gertraude Pfeiffer (b. 1938). They had five children before the marriage collapsed in 1985. The following year he married a third time, Sabine Henning. He seems to have had financial difficulties and his business collapsed. The solution he found was to commit double-suicide with his third wife. They sat in his Mercedes Benz pointed guns at each other and fired. Ghastly.

There are other Coburgs, a Catholic branch that started with the marriage of Prince Ferdinand of Saxe-Coburg-Saalfeld and Princess Antonia von Kohary. This was a magnificent marriage because Antonia was one of the richest heiress of her time. Through the alliance, Ferdinand acquired not just considerable properties, but also became the administrator of a phenomenal fideikomiss (trust) set up by his father-in-law, Fürst Franz von Kohary, a councilor of Emperor Franz I of Austria.

Ferdinand and Antonia had four children: Ferdinand, August, Victoire and Leopold. Ferdinand (1816-1885) was married off to Queen Maria II of Portugal and their children formed a revitalized Portuguese Royal Family. Their great-grandson Manoel II was Portugal's last king. He succeeded

A rare photo of various Coburgs. From the left: Prince Rainer of Saxe-Coburg and Gotha; Grand Duchess Kira Kirillovna of Russia, Aunt Bylla, Princess Klementine and her brother Prince Philipp-Josias of Saxe-Coburg and Gotha; unidentified gentleman; and Uncle Hubertus Coburg.

his father King Carlos in 1908 after a regicide that not only took the monarch's life but also that of his eldest son Crown Prince Luis Filipe. Two years later enemies of the monarchy overthrew the king and the country became a republic. Manoel II died in 1932 without any children from his marriage to the former Princess Auguste Viktoria of Hohenzollern. It was then that the branch of the Dukes of Braganza inherited the rights to the throne. Our cousin Duarte, the current Duke of Braganza, happens to also be a descendant of Ferdinand and Antonia Coburg. Duarte's grandfather, Prince Pedro de Alcantara of Brazil was a grandson of Victoire of Saxe-Coburg and Gotha, only daughter of Ferdinand and Antonia.

Ferdinand and Antonia's second son, August (1818-1881), married another phenomenally wealthy heiress, Princess Clémentine d'Orléans, the youngest daughter of King Louis Philippe of the French and his wife Marie-Amélie, a daughter of King Ferdinando I of the Two Sicilies. August and Clémentine settled in Paris until her father was overthrown in 1848. Three of their children were born in France (Philipp, Ludwig August and Clotilde). Their fourth daughter, Amalie, was born in Coburg where her parents sought refuge in 1848, while the youngest child, Ferdinand, was born in Vienna.

King Ferdinand of Bulgaria was a passionate botanist and enjoyed spending time with nature.

My cousin King Simeon is a grandson of August and Clémentine's youngest son, who in 1887 was elected as Prince of Bulgaria. Ferdinand, a true Coburg, was an extremely ambitious young man who would not avoid the challenge of becoming the founder of a new royal dynasty in Bulgaria. He married his cousin Princess Marie Louise of Bourbon-Parma and with her fathered four children. His eldest, Boris III, was Simeon and Marie Louise's father. Ferdinand's youngest daughter, Nadejda, was the mother of my Württemberg cousins.

Ferdinand joined the Central Powers during the First World War. He lost, and he lost big. Weeks before the German Empire and Austria-Hungary signed the armistice that led to the revolution that topple Grandfather Coburg and all the other ruling German sovereigns, Ferdinand was forced off the Bulgarian throne. Eventually, he settled in Schloß Burglaßschloßen, his brother Philipp's Coburg residence. When he died in 1948, King Ferdinand was buried in the Kohary Gruft, the burial crypt built by the Catholic

King Boris III and Queen Giovanna of Bulgaria with their children, Princess Marie Louise and future King Simeon.

With my cousin King Simeon of Bulgaria at Schoß Friedrichshof.

Coburgs under the Church of St. Augustin, located behind the Edinburgh Palais.

Prince Philipp inherited the bulk of the Coburg and Kohary properties in 1881. He had married another Coburg, Princess Louise of Belgium, eldest daughter of King Leopold II. This was a disastrous marriage and Philipp and Louise ended up separating and eventually divorcing. Louise seems to have been a bit naughty and her amorous escapades were the talk of all Vienna. Emperor Franz Josef had enough and asked Philipp to put an end to his wife's shenanigans. After forging some bank loan documents and credits, Louise was arrested and sent to a sanatorium, while Philipp was left to pay for her huge debts. Their two children did not have a good life either. The eldest, Prince Leopold, was involved with a disreputable woman who shot him and poured acid over his face before committing suicide. He lingered for months and died during reconstructive surgery to correct the damage his mistress had inflicted on him. Philipp's other child, Dora, was the wife of the Duke of Schleswig-Holstein-Sonderburg-Augustenburg, Ernst-Günther, who was the only brother of Grandmother Coburg and Omo's mother. Ernst-Günther died in 1921 and Dora remained at Schloß Primkenau, in Silesia, until the Red Army

Prince Philipp of Saxe-Coburg and Gotha.

Prince Philipp-Josias of Saxe-Coburg and Gotha.

advanced across Poland and Eastern Germany. She had to flee with what she could carry, much like her Solms relations. She died in 1967 at Schloß Taxis, a property owned by our Thurn und Taxis cousins.

Old Prince Philipp Coburg died in 1921. At his death he had chosen a grandnephew, Prince Philipp-Josias, as his heir. By then, however, the Coburg and Kohary Fideikomiss were under assault by the authorities of the new countries that were born from the collapse of the Austro-Hungarian Empire: Czechoslovakia and Hungary. Furthermore, other members of Philipp-Josias' branch demanded a share of what was left of the fortune he inherited. All these Coburgs irrationally fought in court for decades and by the time lawyers were done, little remained of their once incalculable fortune. They suffered further losses after 1945 when the Communists, who also executed Prince Rainer, Philipp-Josias' older brother, confiscated all the property in Hungary and Czechoslovakia. For some time, Philipp-Josias, accompanied by his wife and their son (Philipp August), lived in the relative security of Portugal. He later returned to Austria and began rebuilding with what he had left. In the Austrian capital they still owned the vast Coburg Palais, while they had several smaller forestry and agricultural estates in Walterskirchen, Gröbming and other locations in the Tyrol. Philipp-Josias died in Vienna in 1985. His wife Sarah also died there in 1994. Their son Philipp August, who I met when he came to visit Coburg, married twice and had children from both his wives. In May 2014, along with Arturo Beéche, we

Prince Philipp August of Saxe-Coburg and Gotha.

were headed to see Philipp August, who was deadly ill. Unfortunately, his condition took a turn for the worse and his son Maximilian called and informed us that his father was in no condition to have visitors. We never saw Philipp August again as he died later that year. His two sons continue farming their lands and they are the last male Coburgs of that branch of our family.

Prince Rainer, Philipp-Josias' brother, married twice. He had one child with his first wife Johanna Károly de Károly-Patty, Johannes Heinrich, and then they divorced. Rainer's second wife was Edith de Kózol and she survived him until 1997.

My cousin Johannes Heinrich was a frequent visitor to Coburg and Grein. I liked him very much and always felt that he was a very unlucky man. He firstly married Baroness Marie-Gabrielle von Fürstenberg (1921-2007) with whom he had a daughter, Felicitas, who has attended many of our family gatherings. Johannes Heinrich and Marie-Gabrielle did not get along and Felicitas was their only child. After divorcing his first wife, he remarried our cousin Mathilde of Saxony, youngest daughter of Friedrich Christian, Margrave of Meißen. From this marriage Johannes Heinrich had one son, Johannes Albert, born in 1969. The family lived in Innsbruck, where Johannes Heinrich had his business. Sadly, his son died in a mountaineering accident in August 1987. It was an awful tragedy and not surprisingly the marriage collapsed under the weight of their grief. In later years, Johannes Heinrich and Mathilde made their peace and she accompanied him to several events and family gatherings that I hosted. He died in 2010. Mathilde lives in Bavaria.

Prince Johannes Heinrich of Saxe-Coburg and Gotha and his ex-wife Princess Mathilde of Saxony. This photo was taken at Schloß Callenberg in 2001.

In 2001, I organized an exhibition to commemorate the centennial of Queen Victoria's death. With that in mind, Carin and I invited several Coburg descendants. From left: Ferdinand and Alexander Württemberg; Michael Benedict Weimar; Carin, Moritz Hesse; me, Sophie Württemberg; Georg Friedrich Prussia, Prince Michael of Kent; Hubertus; and Andreas Leiningen. The group included others, among them my cousin Irina with her husband and some of their children, but they are not visible here.

Moritz Hesse and Queen Silvia dancing at my sixtieth birthday.

Three other cousins have always been kind enough to attend many of our gatherings in Coburg and Greinburg: the late Landgraf Moritz of Hesse, and Fürst Andreas and Fürstin Alexandra of Leiningen.

Andreas and Alexandra Leiningen share a very interesting characteristic: they are the last descendants of Queen Victoria to marry each other. Andreas is in fact a descendant of Queen Victoria and her two half-siblings. Alexandra descends from Queen Victoria and her half-sister Fürstin Feodora of Hohenlohe-Langenburg. As a young man learning the forestry industry, I lived for some time with Andreas' parents in Amorbach. Alexandra is the sister of Prince Ernst August of Hannover, the estranged husband of Princess Caroline of Monaco. Like us, the Hannovers are an old branch of the English Royal Family. Their branch broke off in 1837 when Queen Victoria succeeded King Wiliam IV. Since Hannover, also ruled in personal union by the King of England, did not have female succession, the throne went to the Duke of Cumberland, Queen Victoria's uncle. King Ernst August ruled Hannover until his death in 1851, when he was succeeded by blind King Georg V, who lost the throne to the Prussians in 1866. Although the Hannovers have not ruled since then, they have remained one of royal Germany's most prominent dynasties.

Moritz was the grandson of Princess Margarete of Prussia, a first cousin of Grandfather Coburg as they were grandchildren of Queen Victoria. Moritz was a very elegant and extremely refined man, and perhaps one of the most popular members of the Gotha. As a grandson of King Vittorio Emanuele III of Italy, he was also a first cousin of King Simeon of Bulgaria. In 2001 Moritz loaned us some historical pieces that we included in our very successful exhibition to commemorate the centennial of Queen Victoria's death. He was married to Princess Tatiana of Sayn-Wittgenstein-Berleburg, with whom he had four children before they divorced. She is one of the sisters of Fürst Richard who is married to Princess Benedikte of Denmark, a first cousin of my first cousin King Carl XVI Gustaf. Moritz died in 2013 and his funeral was yet another opportunity for the royal mob to get together at his family's marvelous hotel Schloß Friedrichshof.

Interestingly, at Moritz's funeral, which I attended accompaniued by Hubertus and Kelly, I saw many of our cousins. King Simeon was there and Count Hans Veit

Fürst Andreas and Fürstin Alexandra of Leiningen at our son Hubertus' wedding.

Toerring-Jettenbach, another delightful and very funny man, took a picture of us which Arturo Beéche decided to use in this book (page 206). Hans Veit is one of the nicest people I know. He has been a guest at many of our hunts and is also an avid photographer. At Moritz's funeral he took countless photos. *"Why are you taking so many photos,"* I asked him. *"Ah, they are for our friend Arturo,"* he replied. I laughed heartily for even there my collaborator's presence was felt. Last year, Arturo Beéche and I went to Munich to visit some of my friends. We went to Andreas and Luise Hohenlohe-Langenburg's home and had a nice visit with them and their daughter, son-in-law and granddaughters. Earlier, Andreas had joined us for lunch in Munich, along with Hans Veit. To my surprise Hans Veit arrived at the restaurant, located in his family's old town palace across the Residenz, on a Vespa! He is convinced that the agile motorcycle is a great solution for avoiding traffic and parking in the center of Munich. How clever!

Count Hans Veit Toerring-Jettenbach and Carin during after one of our hunts.

I cannot leave without mentioning my cousin Countess Amélie zu Castell-Castell, who is married to Oscar Ritter von Miller zu Aicholz. Amélie is one of the children of Princess Alexandrine Louise of Denmark (1914-1962), a first cousin of both my parents since her mother, Helena, was a sister of Grandmother Coburg and Omo.

With such a large family as ours, one could spend months writing about them. I have tried to mention those I have frequent contact with

Adridand and Claudia surround Beatrice on her wedding day. (1978)

My sister Beatrice.

Beatrice and my nephew Friedrich-Constantin Saxe-Meiningen.

Claudia, Trudi and Beatrice.

here in Coburg or at Greinburg. I hope that if I forgot to mention someone, that they will find it in their heart to forgive me.

As I prepare to bid farewell to you all, let me share some parting words of wisdom. These are life lessons that I have learned …

I fervently believe that one has to be more in the property, just like my Uncle the Duke of Schleswig-Holstein once said. One also must have a good and honest connection to the people and always be respectful. Treat them as normal persons. Large landowners must be humble and approachable; we must be fair and thankful. Our family motto reminds us of that. We must remain true and loyal (faithful) to all those who work for us and the people who provide us with help and assistance.

If you have a negotiation you have to be able to look at the person in the eye and be fair to both sides. You see each other two times in life … therefore you must always stick to what you have agreed. Keep your word. Do not distrust people from the beginning … do not be suspicious of people until they prove you wrong. I had to learn to be open to new ideas. I have trusted everyone I have met and have always given the benefit of the doubt. Some 95% of those I have dealt with have proven worthy of my trust. That's a very good record!

I did not want to be everyone's darling … I am myself. I became good friends with the authorities in Thüringen because I knew that they were there to do a job, just as I was. Both sides conducted negotiations with respect and in the end we all came out satisfied at the other end. They made me honorary citizen of the city of Gotha because of what I achieved and the authorities appreciated my willingness to find a solution. I was honest and thoughtful. Sometimes in life, two people meet who know what their responsibility is … they work together with respect and these two people meet and do something that is positive for future generations. It is important that you always be honest and negotiate in good faith, fairness and with morality. The beautiful museum in Gotha, where the ducal collections now occupy a prominent position, was possible because I negotiated smartly and fairly. I knew what I would be fine with claiming and what I ought to let go. For me it was important that they mention where the art came from, so everyone would know how much we were willing to give up. In the end, we all benefited from the agreement!

With our children at Schloß Greinburg.

A few years ago I was quite ill. I was sick with blood poisoning. They tested me for Parkinson's and I tested positive. I felt that it was perhaps the best time to retire. Healthwise, I recovered. I feel better now, much, much better … and I have years left to live. I miss my business; I miss being involved in an active role in our family business. I feel like a sail boat ready to go, but that is no longer allowed to go for an outing. It is what is and nothing can be done about it – the new generation is in charge and my son is doing a great job!

I feel that youngsters today have a different approach to the way we used to carry out our business. I am extremely confident

Stephanie and Alex on their brother Hubertus' wedding day.

With my sister Vickie.

Alex and Hubertus.

With Alexandra Leiningen and Michael Benedict and Dagmar Saxe-Weimar.

With Carin at our son Hubertus' wedding.

Chapter XVIII – Happy Hour ...

that my son Hubertus' approach will continue bringing us untold benefits. I trust that the excellent education that he received has enabled him to be well perepared for the task he assumed. I am confident that he will be an excellent administrator of our legacy. I rest assured that Hubertus will do a fine job!

As for my parting words to you all ... Perhaps life has changed too quickly and I am a relic of a bygone era. In the electronic era, there is no respect or attention to cultural endeavors. Youngsters today want instant satisfaction at their fingertips. I feel that electronics are in many cases robbing us of our humantiy. Do not get me wrong – I love how electronic devices have made the world smaller and in many cases brought us

With Carin, my life's companion ...

closer together. However, I do not think that the new generations have a deep connection with their history, with the past. Youngsters these days have abandoned reading and I fear that books such as this one, will soon become a thing of the past. In today's world, all emphasis is placed on making money, while people pay little attention to the history surrounding us. I hope, perhaps against all hope that the new generations one day get what we represent, and I am not talking just about my children, but about those of my fellow Heads of House. Maybe my time has passed and now I get to watch, lean back and wonder if I had done the same. The world has changed too quickly, but I do render respect to our past.

We are nearly at the end of our time together. Before I put down the pen, actually, stop clicking the keyboard, I want to express my sincere appreciation to Arturo Beéche for helping me write this book. His assistance has been invaluable, as was his diligence in seeing this project through. We first met many years ago in Coburg. Since then we have collaborated in various projects and I hope that we will be involved in some more. I consider him a very good friend and sincerely wish to thank him for assisting me in reaching the end of this very long journey.

Hence, as I leave you to return to our cocktail hour, I can look back and smile. The Coburgs are back. We have regained our position among the other former ruling dynasties of Europe. We are no longer absent. Our winter came to an end under my direction. We are here to stay and we managed to do so because ... *I did it my way!*

I did it my way ...

Hubertus, Alexander and Stephanie, our children, our legacy ...

ENDNOTES

1. Viktoria Luise Gräfin zu Solms-Baruth, *Memories of My Life for My Children, Grandchildren and Great-Grandchildren.*
2. Franz Josef Fürst zu Hohenlohe-Schillingsfürst, *Monarchen – Edelleute – Bürger: die Nachkommen des Fürsten Carl Ludwig zu Hohenlohe-Langenburg, 1762-1825*, p. 62.
3. Ibid., p. 74.
4. Ibid., p. 75.
5. Solms-Baruth, *Memories ...*
6. Ibid.
7. Ibid.
8. Ibid.
9. Ibid.
10. Ibid.
11. Ibid.
12. Ibid.
13. Ibid.
14. http://www.schloss-callenberg.com/englisch/castle-history/
15. Ibid.
16. Arturo E. Beéche, *The Coburgs of Europe*, p. 21.
17. Ibid., p. 126.
18. Ibid.
19. Ibid., p. 127.
20. Marlene Eilers Koenig, *Queen Victoria's Descendants* (2nd edition), p. 160.
21. Solms-Baruth, *Memories ...*
22. Ibid.
23. Ibid.
24. Ibid.
25. Ibid.
26. Ibid.
27. Ibid.
28. Ibid.
29. Ibid.
30. Ibid.
31. Ibid.
32. Richard Hough, *Advice to My Grand-daughter: Letters from Queen Victoria to Princess Victoria of Hesse*, p. 144.
33. Beéche, *The Coburgs of Europe*, p. 119.
34. Ibid., p. 18.
35. Ibid., p. 19.
36. Ibid., p. 20.
37. Ibid.
38. Ibid.
39. Ibid., p. 23.
40. Ibid., p. 119.
41. Ibid.
42. Ibid.
43. Koenig, p. 161.
44. Eurohistory Archive, Duke of Albany File.
45. Roger Fulford (Ed), *Beloved Mama: Private Correspondence of Queen Victoria and the German Crown Princess 1878-1885*, p. 111.
46. Eurohistory Archive, Duke of Albany File.
47. Charlotte Zeepvat, *Prince Leopold*, p. 173.
48. Ibid., p. 174.
49. Fulford (Ed), *Beloved Mama*, p. 162.
50. Hough, *Advice to My Grand-daughter*, p. 60.
51. Beéche, *The Coburgs of Europe*, p. 118.
52. Hough, *Advice to My Grand-daughter*, p. 68.
53. Beéche, *The Coburgs of Europe*, p. 118.
54. Solms-Baruth, *Memories ...*
55. Eurohistory Archive, Duke of Albany File.
56. Princess Alice, *For my grandchildren*.
57. Theo Aronson, *Princess Alice*.
58. Koenig, p. 146.
59. Beéche, *The Coburgs of Europe*, p. 119.
60. Eurohistory Archive, Duke Carl Eduard of Saxe-Coburg and Gotha File.
61. David Horbury, "Poor Dear Charlie" (Royalty Digest Issue 53).
62. Ibid.
63. Ibid.
64. Ibid.
65. Karina Urbach, *Go Betweens for Hitler*, p. 30.
66. Eurohistory Archive, Duke Carl Eduard of Saxe-Coburg and Gotha File.
67. Princess Alice.
68. Ibid.
69. Princess Alice, p. 90.
70. Ibid., p. 85.
71. The New York Times, October 12, 1905.
72. Beéche, *The Coburgs of Europe*, p. 126.
73. Ibid., p. 127.
74. Viktoria Luise Duchess of Brunswick and Lüneburg, *The Kaiser's Daughter: Memoirs of H.R.H. Viktoria Luise, Princess of Prussia*, p. 160.
75. Ibid.
76. Beéche, *The Coburgs of Europe*.
77. Ibid., p. 136.
78. Urbach, p. 172
79. John C.G. Röhl, *Young Wilhelm: The Kaiser's Early Life*, p. 404.
80. https://en.wikipedia.org/wiki/Kulturkampf
81. Röhl, *Young Wilhelm*, p. 405.
82. Röhl, *Young Wilhelm*, p. 404-405.
83. Karina Urbach, *Go Betweens for Hitler*.
84. Ibid.
85. Beéche, *The Coburgs of Europe*, p. 136.
86. Ibid.
87. Ibid.
88. Ibid., p. 137.
89. The New York Times, April 27, 1940.
90. The New York Times, October 18, 1932.
91. The New York Times, January 27 12, 1947.
92. Ibid.
93. Ibid.
94. Ibid.
95. Ibid.

96. Beéche, *The Coburgs of Europe*, p. 139.
97. Koenig, p. 163.
98. Ibid.
99. Ibid.
100. Solms-Baruth, *Memories ...*
101. Ibid.
102. Princess Alice, p. 280.
103. Ibid, p. 281.
104. Ibid.
105. Ibid.
106. The New York Times, November 30, 1945.
107. Horbury.
108. Koenig, p. 162.
109. Solms-Baruth, *Memories ...*
110. http://www.angelfire.com/realm/gotha/gotha/solms.html
111. Ibid.
112. Ibid.
113. Ibid.
114. Ibid.
115. Solms-Baruth, *Memories ...*
116. Ibid.
117. Ibid.
118. Ibid.
119. Ibid.
120. Ibid.
121. Ibid.
122. Ibid.
123. Ibid.
124. Ibid.
125. Ibid.
126. Eurohistory Archive, Duke Carl Eduard of Saxe-Coburg and Gotha File.
127. Solms-Baruth, *Memories ...*
128. Ibid.
129. Ibid.
130. Ibid.
130. Ibid.
131. Ibid.
132. Ibid.
133. Ibid.
134. Ibid.
135. Ibid.
136. Ibid.
137. Ibid.
138. Ibid.
139. Ibid.
140. Ibid.
141. Ibid.
142.
143.
144.
145. Solms-Baruth, *Memories ...*
146. Ibid.
147. Ibid.
148. Ibid.
149. Ibid.
150. Ibid.
151. Ibid.
152. Ibid.
153. Ibid.
154. Ibid.
155. Ibid.
156. Ibid.
157. Ibid.
158. Ibid.
159. Ibid.
160. Ibid.
161. Ibid.
162. Ibid.
163. Ibid.
164. Ibid.
165. Ibid.
166. Ibid.
167. Ibid.
168. Ibid.
169. Ibid.
170. Ibid.
171. Ibid.
172. Ibid.
173. Ibid.
174. Ibid.
175. Ibid.
176. Ibid.
177. Ibid.
178. Ibid.
179. Ibid.
180. Ibid.
181. Ibid.
182. Ibid.
183. Ibid.
184. Ibid.
185. Ibid.
186. Ibid.
187. Ibid.
188. Ibid.
189. Ibid.
190. Ibid.
191. Ibid.
192. Ibid.
193. Koenig, p. 160.
194. Ibid., p. 164.
195. http://www.angelfire.com/realm/gotha/gotha/saxony.html
196. Koenig, p. 164.
197. Ibid., p. 161.
198. Ibid., p. 162.
199. Ibid., p. 164.

BIBLIOGRAPHY

Albert, Harold A. *Queen Victoria's Sister.* London: Robert Hale, 1967.
Argyll, Duke of. *V.R .I.: Queen Victoria – Her Life and Empire.* London: Harper & Brothers, 1901.
Aronson, Theo. *Crowns in Conflict: The Triumph and Tragedy of European Monarchy 1910-1918.* London: John Murray, 1986.
Aronson, Theo. *Grandmama of Europe: The Crowned Descendants of Queen Victoria.* Indianapolis, IN: Bobbs-Merrill, 1973.
Aronson, Theo. *Princess Alice, Countess of Athlone.* London: Cassell, 1981.
Aronson, Theo. *The Coburgs of Belgium.* London: Cassell & Co., 1968.
Aronson, Theo. *Victoria & Disraeli: The making of a romantic partnership.* London: Cassell, 1977.
Ashdown, Dulcie M. *Queen Victoria's Mother.* London: Robert Hale & Co., 1974.
Ashdown, Dulcie M. *Victoria and the Coburgs.* London: Robert Hale & Co., 1981.
Aspinall, Arthur. (Editor) *The Letters of the Princess Charlotte, 1811-1817.* London: Home and Van Thel, 1949.
Athlone, Princess Alice, Countess of. *For My Grandchildren.* London: Evans Brothers, 1966.
Bachmann, Gertraude. *Herzogin Marie von Sachsen-Coburg und Gotha, geborene Herzogin von Württemberg, 1799-1860.* Coburg: Historischen Gesellschaft Coburg, 1999.
Balansó, Juan. *La familia rival.* 2nd ed. Barcelona: Editorial Planeta, 1994.
Balansó, Juan. *Los Reales Primos de Europa : Quién es quién en el mundo de los tronos, ocupados o vacíos.* Barcelona: Editorial Planeta, 1992.
Battenberg, Marie Princess of. *Reminiscences.* London: George Allen, 1925.
Battiscombe, Georgina. *Queen Alexandra.* Boston, MA: Houghton Mifflin Co., 1969.
Beéche, Arturo E. (Editor) *The Gotha: Still a Continental Royal Family, Volume 1.* East Richmond Heights, CA: Eurohistory.com, 2009.
Beéche, Arturo E. (Editor) *The Grand Duchesses: Daughters and Granddaughters of Russia's Tsars* Oakland, CA: Eurohistory.com, 2004.
Beéche, Arturo E. (Editor) *The Grand Dukes: Sons and Grandsons of Russia's Tsars since Paul I.* East Richmond Heights, CA: Eurohistory.com, 2010.
Beéche, Arturo E. (Editor) *The Other Grand Dukes: Sons and Grandsons of Russia's Grand Dukes.* East Richmond Heights, CA: Eurohistory.com, 2012.
Beéche, Arturo E. *Dear Ellen – Royal Europe Through the Photo Albums of H.I.H. Grand Duchess Helen Vladimirovna of Russia.* East Richmond Heights, CA: Eurohistory.com, 2011.
Beéche, Arturo E., and Ilana D. Miller. *Royal Gatherings: Who is in the Picture? – Volume I: 1859-1914.* East Richmond Heights, CA: Eurohistory.com, 2012.
Beéche, Arturo E., and Ilana D. Miller. *Royal Gatherings: Who is in the Picture? – Volume II: 1914-1939.* East Richmond Heights, CA: Eurohistory.com, 2015.
Beéche, Arturo E., and Prince Michael of Greece and Mrs. Helen Helmis-Markesinis. *The Royal Hellenic Dynasty.* East Richmond Heights, CA: Kensington House Books (a division of Eurohistory.com), 2007.
Belgium, Princess Louise of. *My Own Affairs.* London: Cassell & Co., 1921.
Belgium, Princess Stephanie of. *I Was To Be Empress.* London: Ivor Nicholson & Watson, 1937.
Benson, Arthur Christopher, and Viscount Esher (Editors). *Letters of Queen Victoria 1837-1861.* Vols. I-III. London: John Murray, 1908.
Blackett-Ord, Carol, and Richard Ormond. *Franz Xaver Winterhalter and the Courts of Europe 1830-70.* London: National Portrait Gallery, 1987.
Brockhoff, Evamaria, et al. *Ein Herzogtum und viele Kronen: Coburg in Bayern und Europa.* Coburg: Haus der Bayerischen Geschichte, 1997.
Brook-Shepherd, Gordon. *Royal Sunset: The Dynasties of Europe and the Great War.* London: Weidenfeld & Nicolson, 1987.
Brook-Shepherd, Gordon. *The Last Empress: The Life and Times of Zita of Austria-Hungary, 1892-1989.* London: HarperCollins, 1991.
Brook-Shepherd, Gordon. *Uncle of Europe: The Social & Diplomatic Life of Edward VII.* New York, NY: Harcourt Brace Jovanovich, 1975.
Brook-Shepherd, Gordon. *Victims at Sarajevo: The Romance and Tragedy of Franz Ferdinand and Sophie.* London: Harvill Press, 1984.
Brunswick and Lüneburg, Viktoria Luise Duchess of. *The Kaiser's Daughter: Memoirs of H.R.H. Viktoria Luise, Princess of Prussia.* Englewood Cliffs, NJ: Prentice-Hall, 1977.
Buchanan, Meriel. *Queen Victoria's Relations.* London: Cassell & Co., 1954.
Buchanan, Meriel. *Victorian Gallery.* London: Cassell & Co., 1956.
Calmes, Christian, and Raymond Reuter. *Jean, Grand-Duc de Luxembourg: un souverain et son pays.* Luxembourg: Éditions Luxnews, 1986.
Cannuyer, Christian. *Les maisons royales et souveraines d'Europe.* Paris: Brepols, 1989.
Cassels, Lavender. *Clash of Generations: A Habsburg Family Drama of the 19th Century.* Newton Abbot, Devon: Victorian Book Club, 1974.
Cecil, Lamar. *Wilhelm II: Emperor and Exile, 1900-1941.* Vol. II. Chapel Hill, NC: The University of North Carolina Press, 1996.
Cecil, Lamar. *Wilhelm II: Prince and Emperor, 1859-1900.* Chapel Hill, NC: The University of North Carolina Press, 1989.
Chaffanjon, Arnaud. *Histoires de Familles Royales: Victoria d'Angleterre – Christian IX de Danemark et leurs descendances de 1840 à nos jours.* Paris: Ramsay, 1980.
Chambers, James. *Charlotte & Leopold: The True Story of the Original People's Princess.* London: Old Street Publishing, 2007.
Constant, Stephen. *Foxy Ferdinand, Tsar of Bulgaria.* New York, NY: Franklin Watts, 1980.
Corpechot, Lucien. *Memories of Queen Amélie of Portugal.* Reprint. Ticehurst, East Sussex: Royalty Digest, 1996.
Correia Guedes, Carmina, and Isabel Silveira Godinho. *Growing Up a Prince at Ajuda Palace (1863-1884).* Lisbon: Ministry of Culture, 2004.
Corremans, Luc. *Philippe et Mathilde.* Braine-l'Alleud: Éditions J.M. Collet, 2000.
D'Auvergne, Edmund B. *The Coburgs: The Story of the Rise of a Great Royal House.* London: Stanley Paul & Co., 1911.
da Silveira Godinho, Isabel. *D. Luís – duque do Porto e rei de Portugal.* Lisboa: Palácio Nacional da Ajuda, 1990.
Danneels, Mario. *Paola – de la dolce vita à la couronne.* Bruxelles: Éditions Luc Pire, 2000.

De Fossa, Christophe, and Henri van Daele. *Six Reines*. Bruxelles: Éditions Racine, 1996.
de Launay, Jacques. *Léopold 1er*. Bruxelles: Éditions J.M. Collet, 1982.
de Sagrera, Ana. *Ena y Bee: En defensa de una amistad*. Madrid: Velecío Editores, 2006.
de Sousa, Manuel. *Reis e Rainhas de Portugal*. Mem-Martins: SporPress, 2002.
Defrance, Olivier, and Joseph van Loon. *La fortune de Dora: Une petite-fille de Léopold II chez les nazis*. Bruxelles: Éditions Racine, 2013.
Defrance, Olivier. *La Médicis des Cobourg: Clémentine d'Orléans*. Bruxelles: Éditions Racine, 2007.
Defrance, Olivier. *Léopold 1er et le clan Cobourg*. Bruxelles: Éditions Racine, 2004.
Del Priore, Mary. *O príncipe maldito: traição e loucura na família imperial*. Rio de Janeiro: Editora Objetiva, 2006.
Dimitroff, Pashanko. *Clémentine d'Orleans, Princess Augustus of Saxe Coburg: King-Maker Inveterate*. Sofia: Ascent 96, 1997.
Downer, Martyn. *The Queen's Knight: The extraordinary life of Queen Victoria's most trusted confidant*. London: Bantam Press, 2007.
Duff, David. *Alexandra, Princess and Queen*. London: Collins, 1980.
Duff, David. *Edward of Kent: Father of Queen Victoria*. London: Stanley Paul, 1938.
Dufoux, Georges. *Une dynastie mythique: Les Saxe-Cobourg-Gotha*. Fontainebleau: self-published, 2000.
Dujardin, Vincent, and Michel Dumoulin and Mark Van den Wijngaert. *Léopold III*. Bruxelles: Éditions Complexe, 2001.
Dumont, Georges-Henri. *La Dynastie Belge*. Braine-l'Alleud: Éditions J.M. Collet, 1994.
Ed. by the Chancellery of H.M. the King of the Bulgarians. *Libro Blanco – Al servicio de su patria*. Madrid: Imprenta «El Economista», 1969.
Eilers, Marlene A. *Queen Victoria's Descendants*. 1st ed. New York, NY: Atlantic International Publications, 1987.
Eilers, Marlene A. *Queen Victoria's Descendants*. 2nd ed. Falköping: Rosvall Royal Books, 1997.
Emerson, Barbara. *Leopold II of the Belgians: King of Colonialism*. New York, NY: St. Martin's Press, 1979.
Enache, Nicolas. *La Descendance de Marie-Thérèse de Habsburg, Reine de Hongrie et de Bohême*. Paris: L'Intermédiaire des Chercheurs et Curieux, 1996.
Enache, Nicolas. *La Descendance de Pierre le Grand, Tsar de Russie*. Paris: Sedopols, 1983.
Fenyvesi, Charles. *Splendor In Exile: The Ex-Majesties of Europe*. Washington, D.C.: New Republic Books, 1979.
Finestone, Jeffrey and Robert Massie. *The Last Courts of Europe: A Royal Family Album, 1860-1914*. New York, NY: Vendome Press, 1981.
Frankland, Noble. *Witness of a Century: the life and times of Prince Arthur, Duke of Connaught, 1850-1942*. London: Shepheard-Walwyn, 1993.
Friedrich, Otto. *Ketschendorf: Die Geschichte zweier Schlösser und ihrer Bewohner*. Coburg: Druck- und Verlaghaus A. Rossteutscher, 1973.
Fulford, Roger. (Editor) *Beloved Mama: Private Correspondence of Queen Victoria and the German Crown Princess 1878-1885*. London: Evans Brothers, 1981.
Fulford, Roger. (Editor) *Darling Child: Private Correspondence of Queen Victoria and the German Crown Princess 1871-1878*. London: Evans Brothers, 1981.
Fulford, Roger. (Editor) *Your Dear Letter: Private Correspondence of Queen Victoria and the Crown Princess of Prussia 1865-1871*. New York, NY: Charles Scribner's Sons, 1971.
Gelardi, Julia P. *From Splendor to Revolution: The Romanov Women, 1847-1928*. New York, NY: St. Martin's Press, 2011.
Genealogisches Handbuch des Adels: Fürstliche Häuser Band XIX. Limburg: C.A. Starke Verlag, 2011.
Germany, Crown Prince Wilhelm of. *Memoirs of the Crown Prince of Germany*. Uckfield, East Sussex: The Naval & Military Press, 2005.
Glassheim, Eagle. *Noble Nationalists: The Transformation of the Bohemian Aristocracy*. Cambridge, MA: Harvard University Press, 2005.
Greece, Prince Nicholas of. *My Fifty Years: The Memoirs of Prince Nicholas of Greece*. Annotated and expanded by Arturo E. Beéche. East Richmond Heights, CA: Eurohistory.com, 2006.
Grey, C. *Queen Victoria's Memoirs of The Prince Consort: His Early Years*. New York, NY: Harper & Bros., 1868.
Groueff, Stephane. *Crown of Thorns: The Reign of King Boris III of Bulgaria, 1918-1943*. Lanham, MD: Madison Books, 1987.
Grützner, Günter, and Manfred Ohlsen. *Schloss Cecilienhof und das Kronprinzenpaar*. Berlin: Museums- und Galerie-Verlag, 1991.
Hall, Coryne & Arturo E. Beéche. *APAPA: King Christian IX of Denmark and His Descendants*. East Richmond Heights, CA: Eurohistory.com, 2013.
Hamann, Brigitte. *Die Habsburger – Ein biographisches Lexikon*. München: Piper, 1988.
Hochschild, Adam. *King Leopold's Ghost: A Story of Greed, Terror, and Heroism in Colonial Africa*. New York, NY: Houghton Mifflin, 1998.
Hoffmeister, Hans; Wahl, Volker; et al. *Die Wettiner in Thüringen*. Arnstadt: Rhino Verlag, 1999.
Högel, Klaus-Peter, and Richard Kurdiovsky. *Das Palais Coburg*. Wien: Verlag Christian Brandstätter, 2003.
Hohenlohe-Langenburg, Feodora, Princess of. *Letters from 1828 to 1872*. London: Spottiswoode & Co., 1874.
Hohenlohe-Schillingsfürst, Franz Josef Fürst zu. *Monarchen – Edelleute – Bürger: die Nachkommen des Fürsten Carl Ludwig zu Hohenlohe-Langenburg, 1762-1825*. Neustadt a. d. Aisch: Verlag Degener, 1963.
Hough, Richard. *Advice to My Grand-daughter: Letters from Queen Victoria to Princess Victoria of Hesse*. New York, NY: Simon & Schuster, 1975.
Hough, Richard. *Victoria & Albert*. London: Richard Cohen Books, 1996.
Italy, Marie José, Queen of. *Albert et Élisabeth de Belgique: mes parents*. Bruxelles: Le Cri édition, 2000.
Jagow, Kurt. (Editor) *Letters of the Prince Consort, 1831-1861*. New York, NY: E.P. Dutton & Co., 1938.
Jonas, Klaus. *The Life of Crown Prince William*. Pittsburgh, PA: University of Pittsburgh Press, 1961.
Judtmann, Fritz. *Mayerling: The Facts Behind the Legend*. London: George C. Harrap & Co., 1971.
Katz, Robert. *The Fall of the House of Savoy*. London: George Allen & Unwin, 1972.
Kerckvoorde, Mia. *Charlotte: La passion et la fatalité*. Bruxelles: Éditions Racine, 2001
Kerckvoorde, Mia. *Louise-Marie d'Orléans: La reine oubliée*. Bruxelles: Éditions Racine, 2001.
Kerckvoorde, Mia. *Marie-Henriette: Une amazone face à un géant*. Bruxelles: Éditions Racine, 1998.
King, Greg, and Penny Wilson. *Gilded Prism: The Konstantinovichi Grand Dukes & the Last Years of the Romanov Dynasty*. East Richmond Heights, CA: Eurohistory.com, 2006.
King, Greg. *Twilight of Splendor: The Court of Queen Victoria during Her Diamond Jubilee Year*. Hoboken, NJ: John Wiley & Sons, 2007.
Kirschen, Gilbert. *L'Education d'un Prince: Entretiens avec le Roi Léopold III*. Bruxelles: Didier Hatier, 1984.

Koninckx, Christian. *Astrid 1905-1935*. Bruxelles: Éditions Racine, 2005.
Korneva, Galina & Tatiana Cheboksarova. *Russia & Europe: Dynastic Ties*. East Richmond Heights, CA: Eurohistory.com, 2013.
Korneva, Galina & Tatiana Cheboksarova. *Grand Duchess Marie Pavlovna*. East Richmond Heights, CA: Eurohistory.com, 2014.
Lage Cardoso, Eurico C. E. D. *Manuel II: o rei patriota*. Lisboa: self-published, 2003.
Lage Cardoso, Eurico C. E. D. *Pedro V – O Esperançoso: Vida e Obra de um Rei Inesquecível*. Lisboa: self-published, 2006.
Lamont-Brown, Raymond. *Edward VII's last loves: Alice Keppel & Agnes Keyser*. Stroud, Gloucestershire: Sutton, 1998.
Lee, Sir Sidney. *King Edward VII: A Biography, from birth to accession*. New York, NY: Macmillan Co., 1925.
Lee, Sir Sidney. *King Edward VII: A Biography*. New York, NY: Macmillan Co., 1927.
Longford, Elizabeth. *Queen Victoria: Born to Succeed*. New York, NY: Harper & Row, 1964.
Lorenz, Sönke, and Dieter Mertens and Volker Press. *Das Haus Württemberg: Ein biographisches Lexikon*. Stuttgart: Kohlhammer, 1997.
Madol, Hans Roger. *Ferdinand of Bulgaria: The Dream of Byzantium*. London: Hurst & Blackett, 1933.
Magnus, Philip. *King Edward the Seventh*. New York, NY: E.P. Dutton & Co., 1964.
Mandache, Diana. *Dearest Missy: The Letters of Marie Alexandrovna and of her daughter, Marie, Crown Princess of Romania 1879-1900*. Falköping: Rosvall Royal Books, 2011.
Marie Louise, Princess. *My Memories of Six Reigns*. London: Evans Brothers, 1956.
Masuy, Christine. *Princesses de Belgique: Laeken, les femmes de l'ombre*. Bruxelles: Éditions Luc Pire, 2001.
Mateos Sáinz de Medrano, Ricardo. *Estoril: Los años dorados*. Madrid: La Esfera de los Libros, 2012.
Mattachich, Comte Geza. *Folle Par Raison D'État: La Princesse Louise de Belgique*. Bruxelles: Le Cri édition, 1998.
Mead Lalor, William. *Royalty between the wars*. Falköping: Rosvall Royal Books, 1999.
Montgomery-Massingberd, Hugh. *Burke's Guide to the Royal Family*. London: Burke's Peerage, 1973.
Nikolaev, N.P. ; et al. *La destinée tragique d'un roi ; la vie et la règne de Boris III, roi des Bulgares (1894-1918-1943)*. Uppsala: Almqvist & Wiksells, 1952.
Nobre, Eduardo. *Amélia, Rainha de Portugal*. Lisboa: Quimera Editores, 2006.
Nobre, Eduardo. *Família Real: Álbum de fotografías*. Lisboa: Quimera Editores, 2002.
Nobre, Eduardo. *Paixões Reais*. Lisboa: Quimera Editores, 2002.
Noel, Gerard. *Ena: Spain's English Queen*. London: Constable & Co., 1984.
Packard, Jerrold M. *Victoria's Daughters*. New York, NY: St. Martin's Press, 1998.
Palmer, Alan. *Crowned Cousins: The Anglo-German Royal Connection*. London: Weidenfeld & Nicolson, 1985.
Paoli, Dominique. *Clémentine, Princesse Napoléon*. Bruxelles: Éditions Racine, 1998.
Paoli, Dominique. *Fortunes & Infortunes des princes d'Orléans : 1848 - 1918*. Paris: Éditions Artena, 2006.
Pellender, Heinz. *Chronik der Stadt und der Veste Coburg, der Herren und Herrscher über Coburg und das Coburger Land*. Coburg: Fiedler-Verlag, 1997.
Petropoulos, Jonathan. *Royals and the Reich: The Princes von Hessen in Nazi Germany*. New York, NY: Oxford University Press, 2006.
Plumtree, George. *Edward VII*. London: Pavilion Books, 1995.
Pollock, Kassandra. *Maria Pia of Portugal*. East Richmond Heights, CA: Eurohistory.com, 2015.
Ponsonby, Sir Frederick. *Recollections of Three Reigns*. London: Eyre & Spottiswoode, 1951.
Pope-Hennessy, James. *Queen Mary*. London: George Allen & Unwin, 1959.
Priesner, Rudolf. *Herzog Carl Eduard zwischen Deutschland und England: Eine tragische Auseinandersetzung*. Gerabronn: Hohenloher Druck- und Verlaghaus, 1977.
Ramm, Agatha. (Editor) *Beloved and darling Child: Last Letters between Queen Victoria and Her Eldest Daughter, 1886-1901*. London: Alan Sutton, 1990.
Richardson, Joanna. *George IV: A Portrait*. London: Sidgwick & Jackson, 1966.
Richardson, Joanna. *My dearest Uncle: Leopold I of the Belgians*. London: Jonathan Cape, 1961.
Richardson, Joanna. *Victoria & Albert: a study of a marriage*. London: Dent and Sons, 1977.
Röhl, John C. G. *The Kaiser and His Court: Wilhelm II and the Government of Germany*. New York, NY: Cambridge University Press, 1996.
Röhl, John C.G. *Young Wilhelm: The Kaiser's Early Life 1859-1888*. (3rd edition) Cambridge: Cambridge University Press, 2014
Romania, Marie Queen of. *The Story of My Life*. New York, NY: Charles Scribner's Sons, 1934.
Rose, Kenneth. *King George V*. New York, NY: Alfred A. Knopf, 1984.
Rusk, John. *The Beautiful Life and Illustrious Reign of Queen Victoria*. Minneapolis, MN: Creore & Nickerson, 1901.
Sachsen, Albert Prinz von. *Die Albertinischen Wettiner: Geschichte des Sächsischen Königshauses 1763-1932*. Gräfelfing: E. Albrecht Verlags-KG., 1995.
Sachsen, Albert Prinz von. *Die Wettiner in Lebensbildern*. Graz: Verlag Styria, 1995.
Salway, Lance. *Queen Victoria's Grandchildren*. London: Collins & Brown, 1991.
Sandner, Harald. *Das Haus Sachsen-Coburg und Gotha – 1826 bis 2001*. Coburg: Neue Presse, 2001.
Sandner, Harald. *Ein Herzogtum in aller Welt: Wie das "Haus Coburg" die Throne Europas eroberte*. Coburg: Tourismus & Congress Service, 2001.
Saxe-Coburg-Gotha and Other European Houses. Amsterdam: Sotheby's, 2004.
Saxe-Coburg-Gotha, Ernest Duke of. *Memoirs of Ernest II Duke of Saxe-Coburg-Gotha*. Vols. I and II. London: Remington & Co., 1888.
Saxe-Coburg-Saalfeld, Augusta Duchess of. *In Napoleonic Days – Extracts from the Private Diary of Queen Victoria's Maternal Grandmother*. London: John Murray, 1941.
Shoberl, Frederic. *House of Saxony*. London: R. Ackermann, 1816.
Solms-Baruth, Viktoria Luise Gräfin zu. *Memories of My Life for My Children, Grandchildren and Great-Grandchildren*. Unpublished.
St Aubyn, Giles. *Edward VII: Prince & King*. New York, NY: Atheneum, 1979.
Stéphany, Pierre, and Henri van Daele. *Six Rois*. Bruxelles: Éditions Racine, 1995.
Tuchman, Barbara W. *The Guns of August*. New York, NY: Macmillan Co., 1962.
Tuscany, Luisa of. *My Own Story*. London: Eveleigh Nash, 1911.
Urbach, Karina. *Go Betweens for Hitler*. Oxford: Oxford University Press, 2015.

Valynseele, Joseph. *Les prétendants aux trones d'Europe*. Paris: self-published, 1967.
van der Kiste, John. *Edward VII's Children*. Gloucester: Sutton, 1989.
van der Kiste, John. *Queen Victoria's Children*. Gloucester: Sutton, 1986.
von Stockmar, Baron E. *Memoirs of Baron Stockmar. Vols. I-II*. London: Longmans & Co., 1872.
von Wangenheim, Rita. *Baron Stockmar: Eine coburgisch-englische Geschichte*. Coburg: Hirsch-Verlag, 1996.
Weber, Patrick. *Amours royales et princières: Mariages, liaisons, passions et trahisons de la cour de Belgique*. Bruxelles: Éditions Racine, 2006.
Wiedau, Kristin. *Eine adelige Kindheit in Coburg: Fürstenerziehung und Kunstunterweisung der Prinzen Ernest und Albert von Sachsen-Coburg und Gotha*. Coburg: Kunstsammlungen der Veste Coburg, 2001.
Wilpert, August. *Short history of the Catholic, so called "Kohary" line of the Ducal House of Saxe-Coburg and Gotha*. By order of H.H. Princess Edith of Saxe-Coburg and Gotha. Munich: unpublished, 1990.
Wrangel, Comte F.U. *Les Maisons Souveraines de l'Europe. Vols. I and II*. Stockholm: Collection Hasse-W. Tullberg, 1907.
Zeepvat, Charlotte. *Prince Leopold: The Untold Story of Queen Victoria's Youngest Son*. Stroud, Gloucestershire: Sutton Publishing, 1998.
Zeepvat, Charlotte. *Queen Victoria's Family: A Century of Photographs*. Stroud, Gloucestershire: Sutton Publishing, 2001.
"The Wedding of Hereditary Prince Hubertus of Saxe-Coburg & Gotha and Ms. Kelly Rondestvedt – Coburg, May 23, 2009." Programme.

Newspapers, Magazines

The Illustrated London News (Various years)
The Graphic (Various years)
Eurohistory 1997-2015
Royalty Digest 1992-2005
Time Magazine (Various years)
Newsweek (Various Years)
Black and White (Various years)
The Sketch (Various years)
The Strand Magazine (Various Years)
Die Gartenlaube (1853)
The Times of London

Online Sources:

Austrian National Archive: www.obn.ac.at
Bulgarian Royal Family: www.kingsimeon.com
The Online Gotha: www.angelfire.com/realm/gotha/gotha/gotha.htm
The New York Times 1851-1997: www.nyt.com

INDEX

A
Ambler, John 194

Anhalt
Leopold Friedrich, Hereditary Prince of 47
Elisabeth, Hereditary Princess of (née Hesse-Kassel) 47

Aretz, Dr. Jürgen ix, 172-173
Aufsess, Baron Hans Max von und zu 156

Austria-Hungary
Clotilde, Archduchess of (née Saxe-Coburg & Gotha) 205
Franz II (I), Holy Roman Emperor, Emperor of 84, 204
Franz Joseph, Emperor of 12, 175, 206
Josef, Archduke of 199
Karl, Emperor of 60, 162
Otto, Crown Prince of 162
Regina, Archduchess of (née Saxe-Meiningen) 162
Rudolf, Crown Prince of 175
Stephanie, Crown Princess of (née Belgium) 174
Zita, Empress of (née Bourbon-Parma) 60, 162

B
Baden
Friedrich I, Grand Duke of 34
Karl Leopold, Grand Duke of 34
Louise, Grand Duchess of (née Prussia) 34
Ludwig II, Grand Duke of 34
Sophie, Grand Duchess of (née Sweden) 34

Battenberg
Beatrice, Princess of (née United Kingdom) 44, 48
Louis, Prince of 49
Victoria, Princess of (née Hesse and by Rhine) 25, 49-50

Bauscher, Ulf 175

Bavaria
Amalie, Duchess in (née Saxe-Coburg & Gotha) 205
Leopold, Prince of 196-197

Beéche, Arturo 67, 80, 137, 189, 200, 207, 209, 211

Belgium
Albert II, King of 201
Baudouin, Prince of 38
Baudouin, King of 201
Fabiola, Queen of (née Mora y Aragón) 201
Leopold I, King of (né Saxe-Coburg-Saafeld) 27-28, 37, 46-48
Leopold II, King of 38, 206
Leopold, Prince of 38
Louis Philippe, Prince of 37
Louise-Marie, Queen of (née Orléans) 28, 37, 47
Louise, Princess of (formerly Saxe-Coburg & Gotha) 206
Paola, Queen of (née Ruffo di Calabria) 201
Philippe, Count of Flanders 38

Beveridge
    Michael 187
    Victoria 187
Bismarck, Otto von 34, 68-69

Brazil
Pedro II, Emperor of 38
Pedro de Alcantara, Prince of 205

Brezhnev, Leonid 165

Brockdorff
    Baron Christian-Jasper von 87
    Baroness Donata von (née Solms-Baruth) 87
Brown, Capability 46

Brünswick
Viktoria-Luise, Duchess of (née Prussia) 65

Brünswick-Wolfenbüttel
Anton Ulrich, Duke of 27
Ferdinand Albert II, Duke of 27

Bock, General Field Marshal Fedor von 88
Boelke, Superintendent 23

Bonaparte
Napoleon, Emperor of the French 27-28

Bulgaria
Boris III, King of 38, 205
Ferdinand, King of (né Saxe-Coburg & Gotha) 38, 60, 205
Giovanna, Queen Mother of (née Savoy) 199
Margarita, Queen of (née Gómez-Acebo y Cejuela) 178, 197, 199
Marie Louise, Princess of (née Bourbon-Parma) 205
Marie-Louise, Princess of (formerly Leiningen) 197
Simeon, King of vii, 178, 197, 199, 205, 208-209

C
Cambridge
Alexander, Earl of Athlone (né Teck) 37, 59, 67, 70, 78-79
Lady May 73

Castell-Rüdenhausen
Bertram, Count zu 77, 163
Clementine, Countess zu (née Solms-Sonnenwalde) 22
Conradin, Count zu 77, 163
Friedrich, Count zu 159
Friedrich-Wolfgang, Count zu 77
Victoria, Countess zu 77, 163

Ceausescu, Nicolae 166
Chalwinberch, Thiemo de 8
Chrobok, Bronislaw 197
Clary, Count Mundi 109, 111
Clive, Lord 46

D
Denmark
Alexandrine Louise, Princess of, Countess zu Castell-Castell 209
Christian IX, King of 2
Christian X, King of 58
Frederik V, King of 27
Harald, Prince of 58
Helena, Princess of (née Schleswig-Holstein-Sonderburg-Glücksburg) 58, 209
Ingrid, Queen of (née Sweden) 73

Diesbrück, Heike 159
Diestel, Peter-Michael 169

Dietrichstein
Anna, Countess of (née Meggau) 29
Ludwig Sigismund, Count of 29

E
Entz, Dr. 115, 121

F
France
Henri, Count of Paris 199
Isabelle, Countess of Paris (née Orléans-Braganza) 199
Louis-Philippe, King of the French 47, 205
Marie-Amélie, Queen of the French (née Two Sicilies) 205
Victoire, Duchess of Nemours (née Saxe-Coburg & Gotha) 204-205

Fricke, Dr. 7, 22

G
Germany
Augusta-Viktoria, German Kaiserin (née Schleswig-Holstein-Sonderburg-Augustenburg) 2, 18, 57- 59, 136
Friedrich III, German Kaiser 69, 84
Victoria, German Kaiserin (née United Kingdom) 44, 50, 56, 69
Wilhelm I, German Kaiser 34, 69, 84
Wilhelm II, German Kaiser 2, 12, 18, 25, 35-36, 44, 51-52, 55-60, 65, 69-70, 84, 136

Goering, Hermann 1, 89
Grains
    Hans Ludwig 87
    Victoria Caroline (née Solms-Baruth) 87

H
Hannover
Caroline, Princess of (née Monaco) 208
Ernst August I, King of 208
Ernst August, Prince of 208
Georg V, King of 208
Friederike, Princess of 47

Hanstein, Alexander von 33
Hardy
    Calvert 131
    Jean (née Whitten) 128, 131
    Philip 128, 131
Harten, Gerd von 97
Heideloff, Carl Alexander von 11

Henneberg
Berthold VII, Count of 8
Poppo VII, Count of 8

Hesse-Kassel
Margarete, Landgrafin of (née Prussia) 208
Moritz, Landgraf of 208-209

Hesse and by Rhine
Alice, Grand Duchess of (née United Kingdom) 44, 48-49, 106
Ernst Ludwig, Grand Duke of 44
Ludwig IV, Grand Duke of 48, 50

Himmler, Heinrich 89
Hitler, Adolf 16, 38, 65-71, 80-81, 88-90, 93, 95, 116, 136
Hoeft, Herta 22

Hohenlohe-Langenburg
Andreas, Prince zu 200, 209
Ernst, Fürst zu 2, 158
Ernst, Hereditary Prince of 55, 58
Feodore, Fürstin zu (née Leiningen) 1-2, 58, 158, 208
Kraft, Fürst zu 200-201
Luise, Princess zu (née Schönburg-Waldenburg) 200, 209
Philipp, Fürst zu 200

Hohenzollern
Birgitta, Princess of (née Sweden) 74, 145, 192, 196
Johann Georg, Prince of 145, 192, 196

Hunt von Sternberg, Hermann 8

I
Italy
Elena, Queen of (née Montenegro) 199
Vittorio Emanuele III, King of 199, 208

J
John Paul I (pope) 165
John Paul II (pope) 165-166

K
Kaltenbrunner, Ernst 89
Knobelsdorff
    Christoph von 145
    Georg Wenzeslaus von 18
    Hanko von 145-146, 156
Kohary, Franz, Fürst von 204

L
Leiningen
Alexandra, Fürstin zu (née Hannover) 208
Andreas, Fürst zu 208
Eilika, Fürstin zu (née Oldenburg) 158
Ernst, Fürst zu 34
Karl, Fürst zu (1763-1814) 27, 158
Karl, Fürst zu (1898-1946) 13
Marie, Fürstin zu (née Baden) 34
Marie Kirillovna, Fürstin zu (née Russia) 13
Mechtilde, Princess zu 175
Melita, Princess zu 158
Stephanie, Princess zu 174

Liszt, Franz 33

Luxembourg
Adolphe, Grand Duke of (né Nassau) 52
Jean, Grand Duke of 201
Josephine-Charlotte, Grand Duchess of (née Belgium) 201

M
Magnuson, Tord 194

Mensdorff-Pouilly
Emmanuel, Count of 27
Sophie, Countess of (née Saxe-Coburg-Saalfeld) 27

Miller zu Aicholz
    Amélie von (née Castell-Castell) 209
    Oscar Ritter von 209
Moore, Grace 74
Mountbatten of Burma, Lord (né Battenberg) 49
Mussolini, Benito 67

N
The Netherlands
Alexander, Prince of 106
Bernhard, Prince of (né Lippe-Biesterfeld) 74, 76, 105, 107
Emma, Queen of (née Waldeck und Pyrmont) 105-106
Heinrich, Prince of (né Mecklenburg-Schwerin) 107
Juliana, Queen of 76, 107
Maurits, Prince of 106
Sophie, Queen of (née Württemberg) 106
Willem III, King of 48, 105-106
Willem, Prince of Orange 106
Wilhelmina, Queen of 52, 76, 106-107

O
Oldenburg
Sophie Charlotte, Duchess of (formerly Prussia) 59

P
Patton, General George 78, 95
Paul VI (pope) 165
Pezold, Rüdiger von 156-157, 171-172

Pleß
Conrad, Count von Hochberg, 87-88, 93
Daisy, Fürstin of (née Cornwallis-West) 86
Hans Heinrich XI, Fürst of 87

Portugal
Auguste Viktoria, Queen of (née Hohenzollern) 205
Carlos, King of 205
Duarte, Duke of Braganza 199, 205
Ferdinand II, King Consort of (né Saxe-Coburg & Gotha) 27, 37, 192, 204
Luis Filipe, Crown Prince of 205
Manoel II, King of 199, 204
Maria II, Queen of 192, 204
Pedro V, King of 37

Prussia
August, Prince of 27
August Wilhelm, Prince of 57-58, 66, 136
Cecilie, Crown Princess of (née Mecklenburg-Schwerin) 60
Eitel Friedrich, Prince of 57, 59
Friedrich the Great, King of 18, 27
Kira Kirillovna, Princess of (née Russia) 13
Wilhelm, Crown Prince of 57, 59-60

R
Rasputin, Grigorii 45

Reuß
Heinrich IV, Prince 18
Heinrich XIV, Prince 18
Marie-Louise, Princess (née Salm-Horstmar) 18

Romania
Carol II, King of 199
Marie, Queen of (née Saxe-Coburg & Gotha) 15

Russia
Alexander II, Emperor of 35
Alexandra Feodorovna, Empress of (née Hesse and by Rhine) 44-45, 60
Alexis Nikolaevich, Tsesarevich of 44-45
Olga Feodorovna, Grand Duchess of (née Baden) 34
Ivan VI, Emperor of 27
Kirill Wladimirovich, Grand Duke of 13
Konstantin Pavlovich, Grand Duke of 27
Marie Alexandrovna, Empress of (née Hesse and by Rhine) 35
Michael Nikolaevich, Grand Duke of 34
Nicholas II, Emperor of 12-13, 44-45, 57, 60
Vera Konstantinova, Grand Duchess of 53
Victoria Feodorovna, Grand Duchess of (née Saxe-Coburg & Gotha, formerly Hesse) 13, 15, 44
Wladimir Kirillovich, Grand Duke of 13

S
Salm-Horstmar
Otto, Fürst of 18, 86
Rosa, Fürstin of (née Solms-Baruth) 18, 86

Saxe-Coburg
Albert, Duke of 26
Elisabeth-Sophie, Duchess of (née Saxe-Altenburg) 26
Ernst I, Duke of 11, 25-34, 62
Friedrich, Duke of 26
Johann Casimir, Duke of 11
Louise, Duchess of (née Saxe-Gotha) 29-33
Marie, Duchess of (née Württemberg) 33

Saxe-Coburg and Gotha
Adrian, Prince of 43, 107, 141, 143, 154, 162, 181, 183-184
Alexander, Prince of 30-31, 150, 162, 178, 180-181
Alexandrine, Duchess of (née Baden) 34
Alfred, Duke of (né United Kingdom) 13, 35-36, 44-46, 52-53, 55-56, 58-59
Alfred, Hereditary Prince of 25, 35, 38, 52-53
Andreas, Prince of iii, vii-ix, 1, 6-8, 12, 15, 18-19, 23, 30-31, 40, 43, 49, 61, 64, 66, 68-70, 73-74, 76, 80-82, 84, 87, 90-91, 93, 96-100, 102-103, 107-109, 111, 113-116, 118-121, 123-126, 128-129, 131-132, 135, 137-138, 140-147, 149-152, 154, 156-160, 162-163, 167, 169-175, 178, 180-181, 184, 186-187, 189-194, 196-197, 199-201, 204, 207, 209-211
August, Prince of 47, 204-205
August Clemens, Prince of 38
August Leopold, Prince of 38
Carin, Princess of (née Dabelstein) iii, 137, 158-160, 174-175
Carl Eduard, Duke of (né United Kingdom) ix, 1-3, 8, 11-14, 17-18, 20-21, 28, 35-36, 38, 40, 43-46, 49-53, 55-62, 64-72, 76, 78-82, 89-91, 95-96, 99, 103, 116, 119, 124, 136, 138, 140, 163, 168, 171-172, 175, 201, 205, 208
Caroline-Mathilde, Princess of (formerly Castell-Rüdenhausen, Schnirring and Andrée) 3, 8, 11, 59, 76-77, 82, 163
Claudia, Princess of (formerly Schäfer) 43, 107, 141, 154, 161-162, 184
Clementine, Princess of (née Orléans) 47, 205
Daniel 181
Denise, Princess of (née de Muralt) 81, 107, 112, 141-143, 147, 154, 156-157, 159, 184
Edith, Princess of (née de Kózol) 207
Ernst II, Duke of 11, 29, 31, 34-35, 59
Ernst Leopold, Prinz von 72, 202, 204
Felicitas, Princess of 39, 207
Feodora, Prinzessin von (née von der Horst; formerly Plerger von Perglas) 72-73, 204
Friedrich Josias, Prince of 1, 3-6, 8, 12-15, 17, 20-21, 23, 30, 43-44, 61, 74, 76, 81-82, 89-91, 95-99, 104-105, 107, 112, 125, 138, 140-145, 149-150, 154, 156-157, 159-160, 162-163, 168-171, 184, 186, 192
Gertraude, Prinzessin von (née Pfeiffer) 204
Gertrud (née Krieg) 181, 183-184
Hubertus, Prince of (1909-1945) 11, 17, 38-40, 59, 76, 95, 97, 104, 161, 204
Hubertus, Prinz von (b.1961) 204
Hubertus, Hereditary Prince of (b.1975) 31, 150, 160-162, 175, 178, 180, 193, 201, 209-211
Ingeborg, Prinzessin von (née Henig) 204
Johann Leopold, Hereditary Prince of 15, 38, 40, 59, 71-73, 76, 97, 161, 202, 204
Johanna, Princess of (née Károly de Károly-Patty) 207
Johannes Albert, Prince of 39, 207
Johannes Heinrich, Prince of 37, 39, 207
Katharina, Princess of 74, 180, 194
Katrin, Princess of (née Bremme) 142-143, 154, 156-157, 159-160, 162, 175
Kelly, Hereditary Princess of (née Rondestvedt) 178, 180, 201, 209
Lea (née Rinderknecht) 181
Leopold, Prince of (1824-1884) 204
Leopold, Prince of (1878-1916) 38, 206
Ludwig August, Prince of 205
Ludwig Gaston, Prince of 38
Malte, Prinz von 202
Marianne, Prinzessin von 72, 202
Maria Theresia, Prinzessin von (née Reindl) 73
Marie Alexandrovna, Duchess of (née Russia) 35, 45-46, 52-53
Marie-Gabrielle, Princess of (née von Fürstenberg) 207
Peter, Prinz von (b.1939) 72-73, 202
Peter, Prinz von (b.1964) 202
Peter August, Prince of 38
Philipp, Prince of (1844-1921) 38, 60, 205-207
Philipp, Prince of (b.2015) 180
Philipp August, Prinz von 207
Philipp Josias, Prince of 207
Rainer, Prince of 207
Roswitha, Prinzessin von (née Breuer) 202
Sabine, Prinzessin von (née Henning) 204
Sarah, Prinzessin von (née Hálasz) 207
Simon 181

Stephanie, Princess of 4, 31, 160, 174-175, 184
Viktoria-Adelheid, Duchess of (née Schleswig-Holstein-Sonderburg-Glücksburg) 2, 3, 6, 11-12, 17-18, 20-21, 51, 57-59, 61, 66, 77-79, 82, 89-90, 96, 119, 136-138, 140, 144-145, 147, 151, 156-59, 163, 168, 193, 206, 209

Saxe-Coburg-Saalfeld
Antonia, Princess of (née Kohary) 27, 204
Augusta, Duchess of (née Reuß zu Ebersdorf) 27-28, 30, 33
Ferdinand, Prince of 27, 37, 204
Franz Friedrich Anton, Duke of 1, 27, 34, 43
Juliane, Princess of (formerly Russia) 27
Sophie, Duchess of (née Saxe-Hildburghausen) 27

Saxe-Eisenach
Albert, Duke of 25
Christian, Duke of 26

Saxe-Gotha
August, Duke of 29
Caroline-Amalie, Duchess of (née Hesse-Cassel) 29
Friedrich, Duke of 26
Friedrich IV, Duke of 29
Louise-Charlotte, Duchess of (née Mecklenburg-Schwerin) 29

Saxe-Hildburghausen
Ernst, Duke of 26

Saxe-Meiningen
Beatrice, Princess of (née Saxe-Coburg & Gotha) 43, 107, 141, 143, 147, 154, 162, 184, 186-187
Bernhard, Duke of (1649-1706) 26
Bernhard, Duke of (1901-1984) 186
Friedrich, Prince of 162, 186-187
Friedrich Constantin, Prince of 162, 186-187
Konrad, Duke of 186
Margot, Princess of (née Grössler) 186
Maria-Alexandra, Princess of 162, 187
Vera, Princess of (née Schaffer von Bernstein) 186

Saxe-Römhild
Heinrich, Duke of 26

Saxe-Saalfeld
Anne-Sophie, Duchess of (née Schwarzburg-Rudolstadt) 27
Christian-Ernst, Duke of 26-27
Ernst-Friedrich, Duke of 27
Franz Josias, Duke of 26-27
Friedrich-Josias, Prince of 27
Johann Ernst, Duke of 26
Sophie-Antoinette, Duchess of (née Brünswick-Wolfenbüttel) 27

Saxe-Weimar
Wilhelm, Duke of 25

Saxony
Friedrich Christian, Margrave of Meißen 207
Mathilde, Princess of (formerly Saxe-Coburg & Gotha) 39, 207

Sayn-Wittgenstein-Berleburg
Benedikte, Furstin zu (née Denmark) 209
Hubertus, Prince zu 87, 191
Irina, Princess zu (née Solms-Baruth) 87, 191
Richard, Furst zu 209
Tatiana, Princess zu (formerly Hesse) 209

Schäfer
    Christina 161, 184
    Gion 161, 184
    Gianetta 161, 184

Schleswig-Holstein-Sonderburg-Augustenburg
Adelheid, Duchess of (née Leiningen) 2
Dorothea "Dora," Duchess of (née Saxe-Coburg & Gotha) 18, 206-207
Ernst-Günther, Duke of 18, 206
Friedrich, Duke of 2
Helena, Princess of (née United Kingdom) 50

Schleswig-Holstein-Sonderburg-Glücksburg
Alexandra Viktoria, Princess of (formerly Prussia) 58, 66, 136-137
Alfred, Prince of 13
Christoph, Duke of 13
Friedrich, Duke of 2, 13, 47, 58, 90, 137, 144, 152, 210
Friedrich Ferdinand, Duke of 2, 18, 58
Hans, Prince of 13
Marie Melita, Duchess of (née Hohenlohe-Langenburg) 2, 13, 58
Karoline Mathilde, Duchess of (née Schleswig-Holstein-Sonderburg-Augustenburg) 2, 18, 47, 58, 206

Schnirring
    Calma 77, 163
    Dagmar 77, 163
    Max 77
    Michael 77
Silfverschiöld, Baron Nils August 196

Solms-Baruth
Adelheid, Fürstin zu (née Schleswig-Holstein-Sonderburg-Glucksburg) 18, 22, 58, 86
Anna, Countess zu (née Hochberg) 18, 93, 109
Caroline-Mathilde, Countess zu (née Schleswig-Holstein-Sonderburg-Glucksburg) 3-6, 17-22, 58, 84, 86-93, 95-96, 98, 100, 109, 111-112, 114-115, 118, 120-121, 123-124, 136, 158, 191, 206, 209
Christian, Count zu 87, 191
Elisabeth-Charlotte, Countess zu (née von Kerssenbrock) 86
Friedrich-Hans, Count zu 19, 22, 86-92, 95-96, 100, 107-109, 115, 121, 124, 191
Friedrich I Hermann, Fürst zu (1821-1904) 84
Friedrich II Hermann, Fürst zu (1853-1920) 18, 86

Friedrich Hermann, Fürst zu (1886-1951) 18, 22, 58, 86, 88-89, 95
Gerta, Countess zu (née Staël von Holstein) 86, 191
Hans Georg, Count zu iii, 3-5, 17-20, 22, 84, 86-93, 95-96, 98, 100, 102, 109, 113-15, 118, 120, 190
Henriette, Countess zu (née Reuß) 87
Hermann, Count zu 18, 86, 93
Huberta, Countess zu 87, 191
Hubertus, Count zu 19, 20, 86, 90, 100, 115, 121, 124, 160-161, 191
Johann-Georg, Count zu 86
Louise, Fürstin zu (née Hochberg) 18, 86
Melissa (née Butler) 191
Oda, Countess zu (née Stolberg-Wernigerode) 87, 191
Rupprecht, Count zu 87

Spain
Alfonso XIII, King of 44-46
Alfonso, Prince of Asturias 45
Beatriz, Infanta of 45
Fernando, Infante of 45
Gonzalo, Infante of 45
Jaime, Infante of 45
Juan, Count of Barcelona 45-46, 199
Juan Carlos I, King of 44, 46
Maria, Countess of Barcelona (née Bourbon-Two Sicilies) 199
Maria Cristina, Infanta of 45
Victoria Eugenia, Queen of (née Battenberg) 45

Spence, Sandra 152, 158
Stoeckel, Dr. 1, 5
Stoecker, Adolf 69
Stoiber, Edmund 169

Sweden
Bertil, Prince of 75
Carl XVI Gustav, King of ix, 15, 74-75, 129, 145, 156, 178, 191-194, 196, 209
Carl Johan, Prince of 75
Princess Christina, Mrs. Magnuson 74, 145, 192, 194
Princess Désirée, Baroness Silfverschiöld 74, 196
Gustav V, King of 67, 74, 107
Gustav VI Adolf, King of 3, 47, 74-75, 145
Gustav Adolf, Prince of 3, 15, 47, 73-75, 79, 105, 107
Lilian, Princess of (née Davies; formerly Craig) 75
Louise, Queen of (née Battenberg) 49, 74-75, 145
Madeleine, Princess of 74, 145, 193
Margaret, Crown Princess of (née United Kingdom) 74
Princess Margaretha, Mrs. Ambler 74, 145, 194
Sibylla, Princess of (née Saxe-Coburg & Gotha) 3, 13, 15, 47, 59, 67, 73-75, 81-82, 98-99, 105, 107, 142, 145, 157, 161, 163, 175, 194
Sigvard, Prince of 75
Silvia, Queen of (née Sommerlath) ix, 178, 192-193, 197
Victoria, Queen of (née Baden) 47
Victoria, Crown Princess of 74, 193

T
Taubin
> Jack 187
> Keith 187
> Todd 187, 189

Toerring-Jettenbach
Count Hans Viet 209

Treitschke, Heinrich von 69

Two Sicilies
Ferdinando I, King of 205

U
United Kingdom
Adelaide, Queen of (née Saxe-Meiningen) 2
Alastair of Connaught, Prince 37
Albert, Prince Consort of (né Saxe-Coburg & Gotha) 27, 29, 31, 34, 35, 40, 44, 200
Albert Victor, Duke of Clarence 38
Alexandra of Fife, Princess 37
Alice of Albany, Countess of Athlone 12, 14, 25, 37, 49-52, 56-57, 59, 60, 62-63, 70, 73, 78-80, 106, 163
Andrew, Duke of York 200
Arthur, Duke of Connaught 35-37, 46, 52, 55, 59, 67, 73-74
Arthur of Connaught, Prince 35-38, 52, 55, 59
Charles, Prince of Wales 200-201
Charlotte, Princess of Wales 28, 46, 48
Edward VII, King of 35, 38, 46, 49-50, 55
Edward VIII, King of (later Duke of Windsor) 67, 70-71
Edward, Duke of Kent and Strathearn 28, 47
Edward, Earl of Wessex 200
Elizabeth II, Queen of 39, 49, 73, 200-201
George V, King of 12, 59, 67, 70-71, 91, 201
Helene, Duchess of Albany (née Waldeck und Pyrmont) 25, 43, 48- 52, 55-56, 62-63, 105
Henry, Duke of Gloucester 39
Leopold, Duke of Albany 40, 43-44, 46-49, 63, 73
Louise, Duchess of Fife 37
Mary, Queen of (née Teck) 12, 70
Michael of Kent, Prince 201
Philip, Duke of Edinburgh 200
Victoria, Duchess of Kent (née Saxe-Coburg-Saalfeld, widow Leiningen) 1, 27, 158
Victoria, Queen of 1, 8, 11, 13, 25, 27, 29, 35-36, 40, 43-44, 46-51, 55-56, 58, 63, 67-68, 91, 106, 123, 125, 158, 200, 208-209
William IV, King of 2, 208
William of Gloucester, Prince 39

V
Voights, Herr 138, 140, 144, 156, 163, 168

W
Wachtmeister, Count Carl Gustaf 156, 172

Waldburg zu Wolfegg und Waldsee
Countess Eilika (née Solms-Baruth) 87
Count Jakob 87

Waldeck und Pyrmont
Georg Viktor, Fürst of 47-48
Helene, Fürstin of (née Nassau) 48, 52
Wittekind, Fürst of 52

Walesa, Lech 165
Whitten
- Bertha (née Babb) 111, 125-126, 128-129, 131, 134-135, 140-141
- Frank Sandusky 128, 134, 140
- Kay 128
- Richard iii, v, 40, 87, 92, 100, 103, 108-109, 111-116, 118-121, 123-126, 128-129, 131-135, 138, 141-144, 149, 151-152, 156, 160, 187, 189-190
- Victoria iii, 114, 116, 120-121, 123, 126, 129, 131, 133, 135, 140-141, 151, 184, 187, 189, 190
- Viktoria-Luise (née Solms-Baruth, formerly Saxe-Coburg & Gotha) iii, v, 1, 3-8, 16-23, 39-40, 44, 51, 76, 81, 84, 86-93, 96-100, 102-104, 108-109, 111-116, 118-121, 123-126, 128-129, 131-138, 140-144, 147, 149-152, 158, 160, 170, 187, 189-190

Wied
Pauline, Fürstin zu (née Württemberg) 52

Wimmler, Maria 116, 118, 121

Windsor
Lord Nicholas 201
Lady Nicholas (née Doimi de Frankopan) 201

Württemberg
Albrecht Ferdinand, Duke of 199
Alexander, Duke of (1771-1833) 27
Alexander, Duke of (1804-1881) 47
Alexander, Duke of (b.1933) 199
Antoinette, Duchess of (née Saxe-Coburg-Saalfeld) 27, 47
Charlotte, Queen of (née Schaumburg-Lippe) 52
Eugen, Duke of 199
Ferdinand, Duke of 199
Marie, Duchess of (née Orleans) 47
Marie, Queen of (née Waldeck und Pyrmont) 49
Nadejda, Duchess of (née Bulgaria) 199, 205
Sophie, Duchess of 199, 200
Wilhelm II, King of 48-49, 52, 56

The Coburgs of Europe

A royal biography of the Saxe-Coburg & Gotha dynasty and all its branches in Great Britain, Belgium, Portugal, Bulgaria and Coburg.

Queen Victoria and the Prince Consort were both Coburgs and they feature prominently in the storyline of each of the dynasty's branches.

It includes more than 500 photos of the various Coburg branches.

The price of this hardback book is: USA price: $48.95 + shipping ($8 in the USA – $26.00 overseas). WE SHIP WORLDWIDE!

To order by phone: (510) 236-1730 or email: books@eurohistory.com

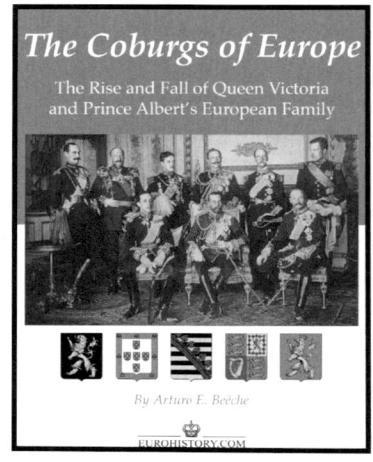

APAPA

King Christian IX of Denmark and His Descendants

The history of King Christian IX of Denmark, the Father-in-law of Europe, and his descendants. Covering the last 150 years of the royal and imperial houses of: Denmark, Norway, Great Britain, Greece, Romania, Russia, Hanover, Baden, Mecklenburg-Schwerin and many other related dynasties and princely houses.

The authors have handsomely documented their writings with nearly 450 exquisite and rare photos of King Christian IX and his wife Louise and their descendants.

USA price: $48.95 plus shipping ($8.00 in the USA – $26.00 overseas).

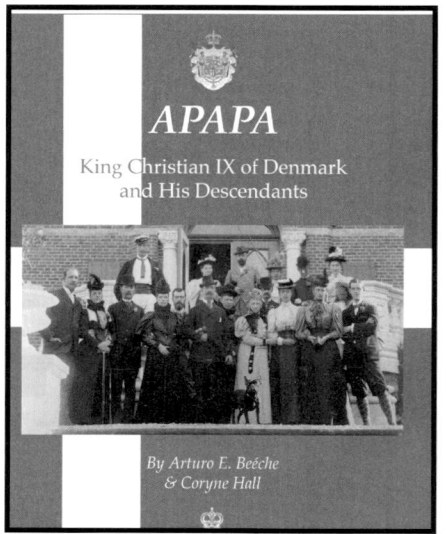

Royal Gatherings

Who is in the Picture? – Volume I

Inspired by a very popular feature inside the pages of EUROHISTORY, Ilana D. Miller and Arturo E. Beéche wrote a book on royal gatherings that happened between 1859-1914. Spanning many of Europe's royal families, Royal Gatherings tells the story behind 38 group photos of royals from King Francesco II of the Two Sicilies, to the wedding of Prince Heinrich of Prussia, and the Assassination of Archduke Franz Ferdinand of Austria.

Royal Gatherings' 176 pages are filled with more than 250 unique photographs, most of them from the Eurohistory Archive and some from private royal collections.

The book sells for $43.95 plus shipping ($8.00 in the USA – $26.00 overseas). Order by Phone: 510-236-1730 or email at: books@eurohistory.com

Russia and Europe – Dynastic Ties

Authored by Galina Korneva and Tatiana Cheboksarova, it includes nearly 600 photos, an overwhelming majority among them collected from the main archives of Russia and several European countries. The moment captured by these original photos is able, often times, to tell the reader far more about the unique world of royalty and aristocracy than countless pages of text. The authors also relied on important information obtained from Russian and foreign periodicals, memoirs and scientific literature. The English-language version of this book was expanded with contributions written by Arturo Beéche, founder and publisher of Eurohistory.

The price of this hardback book is: USA price: $49.95 + shipping ($8 in the USA – $26.00 overseas). WE SHIP WORLDWIDE!

To order by phone: (510) 236-1730 or email: books@eurohistory.com

The Royal Hellenic Dynasty

This is the English-language version of Elleniki Dynazteia published in 2003. The book made an indelible impression on collectors of royal books back then. Due to its widespread acclaim, Eurohistory negotiated for the publication of the book in English as: The Royal Hellenic Dynasty, a book filled with more than 160 photographs of the Greek royal family from between 1863-1950. The Royal Hellenic Dynasty draws an exquisite selection of photos from the private collection of Mrs. Eleni Helmis-Markesinis. The captions were written by Prince Michael of Greece and translated by him and Arturo Beéche, Eurohistory's founder. The book is in the usual coffee-table format, hardback with dustjacket and printed in glossy paper.

Price: $29.95, plus shipping ($8 shipping and handling in the USA. International shipping and handling available for $26.00).

Dear Ellen

Royal Europe Through the Photo Albums of Grand Duchess Helen Vladimirovna of Russia

With special access to the Grand Duchess' private photo albums, as well as images from the Eurohistory Archive and the private collections of the grand duchess' descendants, the author built a photographic journey covering the lives of Helen and her husband, Prince Nicholas of Greece. The book also includes the galaxy of royalty in which the prince and his wife lived. Four of the grandchildren of Helen and Nicholas actively cooperated with the author bringing to light untold family stories and helping reconstruct the lives of two unique royal personages, now nearly forgotten.

Hardbound, glossy paper and contains more than 350 unique photographs, as well a massive several family tree showing Helen and Nicholas in the context of both their families. The book sells for $43.95 plus shipping ($8.00 in the USA – $26.00 overseas). Order by Phone: 510-236-1730 or email at: books@eurohistory.com

ROYAL GATHERINGS, Volume II

The authors have analyzed thirty-six photos taken at royal gatherings between 1914–1939. Each photo has its own chapter in which the authors provide short biographies of the royal personages featured in the photo. Co-authored by Ilana D. Miller and Arturo E. Beéche, it promises to be an excellent addition to Eurohistory's growing library of unique titles. Ranging from the Russian Imperial Family's visit to their Romania cousins in June 1914, to the wedding of the Duke of Spoleto and Princess Irene of Greece in July 1939, ROYAL GATHERINGS, Volume II, examines 36 group photos taken at various royalty get-togethers between those years. The book contains more than 330 photos, as well as an extensive family tree that includes most of the royalties discussed in the book. ROYAL GATHERINGS, Volume II is 248-long glossy pages and hardbound. Cost: $48.95 + Shipping ($8.00 in the USA, $26.00 overseas).

Grand Duchess Marie Pavlovna

– Using rare archival information obtained from various Russian sources, as well as sources in Europe and the United States, renowned Russian authors Galina Korneva and Tatiana Cheboksarova have pieced together the first biography of Grand Duchess Marie Pavlovna, the indomitable "Aunt Miechen." Daughter-in-law, sister-in-law and amiable aunt of Russia's last three stars, Marie Pavlovna enjoyed an enviable position in the highest echelons of pre-Revolutionary Russian society and cultural life. A patron of the greatest jewelers and designers of her time, Marie Pavlovna also spent considerable efforts on endless charities. Her energy was legendary, as was her traveling, spending and meddling in the highest affairs of the empire. This is a spell-binding biography. Illustrated with more than 400 photos, many donated by her descendants, this biography promises to be unequaled!

Grand Duchess Marie Pavlovna is 248-long glossy pages and hardbound. Cost: $48.95 + Shipping ($8.00 in the USA, $26.00 overseas). *To order call our office (510.236.1730) or email us at: books@eurohistory.com – You may also send a check in US$ payable to "Eurohistory" to our address: EUROHISTORY, 6300 Kensington Avenue, East Richmond Heights, CA 94805 USA*

Maria Pia – Queen of Portugal

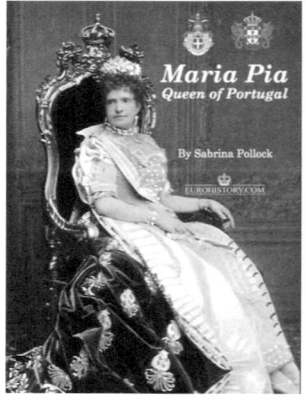

This unique volume is authored by the talented Sabrina Pollock, a regular contributor to Eurohistory.

This is the first English-language biography of little-known Queen Maria Pia, wife of King Luis I. The author conducted extensive research in Portugal, Italy and Germany. This effort allowed Ms Pollock access to previously untapped sources, thus making her book even weightier! The book is handsomely illustrated with a selection of images obtained by the author and publisher, many of these photos never having been published before. Cost: $43.95 + Shipping ($8.00 in the USA, $26.00 overseas).

To order call our office (510.236.1730) or email us at: books@eurohistory.com – You may also send a check in US$ payable to "Eurohistory" to our address: EUROHISTORY, 6300 Kensington Avenue, East Richmond Heights, CA 94805 USA